Sodomy and Interpretation

SODOMY AND INTERPRETATION

Marlowe to Milton

Gregory W. Bredbeck

Cornell University Press

Ithaca and London

First published 1991 by Cornell University Press.

International Standard Book Number 0-8014-2644-8 (cloth)
International Standard Book Number 0-8014-9945-3 (paper)
Library of Congress Catalog Card Number 91-55066
Printed in the United States of America
Librarians: Library of Congress cataloging information appears on the last page of the book.

♾ The paper in this book meets the minimum requirements of the American National Standard for Information Sciences—Permanence of Paper for Printed Library Materials, ANSI Z39.48-1984.

For Phyllis Rackin

Contents

Preface

When this book began, it seemed to be an isolated and risky endeavor. Nobody would outright deny the interest of the project, but neither would anybody outright endorse it. It seemed that I was treading a fine line between an expansion of gender studies and a lapse into the unconscionable. Happily, I find the book entering the world as a member of a community. The growth of gay and lesbian history, the development of a queer theoretical practice, and the emergence of a radical lavender left within the academy, while not necessarily making the project possible, have all in some way contributed to my ability to realize it fully. It would be both morally and politically irresponsible not to mention the names of those whose works played a central role in these developments: John Boswell, Alan Bray, Louis Crompton, Robert K. Martin, Kenneth Plummer, James Saslow, and Jeffrey Weeks, among others. I have also been influenced by the pioneering theoretical work of Sue-Ellen Case, Teresa de Lauretis, David Halperin, D. A. Miller, and Eve Sedgwick. I find myself, therefore, an author of a text that resembles Roland Barthes's conception: "not a line of words releasing a single 'theological' meaning . . . but a multi-dimensional space in which a variety of writings, none of them original, blend and clash."[1]

[1]Roland Barthes, *Image Music Text*, ed. and trans. Stephen Heath (New York, 1977), p. 146.

Jean Howard has reminded us that "the best criticism performs two tasks at once: the practical business of reading another text and the critical business of explaining the terms of that reading."[2] Therefore, I want here to outline as succinctly as possible the second part of my critical task, especially since it is conceived in a way that challenges the typical boundaries of Renaissance studies within the academy. For the most part, the originality of this book manifests itself in the way that I choose to negotiate the demilitarized zone marked off within the academy between the opposing camps of construction and essence. I address this issue in more detail in the second section of my introductory chapter, but it is worth addressing it here in a broader sense, if only to suggest how my book attempts to force an arbitration between the two practices arising in response to this rift. The essentialist side of the debate is most likely familiar to everyone, for it is also the stance that has masqueraded under the various guises of liberal humanism, biological determinism, and common sense. A. L. Rowse springs to mind as the essential essentialist. He says in his book *Homosexuals in History*, "My purpose is not theoretical discussion but the more enlightening one of the study of concrete fact, the way men actually are and behave." Empowering this practice is the belief that a historian is able "to get as close as possible to the lives of human beings, lay finger on pulse and heart."[3]

It is not, I think, necessary to rehearse this position in any great detail. Rather, I would like to juxtapose it momentarily to one of the germinal efforts on the other side of the demarcation line, Mary McIntosh's essay "The Homosexual Role." I take up this work again in the penultimate chapter; here I simply want to note the considerable difference between Rowse's "outing" of figures such as Marlowe and Shakespeare, and McIntosh's assertion that such inquiries "are inconclusive not because of lack of evidence but because none of these men fits the modern stereotype of the homosexual."[4] McIntosh's broader point, which has

[2]Jean E. Howard, "The New Historicism in Renaissance Studies," *ELR* 16, 1 (1986): 31.

[3]A. L. Rowse, *Homosexuals in History* (New York, 1977), p. xii.

[4]Mary McIntosh, "The Homosexual Role," in *The Making of the Modern Homosexual*, ed. Kenneth Plummer (London, 1981), p. 36.

become a commonplace in gay studies, is that the homosexual role "only emerged in England towards the end of the seventeenth century."[5] For reasons that I think are unsupported by her argument, McIntosh's work has been used to foster a sort of paranoia of historicization, a phenomenon in which the effort to examine sexual difference in the past, especially as it might relate to the inscription of the subject, is immediately stigmatized as anachronistic. Ironically, this stance comes perilously close to replicating Rowse's essentialism. For if Rowse begins with the assumption that we can trace an atemporal conception of homosexuality throughout history, the other alternative has been to say that because we *cannot* trace this particular concept through history, nothing can be traced. In each instance "the homosexual" is essentialized as the absolute standard of adjudication. "It" is what we must find if we are to find anything at all.

The result of these two essentialisms is that we typically assess the past in terms of "practices," "ideologies," or "powers" and refuse to recognize that these discourses might somehow construct a historical subject. I examine this notion at length in Chapter 3. For my purposes here, however, it is necessary to recognize that the exact correspondence of sexuality, gender, and subjectivity is a defensive illusion that has come to exist in comparatively recent times. Therefore, my governing assumption throughout is this: While it is true that discourses of homoeroticism during the period did not constitute the "role" or "subjectivity" of "the homosexual," it does not follow that they signified nothing; rather, they signified in ways that sometimes serve ulterior constructions of the subject and sometimes demand an exact link between sign and behavior, but just as often do not.

All these theoretical considerations justify what I perceive to be a two-part analysis. First, I am interested in the ways sodomy and its related discourses betray the determinism of sexual language that is taken for granted in our age. During the period in question, "sodomy" meant sodomy. But it also meant bestiality, lesbianism, heterosexual anal intercourse, adultery, minority and alien status, heresy, political insurgence, witchcraft and sorcery,

[5]Ibid., p. 43.

ad infinitum. And yet, while this multivalency disrupts our notions of how sexuality determines meaning, sodomy during that time period did, indeed, exercise a power and force as strong as it does in our own culture, even if different. Thus, while I acknowledge the multivalency of the issues with which I am dealing, I do not dwell on it. Rather, I focus the greater part of my analysis on examples of the *results* or *effects* of sodomitical discourses. In so doing, I hope that readers will be, at times, forced into an interpretive quandary; by sketching the effects, I want readers to have to ask, What is the cause?, and thereby find out that this question in and of itself exposes the historical boundedness of our own desire for deterministic meaning. In other words, attempting to map out systematically the fragmented meaning of sexual difference in the past again imports our own need for determinant meanings. As I think my book bears out, this need has not always existed. I sharpen the politics of this strategy by focusing throughout on examples that relate to male (homo)sexuality. Most of the examples herein beg us to utter the word *homosexual*. And yet, at the same time, they frustrate the ability to do so. My hope, therefore, is that this dilemma will force readers, especially those who perceive themselves to be heterosexual, to feel a general unease about their ability to know what the word *homosexual* means—and thereby give them pause to ponder whether, indeed, we know what it means today. I do not want to make sense of my topic but rather to show how my topic demonstrates that "sense" itself is a form of cultural fascism that seeks to pin down, label, constrain, control, and dismiss in a way that is undermined by history itself. All these desires become most apparent in my linkage of two terms, *sodomy* and *homoeroticism*. While the examples I choose tend to support their linkage, it is also important to recognize that this intervalidation is not exhaustive of all the "meanings" of sodomy within Renaissance culture or of all the ways in which homoeroticism could be signified. Therefore, certain caveats must be kept in mind throughout, the primary ones being that the "sodomy" I study is but one of many, for I choose to study the term only as it is associated with male-male attraction, and that same-sex attraction—homoeroticism—is *not* the same as homosexuality, though at times it may seem to overlap what we mean by "the homosexual."

I also want to have fun, because that is clearly what most of the texts I deal with are doing—they play, toy, and revel in a sort of pre-Barthesian *jouissance*. I want, therefore, to foreground sodomy in order to escape the morbid (white, heterosexual, male) sobriety that has been brought to bear on many of these texts.

I owe a great deal to a great number of people, places, and things. Research for this project was made possible in part by a University of Pennsylvania Penn-in-London Fellowship, a University of Pennsylvania Dean's Fellowship, field and intramural grant funds from the University of California, and a University of California Regents Faculty Fellowship. These funds allowed me to impose myself on several excellent research facilities. I am grateful to the staffs of the British Library, the Folger Shakespeare Library, and the Furness Library and Rare Book Room at the University of Pennsylvania. Perhaps that library's greatest resource is Georgianna Ziegler, to whom I am especially grateful. Bernhard Kendler of Cornell University Press and my two readers for the press, Katharine Eisaman Maus and Michael Lieb, provided helpful insights and moral support.

A brief version of Chapter 5 was presented at the 1988 MLA seventeenth century divisional session, "Gendering the Seventeenth Century," in New Orleans, and I thank session leader Regina Schwartz for the opportunity. Part of Chapter 3 was presented at the 1989 MLA sixteenth century (excluding Shakespeare) divisional session, "Wordplay in the English Renaissance," in Washington, D.C. Moderator Anne Lake Prescott demonstrated more than a passing interest in my work and helped to bolster my confidence immensely. Part of Chapter 2 was presented at the 1990 Riverside Berkeley Shakespeare Festival Conference and benefited from the thoughtful comments of participants. I am especially indebted to Stephen Orgel and Jonathan Crewe. A segment of Chapter 4 was presented at the 1991 version of the same conference. Participants in the East Coast Milton Seminar's 1991 meeting at the Graduate Center of the City University of New York, especially Bill Readings, James

Saslow, and John Shawcross, provided lively commentary on a version of Chapter 5. I thank Jackie DiSalvo and Joseph Wittreich for providing that opportunity, as well as for their stellar hospitality. A shorter version of Chapter 5 titled "Milton's Ganymede: Negotiations of Homoerotic Tradition in *Paradise Regained*," originally appeared in *PMLA* 106 (1991) and is reprinted here in an expanded form by permission of the copyright owner, The Modern Language Association of America. My students at both the University of Pennsylvania and the University of California will notice their influence throughout.

Many generous people have offered time, advice, and friendship. Claude Summers shared his work on Milton with me at a key point. Colleagues at the University of California, Riverside, have made my intellectual development both inevitable and enjoyable; I note especially the support of Philip Brett, Sue-Ellen Case, Susan Foster, John Ganim, Diana Garber, Stephanie Hammer, Deborah Hatheway, George Haggerty, Ralph Hanna, Lesliee Reilly, Sharon Salinger, Margi Waller, and Deborah Willis. The Renaissance scholars at the University of Pennsylvania are surpassed in their intelligence only by their festiveness: of this group, Rebecca Bushnell demonstrated an uncommon willingness to read my work and teach me about things I did not know, Cary Mazer shared his knowledge of theater history and also mentored my pedagogical development, and Maureen Quilligan was a constantly inspirational persona. I learned a lot and gained much support from fellow graduate students at Penn, especially Alyson "Cadbury" Booth, Kim Hall, Gwynne Kennedy, Beth Magnus, Barbara Reibling, and Wendy Wall.

In the less formally institutional modes my debts are even greater. Stuart Curran heads this list, having equally mastered the sometimes contradictory roles of friend, mentor, and idol. He also had the uncommon foresight and grace to say yes to the idea when many, perhaps including himself, doubted the wisdom of it. The influence of Peter Stallybrass and Ann Rosalind Jones lies tacitly beneath all my work and play. Jean Peterson has distinguished herself as a friend constantly willing to teach me about the historicity of transgression in the past and the materiality of it in the present. The gang at Raffles in Philadelphia—

Billy, Bob, Bob, Chris, Donna, Eddy, Joe, John, Miss June, Karl, Lloyd, Mark, Mitzi, Paul, Pete, P. J., Richard, Rob, and Rose—made sure the spirit was willing even when the mind was weak, and the gentlemen at the Queen's Head made a year of research in London as entertaining as it was educational. The immense debt of friendship and knowledge I owe to Joseph Wittreich surpasses the strictures of discourse. I should also acknowledge the support of the late Miss Misha, the most remarkable cat I have had the pleasure to know. It is traditional to dedicate a book to partner or family, but I am not naive enough to believe that such bourgeois sentimentality can surpass the true bond expressed in my dedication.

GREGORY W. BREDBECK

Riverside, California

Sodomy and Interpretation

Lo, I have given thee wings wherewith to fly
Over the boundless ocean and the earth;
Yea, on the lips of many shalt thou lie
The comrade of their banquet and their mirth.
Youths in their loveliness shall make thee sound
Upon the silver lute's melodious breath;
And when thou goest darkling underground
Down to the lamentable house of death
Oh yet not then honor shalt thou cease,
But wander, an imperishable name.

—Theogonis

The one duty we owe to history is to re-write it.

—Oscar Wilde

CHAPTER I

Introduction: History and the Scene of Sodomy

> That homosexuality has been a natural condition of kings, composers, engineers, poets, housewives, and bus drivers, and that it has contributed more than its fair share of beauty and laughter to an ugly and ungrateful world should be obvious to anyone who is willing to peer beneath the surface.
>
> —Martin Grief

> If you removed all of the homosexuals and homosexual influence from what is generally regarded as . . . culture, you would be pretty much left with *Let's Make a Deal.*
>
> —Fran Leibowitz

The Poetics of Renaissance Sodomy

Sodomy during the Renaissance was both done and written; perhaps it was written more interestingly than it was done. Although the act of sodomy is constrained by certain physical exigencies—one can only *do* so much with what one *has*—the discursive encoding of it reveals a vast and sometimes self-contradictory canon of writing that extends from law and lexicography through arcadian romance and mythological poetry, to biblical exegesis and to broadside pornography. Much criticism reduces this transversal canon to its most rarefied or conservatively controlled ideologies.[1] As one critic puts it in a discus-

[1]This statement is made problematic by the growing canon of criticism exploring the dynamics of Renaissance homoeroticism. Early inquiries tended to adopt the strategy I am outlining here; see Alan Bray, *Homosexuality in Renaissance England* (London, 1982). Bray's work has stimulated a multifaceted response that is helping us to understand the issues involved in theorizing sexual difference historically. Some of the more noteworthy examples are James M. Saslow, *Ganymede in the Renaissance: Homosexuality in Art and Society* (New Haven, 1986), which focuses primarily on the Italian Renaissance (for an excellent discussion of the shortcomings of Saslow's approach, see Francis Ames-Lewis, "Ganymede on Dangerous Ground," *European Gay Review* 4 [1990]: 128–134); Joseph Pequigney, *Such Is My Love: A Study of Shakespeare's Sonnets* (Chicago, 1987), which I discuss in Chapter 4; Jonathan Goldberg, *James I and the Politics of Literature: Jonson,*

sion of Shakespeare's *Sonnets*, "Today this legal term for homosexual intercourse [buggery] offends our ears, but its use draws attention to the *abhorrence* with which many Christians of the time (and since) regarded physical intimacies between men."[2] There is certainly a strong degree of moral condemnation in many Renaissance configurations of homoeroticism. However, encodings of homoeroticism during the period also strongly signal their own flaws, the points at which their formulations betray the existence of alternative perspectives and contrasting material experiences behind, around, and within the written word. Moreover, legal and religious discussions of homoeroticism frequently find their demonic counterparts in more transgressive genres; hence, the monstrous buggerers in the law and the church become, in broadsides and pamphlets, very real, fleshly people with very erect penises. These sublimated dynamics are typically ignored by modern criticism, a discipline frequently too concerned with reading the word to question why it was written. Even such an enlightened scholar as Alan Bray, who recognizes a plurality of ways in which one could express homoerotic tendencies during the Renaissance, posits these multiple images of homoeroticism as responses to a monolithic and unavoidable ideological inscription of moral stigmatism. The individual drawn to homosexuality, writes Bray, "was faced with more than the naked fact of that intense disapproval: he had also to contend with its widely accepted integration into the way the scheme of things was understood and into the Christianity of his time. It was this dimension which was the iron in the problem, especially as that view of things was probably something he shared himself."[3] For Bray, the language of Renaissance sodomy

Shakespeare, Donne, and Their Contemporaries (Baltimore, 1983), which discusses in passing James's sexuality, "Sodomy and Society: The Case of Christopher Marlowe," *Southwest Review* 69 (1984): 371–378, and "Colin to Hobbinol: Spenser's Familiar Letters," in *Displacing Homophobia: Gay Male Perspectives in Literature and Culture*, ed. Ronald R. Butters, John M. Clum, and Michael Moon (Durham, N.C., 1989), pp. 107–126; Stephen Orgel, "Nobody's Perfect: or Why Did the English Renaissance Stage Take Boys for Women?", also in *Displacing Homophobia*, pp. 7–30.

[2]C. B. Cox, "Bisexual Shakespeare?" *Hudson Review* 40, 3 (1987): 481. Emphasis mine.

[3]Bray, *Homosexuality in Renaissance England*, p. 63.

is perfectly inscriptive—perfectly able both to construct and to contain its subject.

There is a strong case to be made for this stigmatized reading of Renaissance sodomy. Throughout the course of the Renaissance a large number of derogatory terms became associated with people who engaged in sodomy—pathic, cinaedus, catamite, buggerer, ingle, sodomite[4]—and legal writings of the time express a definite attitude of abhorrence. James I, in advising his son on the ideal tenets of a prince, labels sodomy (along with witchcraft, willful murder, incest, and counterfeiting) one of the "horrible crimes that yee are bound in conscience never to forgive."[5] Edward Coke ascribes sodomy to the realm of "Sorcerers, Sodomers and Hereticks."[6] Francis Meres's *Palladis Tamia* associates sodomy with usury and labels both as sterile practices: "As *Paederastie* is unlawful, because it is against kinde: so usurie and encrease by gold and silver is unlawful, because against nature; nature hath made them sterill and barren, and usurie makes them procreative."[7] And the prosecutor in the trial of Mervin Touchet, the Earl of Castlehaven, who was tried for sodomy in 1631, states, "As for the *Crimen Sodomiticum*, in the second Indictment, I shall not Paraphrase upon it, since *it is of so abominable and Vile a Nature*, that as the Indictment truly expresses it, *Crimen inter Christianos non nominandum*, it is a Crime not to be named among Christians."[8] In all these examples, as in much criticism written about them, homoeroticism is contained within a mythology of the unnatural, the alien, and the demonic.

Because the transcripts of Touchet's trial were widely disseminated near the end of the seventeenth century, they more prop-

[4]Ibid., pp. 13–32.

[5]James I, *The Political Works of James I*, ed. Charles Howard McIlwain (Cambridge, Mass., 1919), 1, p. 20.

[6]Edward Coke, *The Third Part of the Institutes of the Laws of England* (London, 1644), p. 36.

[7]Francis Meres, *Palladis Tamia, or, Wits Treasury Being the Second Part of Wits Commonwealth* (London, 1598), p. 322.

[8]*The Tryal and Condemnation of Mervin, Lord Audley Earl of Castle-Haven, at Westminster, April the 5th 1631* (London, 1699), sig. C2. A similar view is also expounded in an earlier transcript, *The Trial of Lord Audley, Earl of Castlehaven, For Inhumanely Causing his Own Wife to be Ravished, and for Buggery* (London, 1679).

erly belong to the historical dynamics of the Enlightenment than they do to the province of this book.[9] However, the transcripts also display the sort of discursive instability concealed by this demonized rhetoric of sodomy and therefore can provide us with a vivid fruition of the sort of dynamics that, I will claim, in various forms underpin the rhetoric of sodomy throughout the entire Renaissance. For if we look further into Touchet's trial, signals of a different experience emerge. The preface to the trial describes "the Develish and Unnatural Sin of Buggery" and claims that "this sin [is] being now Translated from the Sadomitical Original, or from the Turkish and Italian Copies into English; not only in the infamous example of that Monster Ri[g]by, and other Notorious Sodomites; but also . . . at Windsor."[10] Admittedly, this passage still maintains an ideology of the alien and the unnatural, attributing sodomy to *foreign* languages and *monstrous* men. But the material experience of that "Monster Rigby," a common soldier, probably was not governed by an intense recognition of his *contra naturam* status, for, in contrast to the rhetoric of the preface to *The Tryal of Mervin Touchet*, the broadside account of Rigby's case domesticates his actions by placing them within the recognizable context of urban London and in the process reveals the inadequacies of the discursive triumvirant of "Sorcerer, Sodomer and Heretick." The broadside describes how Captain Edward Rigby was fined one thousand pounds and sentenced to three days in the pillory and one year in jail because he

> did Solicite, Incite, and as well by words as other ways, endeavour to perswade one *William Minton* (of about the Age of Nineteen Years) to suffer him the said *Rigby*, to commit the

[9]For a discussion of the sociopolitical and historical dynamics informing the emergence of texts such as these, see Randolph Trumbach, "Sodomitical Subcultures, Sodomitical Roles, and the Gender Revolution of the Eighteenth Century: The Recent Historiography," and G. S. Rousseau, "The Pursuit of Homosexuality in the Eighteenth Century: 'Utterly Confused Category' and/or Rich Repository?", both in *Unauthorized Sexual Behavior during the Enlightenment*, ed. Robert P. Maccubbin (Williamsburg, Va., 1985).

[10]*Tryal*, sig. A3.

> Crime of *Sodomy* with him the said *Minton*. And the said *Rigby* did also Endeavour and attempt to Commit the Crime of *Sodomy* with him, the said *Minton*; and did also do and perpetrate divers other Enormities and abominable things, with an intent to Commit the Crime of *Sodomy* with the said *Minton*.

It further claims

> that on *Saturday* the Fifth of *November* last, *Minton* standing in St. *James's Park* to see the Fireworks, *Rigby* stood by him, and took him by the hand, and squeez'd it; put his Privy Member Erected into *Minton's* Hand; kist him, and put his Tongue into *Minton's* Mouth, who being much astonish'd at these Actions went from him; but *Rigby* pursued him, and accosted him again.[11]

Minton's response to the situation indicates that elaborate social networks existed both to facilitate and to suppress homoerotic meetings. He arranges a date with Rigby at the George Tavern for the next day and then proceeds to inform constables of the meeting so that Rigby can be caught in the act. The process is described in minute and pornographic detail:

> *Rigby* seemed much pleased upon *Mintons* coming and drank to him in a glass of Wine and kist him, took him by the Hand, put his Tongue into *Mintons* Mouth, and thrust *Mintons* hand into his (*Rigby*) Breeches, saying, *He has raised his Lust to the highest degree, Minton* thereupon askt, *How can it be, a Woman was only fit for that, Rigby* answered, DAM' EM, THEY ARE ALL POCT, I'LL HAVE NOTHING TO DO WITH THEM. Then *Rigby* sitting on *Minton's* Lap, kist him several times, putting his Tongue into his Mouth, askt him, *if he should* F---- *him*, how can that be askt *Minton, ile show you* answered *Rigby, for its no more than was done in our Fore fathers time*; . . . Then *Rigby* kist *Minton* several times, putting his Tongue in his

[11] *An Account of the Proceedings Against Capt. Edward Rigby, At the Session of Goal Delivery, held at Justice-Hall in the Old-Bailey, on Wednesday the Seventh Day of December, 1698* . . . (London, 1698).

> Mouth, and taking *Minton* in his Arms, wisht he might lye with him all night, and that his Lust was provoked to that degree, he -------- in his Breeches, but not withstanding he coul F---- him; *Minton* thereupon said, *Sure you cannot do it here*, yes, answered *Rigby*, I can, and took *Minton* to a corner of the Room, and put his hands into *Mintons* Breeches, desiring him to pull them down, who answered he would not, but he (*Rigby*) *might do what he pleased*; thereupon *Rigby* pulled down *Mintons*, who feeling something warm touch his Skin, put his hand behind him, and took hold of *Rigbys* privy Member, and said to *Rigby, I have new discovered your base inclinations, I will expose you to the World, to put a stop to these Crimes*; thereupon *Minton* went towards the door, *Rigby* stopt him, and drew out his sword, upon which *Minton* gave a stamp with his foot, and cry'd out *Westminister*.

Aside from the wonderful final line, in which Minton invokes the seat of British government to save himself from the sin of sodomy (a role the British government still takes very seriously), several things ring false in this account. Minton's naïveté about the sexual act is discordant with his earlier sophistication about how to arrange an entrapment of Rigby, perhaps suggesting that his ignorance is a strategy to avoid legal responsibility. The discourse also exhibits that while the legal voice may have abhorred homoeroticism, it also had given it enough thought to have formulated a very modern system of culpability—hence, Minton is said to have disclaimed responsibility for the lowering of his pants. But more important than these legal observations are the things the broadside shows us about the language practices of the period. Despite the seemingly modest use of elliptical dashes ("F----"), the text also transmits a very broad and very blatant image of homoerotic behavior; indeed, it is difficult to tell whether the piece is more interested in condemning Rigby's "abominable" behavior or displaying it. Behind the "Sorcerer, Sodomer and Heretick," then, behind the words of condemnation, there exists a much more important picture of homoeroticism, a picture that would be effaced by a criticism too concerned with the official pronouncement of gendered ideology to look for evidence of ruptures within it.

Alan Bray, in *Homosexuality in Renaissance England*, devotes a final chapter to analyzing the sort of social changes demonstrated by cases like that of Rigby. He documents how in the early eighteenth century a new homosexual subculture emerged, one centered primarily in "Molly houses," private meeting places for men where "effeminacy and transvestism with specifically homosexual connotations were a crucial part." As Bray sees it, "there was now a tension that had not existed before. Alongside the old forms of society in which homosexuality had appeared, new meanings were now being attached to homosexuality: it was more than a mere sexual act."[12] It is possible, however, to trace a long and varied genealogy for the "new" tension Bray cites, a lineage that comprises the subject matter of this book. Juxtaposed to the mythologized ideology of the official records of a nobleman's trial, the brutal explicitness of the broadside account of this soldier's actions raises several important issues, not the least of which is the difference between high and low languages.[13] For the critical issue here is not so much Rigby's actions as it is a paradox in articulation, a paradox that demonstrates that the official word as recorded in a transcript deposited

[12]Bray, *Homosexuality in Renaissance England*, pp. 81–114. The emergence of "the homosexual" and "the homosexual subculture" has been the topic of much historical work. The two most formative explications of it within gay studies have been McIntosh, "Homosexual Role," and Michel Foucault, *The History of Sexuality, Vol. 1: An Introduction* (New York, 1980). The broad concern of these studies has been augmented by historically specific case studies in *Unauthorized Sexual Behavior*, ed. Maccubbin. Of particular interest in this collection are Arend H. Huusen, Jr., "Sodomy in the Dutch Republic during the Eighteenth Century," and Michael Rey, "Parisian Homosexuals Create a Lifestyle, 1700–1750: The Police Archives," both of which discuss the dynamics of nascent homosexual subcultures.

[13]The importance of the stratification of discourse in the formation of a culture has been explored by Mikhail Bakhtin, *Rabelais and His World* (Bloomington, Ind., 1984); for the ramifications of this theory in the methodology of the study of Renaissance material culture, see Peter Stallybrass and Allon White, *The Politics and Poetics of Transgression* (Ithaca, 1986). My idea of the placement of sodomy within the Renaissance culture has been centrally informed by their assertion that "a fundamental rule seems to be that what is excluded at the overt level of identity-formation is productive of new objects of desire" (p. 25).

at Westminster differs greatly from the detailed description of material practice displayed on a poster tacked to a pub wall. It is also a potent reminder that history happens not just in castles and manors but also in pubs and brothels, and not just to princes and courtiers but also to soldiers and nineteen-year-old boys. The Rigby case, then, though at the terminal historical edge of the period in question, also foregrounds the fissures and contradictions that, I will claim, are the definitive mark of sodomy and male homoeroticism throughout the Renaissance. Moreover, recognizing these rifts between the ideological and the material and between the high and the low suggests not only a different way of recuperating the past but also a different way of reading "canonical" texts, for literature is produced in a specific historical moment—a moment delineated by the material experience of day-to-day life as well as by the patronage of kings and the pressures of parliamentary edicts.

Renaissance configurations of homoeroticism are uniquely able to expose the historical and social rifts typically concealed in higher discourses, for the language of sodomy throughout the entire Renaissance was a dynamic and fluid field that specifically took as its task defining the unacceptable; hence, the language of sodomy functions both as a demarcation between high and low and as a specification of a point where low transgresses high. Linguistically, the terminology of sodomy gradually changed from a limited and generalized discourse to a copious and specified one. Early Renaissance dictionaries provide a relatively small vocabulary to express the multiple meanings of homoeroticism during the period. Thomas Cooper's *Bibliotheca Eliotae* lists only one word that might serve as an appropriate signifier: "Sodomito, aui, are: to use or comitte the sinne of Sodome afaynste naturae."[14] Unlike Rigby's case, the definition contains no specification of sexual action, no "erect privy member" to indicate clearly an intent to bugger. Sodomy here is part of a broader concern of practices that run "afaynste naturae." The majority of early definitions of sodomy exhibit a similar lack of sexual speci-

[14]Thomas Cooper, *Bibliotheca Eliotae* (London, 1552), sig. TTTiiiiv.

fication. Florio's *A Worlde of Wordes* offers this circular declension of sodomy:

> Sodomia, the naturall sin of Sodomie.
> Sodomita, a sodomite, a buggrer.
> Sodomitare, to commit the sinne of Sodomie,
> Sodomitarie, sodomiticall tricks.
> Sodomitico, sodomiticall.[15]

And even when Cooper's later dictionary, *Thesaurus Linguae Romanae et Britannicae*, allows a more sexually specific signifier, *Catamitus*, to enter the lexicography, it stops short of the blatant physicality of the Rigby broadside: "Catamitus. A boye abused contrary to nature."[16]

The point here is not that sodomy during the early Renaissance was asexual but rather that its lack of sexual specificity allowed the term to be used in unspecified ways, ways that signify broad fields of sexual aberration all additionally stigmatized by the prurience of male-male attraction. When Michael Drayton, in *The Moone-Calfe*, describes the child so sinful that it actually repulses even its father, the devil, he invokes this notion of sodomy to make his point:

> Sodom for her great sin that burning sank,
> Which at one draught the pit infernal drank,
> Which that just God on Earth could not abide,
> Hath she so much the devils terrified:
> As from their seat, them well near to exile,
> Hath Hell new spewed her up after this while:
> Is she new risen, and her sin again
> Embraced by beastly and outragious men.[17]

[15]John Florio, *A Worlde of Wordes, or Most Copious and Exact Dictionarie in Italian and English* (London, 1598), p. 376.

[16]Thomas Cooper, *Thesaurus Linguae Romanae et Britannicae* (London, 1565), sig. R4v.

[17]Michael Drayton, *The Works of Michael Drayton*, ed. J. W. Hebel (Oxford, 1961), 3, p. 174.

But this sodomitical debauchery is a part of a larger schema of sexual decay that is the true subject of the poem. For when the poem presents its "monstrous birth," it does so in terms that reveal an even broader concern with the definition of sexual difference in general:

The birth is double, and growes side to side
That human hand it never can divide;
And in this wondrous sort as they be Twins
Like Male and Female they be *Androgines*. . . .

. . . . A man in show, thereby as to define,
A fem'nine man, a woman Masculine;
Before bred, nor begott; a more strange thing,
Than ever *Nile*, yet into light could bring,
Made as Creation meerely to dispight,
Nor man, nor woman, scarce *Hermaphrodite*.[18]

The early Renaissance canon of satires continually returns to sodomy as a metaphor for sexual plurality or sexual deviance. In *The Scourge of Villanie* John Marston uses the invocation of sodomy several times as an affront to the foppish gallantry of courtiers and dandies:

Seest thou yon gallant in the sumptuous clothes,
How brisk, how spruce, how gorgiously he showes,
Not his French-herring bones, but note no more,
Unlesse thou spy his fayre attendant whore,
That lackyes him. Marke nothing but his clothes,
His new stampt complement, his Cannon othes,
Marke those, for naught but such lewd viciousnes
Ere graced him, save Sodome beastlines.
Is this a *Man*? Nay, an incarnate devill,
That struts in vice, and glorieth in evill.[19]

In this context the invocation of sodomy is truly punning, for it

[18]Drayton, *Works*, 3, pp. 170–171.
[19]John Marston, *The Scourge of Villanie* (London, 1599), sigs. E6v–E7r.

stresses the fact that the one signifier, *sodomy*, carried with it several senses that were all equally valid if slippery referents. Even when alternative nomenclature is used, Marston's satiric conception of homoeroticism relies on the undifferentiated idea of sexual otherness rather than an Adamic linkage of sign ("sodomy") and signified ("male-male eroticism"):

> Alack, alack, what peace of lustfull flesh
> Hath *Luscus* left, his *Priape* to redresse?
> Grieve not good soule, he hath his *Ganimede*,
> His perfum'd she-goat, smooth kembd & high fed.[20]

The satirist later admits that "Yon effeminate sanguine *Ganimede*, / Is but a Bever, hunted for the bed,"[21] but this sexual Ganymede is encased in a broader scheme, "The Cynicke['s]" search "for a *Man*," that also includes "A Mimick Ape," "*Aesops* asse," and "a muckhill over-spred with snow."

The poetics of sodomy revealed in Marston's satires is not so much a system of words designed to articulate a specification of sodomy as it is a specification of sodomy designed to articulate a system of words and ideas—a way to encompass a multitude of sins with a minimum of signs. In the terminology of Renaissance rhetoric, this pattern of signification can best be termed "The *Synechdoche* of the speciall," which, according to Abraham Fraunce's *The Arcadian Rhetoric*, "is when by the speciall we note the generall, so we put a finite number for a great one; so the singular for the plurall."[22] This language pattern remains a dominant trope in Renaissance satires at least though the middle of the 1600s. Edward Guilpin uses it to condemn the theater-goer "who is at every play, and every night / Sups with his *Ingles*, who can well recite. . . ."[23] In the seventeenth century Thomas Middleton uses the trope to deride "this neast of Gallants" who "keepe at

[20]Ibid., sig. C4.

[21]Ibid., sig. F3.

[22]Abraham Fraunce, *The Arcadian Rhetoric*, ed. Ethel Seaton (Oxford, 1950), p. 22.

[23]Edward Guilpin, *Skialethia, or, a Shadowe of Truth in Certaine Epigrams and Satyres* (London, 1598), sig. B1.

every heele a man, beside a French Lackey, (a great Bay with a beard) and an English Page, which filles up the place of an Ingle,"[24] and Richard Middleton employs it in several of his epigrammatic satiric aspersions on Longatoe:

> *Maia's* forsake *Longatoe's* profred love,
> For, drunke of late, he swore no woman kinde
> Should him unto lascivious habit move:
> And then the drunk-proud-foole waxed so kinde,
> He, like a Catamite, kist all men about him,
> While they laught at his follie and did flout him.[25]

The satirist who exhibits perhaps the strongest reliance on this synecdochic sodomy is Richard Brathwait. His dedicatory epistle to *A Strappado for the Divell* clearly reveals the sort of undifferentiated catalogue of otherness to which early Renaissance sodomy belonged:

> To all Userers, Broakers, and Promoters,
> Sergeants, Catch-poles, and Regraters,
> Ushers, Panders, Suburbes Tra-
> ders, Cocknies that have
> manie fathers.
>
> Ladies, Monkies, Parachitoes, Mar-
> mosites and *Catamitoes*, Falls, high
> tires and rebatoes, false-haires
> periwigges, monchatoes: grave Gregorians, and Shee-
> painters.[26]

Brathwait's numerous satires clearly demonstrate that *catamite* is not just one separate signifier but rather is a term that articulates this entire catalogue of meanings. In "An Heroycke Embleme

[24]Thomas Middleton, *The Blacke Booke* (London, 1604), sig. C3.

[25]Richard Middleton, *Epigrams and Satyres* (London, 1608), p. 9.

[26]Richard Brathwait, *A Strappado for the Divell: Epigrams and Satyres Alluding to the Time, with Divers Measures of No Lesse Delight* (London, 1615), sig. A9. Emphasis mine.

upon the Warriour Called Honora," Ganymede is used as one part of a negative catalogue fortifying by contrast the image of the good soldier:

Infuse true resolution in the minde
Of thy professors, that their spirits may finde
What difference there is in honours fight,
Twixt a good Souldier and a carpet-Knight.
His perfume's powder, and his harmonie
Reports of Cannons, for his braverie,
Barded with steele and Iron, for the voice,
Of Amorous Ganimedes, the horrid noise
Of clattering armour, for a Downie bed
The chill cold ground, for pillow to their head,
Tinckt with muske Roses, Target and their shield,
For gorgeous Roomes, the surprise of the field,
For nimble capring, Marching, for the tune
Of moving comforts, striking up a drumme,
For dainties, hunger; thus is honour fed,
With labour got, and care continued.[27]

And in his satire "Upon the Generall Sciolists of Poettasters of Brittannie," he places the catamite within a satirically condemnatory catalogue of British poets: "These are those Babell publique prostitutes, / Lures to damnation, Roman Catamites, Inventresses of pleasures."[28]

In a later volume, *Times Curtaine Drawne*, Brathwait returns to the topic and rearticulates sodomy as a part of the "worlds pleasure" he is attempting to correct:

I doe cashiere all private Parasites,
Ladie-fied Monkeys, lustful Catomytes,
Painting, and pushing, sleeking of the skin,
Pandring of hayre, to let temptation in.[29]

[27]Ibid., p. 9.
[28]Ibid., pp. 31–32.
[29]Richard Brathwait, *Times Curtaine Drawne, or the Anatomie of Vanitie* (London, 1621), sig. F7v.

Lest it be thought that this occurence of homoeroticism is a marginal event in marginal minds, it should also be noted that the same sort of tropical sodomy can be found in one as canonically central as John Donne:

> Why should'st thou (that dost not onely approve,
> But in ranke itchie lust, desire, and love
> The nakednesse and barenesse to enjoy,
> Of thy plumpe muddy whore, or prostitute boy)
> Hate vertue, though shee be naked and bare?[30]

As in the other examples, Donne invokes sodomy not as a specific condemnation of male-male eroticism but as part of a larger attack on undifferentiated debauchery in which "prostitute boy" and "plumpe muddy whore" are equivalent—though prurient—terms.

Against this rhetorical legacy of undifferentiated vice, the pornographically specific tract of Rigby's case does, indeed, seem to indicate a drastic change in the ideology of homoeroticism. The rhetoric of the Rigby case, however, is not the origin of a new discourse but rather the logical culmination of a lengthy process of discursive complication and specification of homoeroticism during the Renaissance. By 1670, when Thomas Blount published his dictionary, *Glossographia*, the sole sodomite of Cooper had fragmented into a full nomenclature encompassing subtle variations of meaning. Blount's definition of sodomy provides the same biblical referent as Cooper's but also includes a vernacular sexual specification:

> Sodomy (sodomia) buggery; so called from the City of *Sodom* in *Judaea*, which for the detestable sin was destroyed with fire from heaven.
>
> Sodomite, an Ingler or Buggerer.[31]

[30]John Donne, *Complete Poetry and Selected Prose*, ed. John Hayward (London, 1962), p. 122.

[31]Thomas Blount, *Glossographia: Or a Dictionary Interpreting the Hard*

Checking the cross-references provided reveals congruous but not identical definitions:

> Ingle (Span. from the Lat. Inguen, i. the groin) a boy kept for Sodomy. See *Ganymede.*

> Buggerie (Fr. *Bougrerie*) is described to be *carnalis copula contra naturam, & haec vel per confusionem Specierum,* a man or a woman with a bruit beast, *vel sexuum*; a man with a man, or a woman with a woman. *See Lev. 13, 22, 23.* This offence committed with mankinde or beast is felony without clergy; it being a sin against God, Nature, and the Law; And in ancient time such offenders were to be burnt by the Common Law. *25 Hen. 8. 6. 5 Eliz. Fitz. Nat. Br. 269.* My Lord *Coke* (*Rep 12. Page 36*) saith, that this word comes from the *Italian, Buggerare,* to bugger.

The further cross-reference reveals yet another gradation of meaning that, in turn, is also the cross-referent for *catamite*:

> Ganymede (Ganymedes) the name of a Trojan Boy, whom *Jupiter* so loved (say the Poets) as he took him up to Heaven, and made him his Cup-bearer. Hence any Boy, loved for carnal abuse, or hired to be used contrary to Nature to commit the detestable sin of *Sodomy,* is called *Ganymede,* or ingle.

> Catamite (catamitus) a boy hired to be abused contrary to nature, *a Ganymede.*[32]

In sheer numbers of words alone, the nomenclature of homoeroticism obviously proliferated during the period. This growth is best seen in the fact that Cooper's early definition of Ganymede carried none of Blount's vernacular implications with it: "Ganimedes: a Trojan chylde, which feigned to bee ravyshed of Jupiter, and made his butlar."[33] Blount, of course, is not responsible

---

Words of Whatsoever Language, Now Used in our Refined English Tongue (London, 1670), p. 596.

[32]Ibid., pp. 288, 92–93.

[33]Cooper, *Bibliotheca,* sig. Iiiii4v.

for the expanded meaning of Ganymede, for even as early as 1595, in Marlowe's *Hero and Leander*, the sexualized meaning of the myth is fully operative.[34] Clearly, the process of discursive proliferation occurred throughout the Renaissance, not just at its end. But perhaps what is most interesting about Blount's lexicography is the way it establishes a range of sexual subject positions within the field of homoeroticism. Only one term, *buggery*, carries with it the import of legal sanction, suggesting that the other terms are vernacular or idiomatic usages. Moreover, the three terms *Ganymede*, *catamite*, and *ingle* suggest three separate modes of homoerotic interaction: a boy "loved for carnal abuse"; a boy "hired to be abused contrary to nature"; a boy "kept for Sodomy." Roughly speaking, these three terms define a range of meanings analogous to those of *lover*, *hustler*, and *kept boy* in the modern gay idiom.[35]

Legal discourses of the Renaissance exhibit a similar proliferation and specification of homoeroticism. The longest-standing statute on the books dates from the time of Henry VIII and remained at least through the end of the reign of Charles I: "Buggery shall be accounted Felony; And no offender therein shall have his Clergy."[36] However, the interpretation of this statute reveals a growing concern with delineating modes of homoerotic behavior. In 1641 Francis Bacon, in *Cases of Treason*, states that "where a Man committeth Buggery, with Man or Beast, it is Felony"—a category that also includes "where one stealeth certain Kind of Hawks."[37] Yet by the time Serjeant Thorpe presented *His Charge, as it was delivered to the Grand Jury at York Assizes, the Twentieth of March, 1648*, sodomy had become part of a category of misprision of treason that included a wide range of delineated sexual transgressions:

[34]For a full explication of Marlowe's use of the myth, see Chap. 3.

[35]*Lover*: "one's friend in all senses—social, sexual, *etc.*"; *hustler*: "a male prostitute"; *kept boy*: "young lover who is kept, *ie* has all his bills paid for by an older homosexual" (Bruce Rodgers, *Gay Talk: A [Sometimes Outrageous] Dictionary of Gay Slang* [New York, 1972], pp. 128, 111, 120).

[36]Ferdinando Pulton, *A Collection of Statutes Now in Use, With a Continuation of the Statutes Made in the Reign of the Late King Charles the First of Blessed Memory . . . by Thomas Manby* (London, 1670), p. 1548.

[37]Francis Bacon, *Cases of Treason* (London, 1641), p. 304.

> If any commit a Rape, *viz.* have the carnal Knowledge of a Woman, against her Will, or with her Will, if she be under ten Years old.
>
> If any commit Buggery, or Sodomy, a Crime *Inter Christianos non nominandum*, says the Indictment.[38]

By the time of the publication of Edward Coke's last two volumes of the reports, the legal language of sodomy encompassed gradations of differentiation between sodomy and buggery, a subdivision of meaning ascribed to rape, and a specification of the sexual act itself:

> Mich. 5 Jac Regis, Case concerning Buggary.
>
> The Letter of the Statute, 25 H 3. *cap.* 6. If Any Person shall commit the detestable sin of Buggary with Mankind or Beast & c. it is Felony; which Act being Repealed I *Mar.* is revived and made perpetual 5 *Eliz. cap. 17.* and he lose his Clergy.
>
> It appears by antient Authorities of the Law, That this was Felony, but they vary in the punishment. For *Britton*, who writ 5 *Ed. I. Cap.* 17 saith, that *Sorcerers, Sodomers, and Hereticks* shall be burned: *F. N D. 269*; agrees with it. But *Fleta Lib. I. cap. 35. Christiani Apostati, & c.* debent *cumburi*, (this agrees with *Britton*) but *Pecorantes et Sodomitae terra vivi s ffodiantur.* But in the *Mirror* of *Justice*, vouched in *Plow. com.* in *Fogasses* Case, the Crime is more high, for there is called *Crimen laessae majestatis*, a horrible Sin against the King, either Celestiall or Terestrial in three manners: I. By Heresy, 2. By Buggary, 3. By Sodomy. Note, Sodomy is with mankind, and is Felony, and to make that Offence, *Oportet rem penetrare et semen naturae emittere et effundere*; for the *Indictment* is, *Contra ordinationem Creatoris et naturae ordinem rem habiut veneream dictung; puerium carnaliter cognovit*; and so it was held in the Case of *Stafford, Paederastes amator puerorum*, Vide Rot. Parl. 50 Ed. 3. 58. So in a Rape there must be penetration, and emission of Seed, *Side*

[38]Thorpe, *His Charge, as it Was Delivered to the Grand Jury at York Assizes, the Twentieth of March, 1648* (London, 1649), p. 8.

> *Stamf. fol* 44. which Statute makes the Accessary Guilty of Felony.
>
> *West. I. cap.* 34, If a Man ravish a Woman, *II H. 4. 18.* If one Ayd another in a *Rape*, or be present, he is principle in the Buggary, Vide *Levit.* 18.22., *et cap.* 10. 13. I Cor. 6.[39]

Sodomy is now solely a male sexual activity, as it must include penetrating someone and ejaculating. Moreover, sodomy is specifically the misspending of male seed between men; the misspending of seed between men and women becomes rape. Several important issues are raised by Coke's specifications: for example, what has happened to the category of woman-woman sodomy Blount admitted into his definition? But these questions are of less importance to a poetics of Renaissance sodomy than the more general point that Coke's legal discourse clearly demonstrates a remarkably large amplification of the language constraining (and hence defining) homoerotic activity in the Renaissance. Moreover, the entire process of specification demonstrated in legal language and lexicography marks a movement from general demonic condemnation (the mythology of the preface to Touchet's trial) to specific sexuality (the erect privy member of the Rigby broadside).

The change in the language of sodomy during the Renaissance is best thought of as a movement from synecdoche to *ironia*, specifically that subdivision of *ironia* that Fraunce terms *negatio*: "A kinde of pretended omitting or letting slip of that which indeed wee elegantly note out in the verie shewe of praetermission, as when we say; I let this passe; I passe it over with silence."[40] For while the later specifications of sodomitical behavior all serve to constrain and suppress the social status of homoeroticism, they also "elegantly note out" the first linguistic genesis of homoerotic behavior *as* homoerotic behavior. The linguistic model indicated by the difference in semantic status of sodomy between the early and late Renaissance is one in which

[39]Edward Coke, *An exact abridgement of the two last volumes of reports, entitled the 12th & 13th parts* (London, 1670), pp. 36–37.

[40]Fraunce, *Arcadian Rhetoric*, p. 13.

the discursive concern with the documentation of prurience leads to an ever-increasing reification of sexualities and sexual behaviors and, at the same time, creates a linguistic movement from synecdochic articulation to ironic silence. To a certain extent this double dialectic of exclusion/inclusion and sound/ silence operates within the emergence of all gender and sexual matrices in the Renaissance. However, the category of homoeroticism is particularly and peculiarly able to expose the submerged contradictions of power encoded in the evolution of early modern gender meaning, most notably because it suggests that sexual ideology as articulated in high discourses is not an adequate description of the full spectrum of material sexual possibilities.

Throughout the Renaissance homoeroticism is figured and refigured as a slippery category that is at once both a type of sexual meaning and an effacement of sexual meaning. Both synecdoche and *negatio* are *parts* of speech, not *all* of it, and this limited status continually hints at broader experiences motivating these partial articulations of control. Although the rhetoric of sodomy changed considerably in the Renaissance, in all cases the entrance of sodomy into idealized languages of social order somehow also invokes the broader arenas of dissent trying to be controlled. The thesis of this study is that much literature of the Renaissance—much more, at least, than has been recognized—exploits the conflations of high/low and decorum/transgression present in Renaissance homoeroticism and that an examination of the rhetorical interplay of synecdoche and negatio that characterizes the language of sodomy in a number of discursive arenas of the Renaissance can begin to suggest a perspective from which modern critical practice can more fully discover the dynamics influencing the evolution of gender meaning in early modern England.[41] The final goal of such a project is, ideally, to establish a

[41]Throughout this study I continually stress that I am studying homoeroticism as it affects epistemology primarily to demonstrate that I am involved in a process of *interpreting* the past, not simply documenting it. I do this in order to separate my aims from those of the increasing and fascinating field that has come to be known as "gay history"—that is, the "collation" of a homosexual past. The practice of gay history, I feel, sometimes

system in which such a project would be unnecessary. The goal is not so much to establish the place of homoeroticism in a critical practice as it is to use homoeroticism as a way of forging a critical practice that finally effaces the manifest validity of gendered and sexualized meaning altogether by demarcating absolutely its social and historical contingency. Such a goal will not be realized in the chapters that follow. Rather, the more modest purpose here is to demonstrate that the rhetorical and epistemological development of Renaissance sodomy on the one hand marks the birth of modern sexual and gender epistemology as we know it, but on the other hand also encodes the potential for radical disruption of that meaning. This recognition of radical potentiality within the constructs of the Renaissance will not only liberate the past from a critical heritage of interpretation intent on making gender mean

---

risks atemporalizing our current definition of homosexuality by suggesting that it is a valid matrix for redividing the past. But this theoretical stance should not be taken as a derogation of the important and empowering work in the field of gay history; indeed, certain works in the field have greatly influenced my own thinking: K. J. Dover, *Greek Homosexuality* (New York, 1978), and Bernard Sergent, *Homosexuality in Greek Myth* (Boston, 1984), on the classical period; John Boswell, *Christianity, Social Tolerance, and Homosexuality: Gay People in Western Europe from the Beginning of the Christian Era to the Fourteenth Century* (Chicago, 1980), on the early Christian era; Jonathan Katz, *Gay American History: Lesbians and Gay Men in the U.S.A.* (New York, 1976), and Martin Bauml Duberman, *About Time: Exploring the Gay Past* (New York, 1986), on American history. For a representative selection of essays about gay history, as well as an examination of some of the problems of gay historiography, see *The Gay Past: A Collection of Historical Essays*, ed. Salvatore J. Licata and Robert P. Petersen (New York, 1985).

My use of the term *epistemology* to mark a distinction in my own work is itself problematic. As some postmodernists have suggested, the very concept of epistemology presupposes a division between "things" and "concepts" that works against the post-Saussurean conception of phenomenology (Barry Hindess and Paul Hirst, *Modes of Production and Social Formation* [London, 1977], pp. 10–33). But for my purposes I am using the term to indicate that I am studying homoeroticism not for what it *was*, but rather for how it was *thought*. Therefore, my study works within the same general problematics sketched by David M. Halperin (*One Hundred Years of Homosexuality and Other Essays on Greek Love* [London, 1989]) in the classical era and Stephen Orgel ("Nobody's Perfect") in the Renaissance.

one way; it will also suggest, perhaps, the course toward a future free from the tyranny of gendered meaning in general.

Sodomy and Interpretation

My purpose throughout this book is monocular and insistent: to read Renaissance sodomy. But with this said, I must also note that, like Renaissance sodomy itself, my purpose also unravels multivalently. On the simplest level my text is bifurcated because I want to present chapters that contribute to an accumulated argument but that also might be of benefit to readers individually. This structure requires that some pieces of data be repeated in different chapters, especially those from the introduction that are sometimes resituated within different arguments. But my text is double-voiced in another way. Although I continually return to the actual language of the Renaissance to make my points, I have also unavoidably been influenced by current theoretical debates on the interpretation of gender and sexuality. Some of these arise during the course of my arguments (although I have for the most part relegated them to footnotes in the hopes of achieving a narrative coherence), but I would like here to outline some of the dominant problematics that have influenced this work, its position in relation to them, and the effect they may have had on the "historical integrity" of the analysis.

Although my book is in many ways an extended rumination on the question How can we read sodomy?, a prior question this inquiry entails is, *Should* we read sodomy? I do not ask this in the spirit that Jesse Helms or Britain's Clause 28 would ask it. Rather, the latter question, which I do not expressly take up in my text, demands that I situate my own critical stance in relation to the growing industry surrounding the debate between essentialism and constructionism in gender studies. The terms of this debate have been eloquently anatomized and critiqued by Diana Fuss in *Essentially Speaking*, and I refer any reader unfamiliar with the basic premises of the debate to this intelligent work.[42] My

[42]Diana Fuss, *Essentially Speaking: Nature, Feminism, Difference* (London, 1989).

own position is similar to that of Fuss, in that I am primarily a constructionist—that is, I do not believe that there is an atemporal or "natural" basis for meanings, especially those relating to sex, sexuality, and gender. I also believe, however, that this debate in and of itself is ideologically obfuscating. That is, we are forced by it into a series of issues that for the most part can be reduced to the question of the chicken and the egg—and this question *always* plays back into a system of western control that frustrates our abilities to exercise power in the present by continually telling us that the opportunity to enact change resides in a place that is *always already gone*. The debate is, in short, another expression of a system of power that seeks to keep revolution off the streets and in the past. The debate between essentialism and constructionism, therefore, finds its philosophical analogue in that most ideologically manipulative and central document of power, the Bible, and its own focusing of power on a nostalgic origin: "In the beginning. . . ."[43] I agree with Fuss's strong assertion that an overvaluation of the debate in its entirety has "foreclosed more ambitious investigations of specificity and difference by fostering a certain paranoia around the perceived threat of essentialism,"[44] and I have attempted to avoid this paranoia by "risking" to speak of homoeroticism *as* homoeroticism—as a specifically identifiable phenomenon, even as I acknowledge that all the discourses that variously inscribe this phenomenon are necessarily historically bounded and contingent.

My second reason for determining that we *should* speak of sodomy has to do with how the essentialist/constructionist debate has come to restrict our notions of the historicity of sexual difference. For the most part, the desire to maintain a firmly constructionist ideology has been enacted through the triple division of the past along the axes of "race," "class," and "gender." Gender, we are told, must be read through the contingencies of race and class, class through race and gender, race through class and gender. Such a strategy has allowed us to recognize that

[43]Gen. 1:1.
[44]Fuss, *Essentially Speaking*, p. 1.

certain cultural powers maintain their hegemonic status by diversifying along and impregnating through a complex web (Foucault would call it a knot) of meanings. The strategy involved here, I think, must itself be historicized. For while in the early stages of gender and sexual theorization the trivium represented a powerful attempt at coalition politics, it has also demonstrated a trend toward becoming a troika of containment.[45] That is, the increasingly codified *triangulation* of these three terms has resulted in a practice that dilutes the political efficacy of any one of the terms by continually denying any noncontingent power to them. Additionally, the triangle achieved by the intersection of these axes encloses a relatively small area. And the triangle is *never* pink, for one (and, to my purposes, the primary) factor that is displaced by the analytic grid of race, class, and gender is sexual difference.[46] As Tennessee Williams is rumored to have said

[45]This idea has been somewhat anticipated by Cora Kaplan ("Pandora's Box: Subjectivity, Class, and Sexuality in Socialist Feminist Criticism," in *Making a Difference: Feminist Literary Criticism*, ed. Gayle Greene and Coppelia Kahn [London, 1985]). Although Kaplan does not advocate the "strategic essentialist" position that I outline here, she does articulate a strategy of dialectical interplay that, I think, is representative of the multiple axes system at its most productive and radical stage.

[46]My decision to focus on male-male eroticism in some ways betrays the theoretical stance I am professing here. I have chosen to focus on male sexual difference primarily because (a) it reflects my own sexual/political identity, and critical writing is always to some extent an exercise in (self-) identity politics; and (b) to consider both male and female homoeroticism necessitates a consideration of the axis of gender difference, which, as I outline here, is contrary to my primary theoretical goal. However, as Sue-Ellen Case has perceptively noted in a defense of "queer theory" at the 1990 Santa Cruz conference of the same name, to privilege the separatist position that I am here adopting also mimetically reinscribes the man/woman dichotomy by presupposing that it is a binary that governs sexual orientation. My response is simply to note that *not* to privilege separatist position is also to mimetically reinscribe homophobia, which is at its basic level a belief that sexual orientation alone removes the subject from "nature," "society," and other totalizing schemas. Obviously, neither of these stances is an "answer" but, rather, taken together, they serve to delimit the problematic we are attempting to understand as gay, lesbian, or queer theoretical scholars. Even Fuss, who eloquently articulates the polarities of the debate, can offer no real solution (*Essentially Speaking*, pp. 97–112).

when entering a party where Ernest Hemingway was holding court: "There is no place in this room for a faggot."[47] My primary concern with the triangulation of these variables, however, is not that it excludes my sexual position but that, when codified as *the* triangle, these variables also serve again as a system that solidifies white, straight, masculine hegemonic power. I explain it to my students this way: Imagine for a moment that you are a white, straight male—wouldn't it be nice if the only threats to your position were race, class, and gender?

Throughout this book, therefore, I have adopted as my primary inquisitive strategy a well-turned phrase from Eve Kosofsky Sedgwick: "Let's hypothesize that gay/lesbian and antihomophobic inquiry still has a lot to learn from asking the questions that feminist inquiry has learned to ask—but only so long as we don't demand to receive the same answers."[48] Like Sedgwick, I begin by assuming that we need *not* assume that sexual difference is *necessarily* subordinate to or even contingent on these other axes of power. The result is that I have formed an analysis in which I for the most part consciously avoid asking how homoeroticism is diversified along hegemonic axes of power and focus instead on how, if we momentarily posit a strategic essentialism to the nexus of meanings that is homoeroticism, these hegemonic axes begin to shift, mutate, and otherwise lose their tenuous claims to totalitarian validity. In some places this strategy has led to obvious elisions in certain texts. For example, I devote a rather long section to an analysis of the disruption of heteroerotic desire in Christopher Marlowe's *Hero and Leander*. The presence of Leander, it is said, makes "rudest peasant" and "barbarous Thracian soldier" alike melt with passion. Obviously the threat here is not

[47]This problem is strikingly borne out by *Critical Terms for Literary Study*, ed. Frank Lentricchia and Thomas McLaughlin (Chicago, 1990). Even a cursory glance at the chapter of this much heralded anthology titled "Literature, Culture, Politics" (pp. 225–320) reveals that *after* "culture," "canon," and "literary history" come "gender," "race," "ethnicity," and "ideology"—but nothing else. The priorities marked here, as well as the silences inscribed, perfectly support my claims.

[48]Eve Kosofsky Sedgwick, "Across Gender, Across Sexuality: Willa Cather and Others," in *Displacing Homophobia*, ed. Butters, Clum, and Moon, p. 54.

just in the ability of Leander to initiate male-male desire but also in the way this desire transgresses class and occupational divisions.[49] But rather than focus on the fact that the threat of homoerotic desire is here expressed along the axis of class anxiety, I focus instead on the fact that it is presented. In other words, I strike a mark between *what* is presented and the *mode* of representation, believing that there is still much that we can learn by (as pure constructionists would tell us, [ph]allaciously) deploying a conscious and (I hope) responsible degree of essentialism within our inquiry into the constructionism of the past.

The argument breaks down into four segments. In Chapter 2 I analyze how sodomy is integral to the mediation of cultural order as expressed in, first, Shakespeare's *Troilus and Cressida* and, second, the large canon of writings about the life of Edward II. Shakespeare's play, I claim, demonstrates that the construction of the sodomite as an absolute other to social order was, in reality, an effort to give the sodomite a place of utility within the maintenance of social order. This dialectic of exclusion/ inclusion is fully operative in a number of "historical" tracts written about the life of Edward II in the Elizabethan and Jacobean period. I go on to analyze how these tracts constitute an effort to give rise to a coherent narrative of cultural power—and how this effort is exposed and undercut in Marlowe's *Edward II*. The process that sodomy exemplifies in these writings is, I claim, central to the very epistemological basis of how Renaissance

[49]The institutionalization of "race, class, and gender" also in many ways has effaced the historical variability of them. For example, while I am using "class" here in order to demonstrate that I am aware of certain elisions in my argument, it is also true that I recognize an implicit difficulty in speaking of "class" in precapitalist societies. As Marx has argued—and as I agree—class formation is contingent on the various modes of production and material commodification within a culture (see Karl Marx, "The Materialist Concept of History," in *Marxism: Essential Writings*, ed. David McLellan [Oxford, 1988], pp. 3–19). Thus, the very import of "class" from current theorizations of it into the Elizabethan culture that produced *Hero and Leander* may be anachronistic, because the modes of production differed greatly from ours today. A similar complexity can arise with issues of gender and has been explored provocatively by Joan Kelly, *Women, History, and Theory: The Essays of Joan Kelly* (Chicago, 1984), pp. 1–18, 19–50.

culture "thought" political power, and I demonstrate this centrality through a brief analysis of Hobbes's *Leviathan* and its peculiar construction of "Man."

In Chapter 3 I flip the perspective. The representations of Edward II show how orthodox systems rely on a mutability of homoerotic meaning, but other discursive arenas, I claim, practice their own strategic essentialism—momentarily "freeze" the vacillating category of sodomy and thereby watch other more orthodox codes of power spin around it. I focus my argument in this chapter on romances and erotic narratives. Much of this poetry has been marginalized as either overtly precious or trivially aesthetic. However, these poems also expose some very basic contradictions within the language of desire and decorum during the Renaissance, and in several texts the means to this exposition is the representation of homoeroticism. I begin by setting forth this argument as it can be seen in advice epistles from fathers to sons and also in occasional poetry appended to epyllia. Taken together, these texts demonstrate a conception of desire that parallels contemporary poststructuralist theorizations of desire as a system of metaphysics. In Sidney's *Old Arcadia* this metaphysics of desire is demonstrated by the striking of an opposition between the heteroerotic main narrative and a preexisting realm of meaning that is figured through distinctly homoerotic representation. The ability to pinpoint a metaphysics of desire in the Renaissance, I claim, indicates that certain structures that we think of as being definitive of the period were actually in contest—and I demonstrate this point in a final section that contrasts two epyllia, Weever's *Faunus and Melliflora* and Marlowe's *Hero and Leander*. Both poems employ homoerotic imagery, and both take as their primary topic the critique of dynastic (or patrilineal) sexual decorum. Yet there is a decisive difference between the two, for Weever's poem seeks to purify the meaning of heteroeroticism while Marlowe's seeks to undermine it. This difference is also reflected in the contrasting ways in which each poem figures the rhetorical space of homoeroticism. In Weever's poem patrilineal desire is a "given" and homoeroticism is placed within it; in Marlowe's poem homoeroticism is the "given" and patrilineal desire is shown to be a partial and sometimes impotent discourse in relation to it.

In Chapter 4 I move from the realm of cultural poetics to the poetics of the subject. Much energy has been expended on determining how we can read the subject of Renaissance sodomy, and in this chapter I attempt to problematize this issue further by demonstrating that the rhetoric of Renaissance sodomy was not indicative of an absolute otherness but, rather, was viewed as a subjectively inscriptive discourse—but the ways in which it inscribed its subject betray how we usually talk about subjective inscription. My argument focuses primarily on the sonnet sequences of Barnfield and Shakespeare. In each case I argue that what has been thought of as "homosexual" and "gay" in these sequences is not that at all; instead it is part of a more complicated strategy of subject construction. Both sequences "make" homoerotic "sense," but with the end of creating a space of subjectivity that is something else altogether. I suggest that the most appropriate way to think of the subject in these sequences is as a sub*junct*; that is, both sequences inscribe sexual meaning, but to the end of creating a subject only tangentially related to the juncture of these determining discourses. I also attempt in this chapter to place this concept of subjunctivity within broader frames of Renaissance subjectivity, first by situating it within the sonnet tradition as a whole, especially within Sidney's *Apology*, and second by showing it to be analogous to Hamlet's conception of self-meaning in Shakespeare's play.

Finally, in Chapter 5 I suggest that what can be gleaned from the manipulations of the subject in the sonnet tradition is that Renaissance sodomy does not "mean" but, rather, is "negotiated." For in all these analyses the common denominator is a space between what is said and what is meant; by that I mean that we can read an inscriptive ability in the Renaissance rhetoric of sodomy, but this inscription is typically in the service of some ulterior inscription. This multiplicity, I claim, becomes more pronounced as we progress into literature of the later Renaissance. I demonstrate this point through an analysis of Milton's major poetry, especially *Paradise Regained*. Milton's brief epic pointedly engages traditions that had been honed to inscribe sexual difference over the course of a hundred years or so, but with the goal of inscribing an even greater difference. Milton's poem, I claim, speaks the sodomite—but to the end of speaking otherwise. And in this doubleness of speech, we also find, perhaps, a way to a new writing, a means of recuperating the historicity of sexual difference in its own terms and in its own times.

CHAPTER 2

The Authority of Sodomy

> The ass is the secret femininity of males, their passivity.
>
> —Jean-Paul Sartre

> My attitude toward anybody's sexual persuasion is this: without deviation from the norm, progress is not possible.
>
> —Frank Zappa

Constructing Patroclus

In Shakespeare's *Troilus and Cressida*, Thersites, the "scurrilous and deformed" Greek, labels Patroclus as "Achilles' brach," "Achilles' male varlet" and Achilles' "Masculine whore."[1] Coming from the base railer of the Greeks, such gibes are perhaps easily ignored or attributed to the deformities of the cur's mind. Thersites is, after all, the first to call Cressida a whore, the first to associate Pandarus the man with the derogatory term *pander*, and the first to lower Menelaus and Paris from the level of military heroes to the level of "the cuckold and the cuckold-maker" (V.vii.9); the mind of Thersites is as he describes the world of the play: "Lechery, lechery, still wars and lechery! Nothing else holds fashion" (V.ii.193–194). And yet none of these sexual railings have provoked quite the same critical response as Thersites' construction of Patroclus as a catamite. Kenneth Palmer, in annotating the Arden edition of the play, goes to great lengths to erase the homoerotic connotations of these speeches. Using the example of "brach," he states: "In view of Achilles' comment, it seems unlikely that Thersites meant (or was taken to mean) that Pa-

[1]William Shakespeare, *Troilus and Cressida*, ed. Kenneth Palmer (London, 1982), II.ii.116, V.i.14–16. All subsequent citations will be to this edition.

troclus was a catamite."[2] And when Thersites' dialogue achieves an unmistakable sexual connotation with "male varlet," Palmer takes refuge in the fact that even if Thersites actually does mean to suggest a sexual relation between Achilles and Patroclus, "there is no certainty that [his] imputation . . . is correct."[3] Such editorializing, as well as carrying an air of repressive modesty, entirely misses the point of Thersites as a character.[4] As with many Shakespearian railers, the purpose of Thersites is, to borrow from Lear's fool, to "teach thee a speech" (I.iv.113), and the speech he teaches is precisely that which Palmer resists: the political discourse of Renaissance sodomy.

Thersites' edificatory purposes derive from his relationship to satire, a genre that throughout the Jacobean Renaissance almost compulsively returned to the topic of homoeroticism as a mode of social regulation. The prevalence of homoerotic allusions within Renaissance satires is easily documented. Richard Brathwait, for example, dedicates his *Strappado for the Divell* to "Ladies, Monkies, Parachitoes, Mar-/ mosites and Catamitoes."[5] John Donne, in his first satire, returns to these sodomitical tropics to slur the dandy "that dost not onely approve, / But in ranke itchie lust, desire, and love / The nakednesse and barenesse to enjoy, / Of thy plumpe muddy whore, or prostitute boy."[6] Ben Jonson's description of Sir Voluptuous Beast tells how "*Beast* instructs his faire, and innocent wife, / In the past pleasures of his sensuall life. . . . / And how his *Ganimede* mov'd,"[7] and Richard Middleton's *Epigrams and Satyres* describes the drunken Longatoe, who, "like a Catamite, kist all men about him, / While they laught at his follie and did flout him."[8] The writer who is today

[2]Ibid., p. 156.

[3]Ibid., p. 263.

[4]The desire to "read out" the homoerotic possibilities of the play is further refuted by the occurrence of both Achilles and Patroclus in the Renaissance lexicography of homoeroticism; see Cooper, *Bibliotheca*, sig. TTTiii, and Marlowe's *Edward II*, I.iv.395–396.

[5]Brathwait, *Strappado*, sig. A9.

[6]Donne, *Complete Poetry*, p. 122.

[7]Ben Jonson, *Ben Jonson: Works*, ed. C. H. Herford and Percy Simpson (Oxford, 1925–1952), 8, p. 34.

[8]Richard Middleton, *Epigrams*, p. 9.

perhaps the most famous of all the Renaissance satirists, John Marston, also provides the most numerous examples of satire's affinity for sodomitical allusions. *The Scourge of Villanie* attacks at various points "some pedant Tutor" who "in his bed/Should use my frie, like Phrigian *Ganimede*," "Yon effeminate sanguine *Ganimede*" who "is but a bever, hunted for the bed," Luscus, who "hath his *Ganimede*, / His perfum'd she-goat, smooth kembd & high fed," "yon gallant in the sumptuous clothes" who shows a propensity for "Sodome beastlines," and another gallant who has a "*Ganimede* . . . that doth grace / [his] heeles . . . One *who for two daies space / Is closely hyred*."[9]

In all of these examples the recourse to homoeroticism is part of a larger strategy of social exclusion. Through the pejorative display of social deviance, satires such as these attempt to isolate and expel elements that threaten the integrity of orthodox social structures.[10] This essentially conservative purpose is best exemplified in Richard Brathwait's *Placentia*, where the poet describes his self-perceived mission:

I have no Rhetoricke but bluntnesse I,
Nor knew I ever now to face a lye;
As many can, yea, and some great ones too,
As our Court-Apple-Sqires, and fauns can doe:
I doe cashiere all private Parasites,
Ladie-fied Monkeys, lustful Catomytes,
Painting, and pushing, sleeking of the skin,
Pandring of hayre, to let temptation in.[11]

[9]Marston, *Scourge*, sigs. C5, F3, C4, E6v–E7r, p. 51.

[10]More than almost any other genre, satire has provoked prolonged rumination on the relationship between literary production and social purpose. Even Alastair Fowler, who consistently views literature as a self-referential discourse, recognizes that "a radical moral stance is perhaps the most striking feature of the satiric repertoire" (Alastair Fowler, *Kinds of Literature: An Introduction to the Theory of Genres and Modes* [Cambridge, 1982], p. 110) and additionally claims that it is the social referentiality of satire that has made it one of the most frequently censored genres (p. 215). A similar view can also be found in Harry Levin, "The Wages of Satire," in *Literature and Society*, ed. Edward W. Said (Baltimore, 1980), pp. 5, 1–14 passim.

[11]Brathwait, *Times Curtaine Drawne*, sig. F7v.

Or, as he states in *Panedone*,

> O let these Mirrors (I will say no more)
> Which have divulg'd their fame so long before,
> Be Annalls or Records for us to read,
> That as we imitate them, so our seede,
> Carefull preservers of our Memorie,
> May stampe like formes in their posteritie.[12]

In prose his point becomes even more blunt: "When the natures of men are deere perverted, then it is high time for the Satyrist to pen something which may divert them from their impietie, and direct them in the course and progresse of Vertue."[13] For Brathwait, the purpose of the satirist is, as he states in *Times Anatomie*, to create "harsh-tun'd Poems for my countries sake".[14] He is by no means alone in this view. Nicholas Breton prefaces *The Good and the Badde* with an epistle that claims: "I am sure that if you read thorough this Booke, you will finde your description in one place or other: if among the Worthies, holde you where you are, and change not your Carde for a worse: If among the other, mend that is amisse and all will be well."[15] In a similar vein, Thomas Middleton's epistle casts the satirist as a hero:

> And I account him as a Traytor to Vertue, who diving into the deepe of this cunning Age, and finding there such Monsters of nature, such speckled lumps of poyson, an Pandars, Harlots, and Ruffians do figure, if hee rise up silent again, and neither discover or publish them to the civil Ranck of sober and continent Livers, who thereby may shunne those two devouring Gulfes: to wit, of Deceit and Luxury, which swallow up more Mortals, then *Scylla* and *Charibdis*, those two Cormorants & Woolners of the Sea.[16]

[12]Ibid., sig. L5r.

[13]Brathwait, *Nature's Embassie: or, the Wilde-mans Measures* (London, 1621), sig. A2.

[14]Brathwait, *Times Curtaine Drawne*, sig. B3.

[15]Nicholas Breton, *The Good and the Badde, or Descriptions of the Worthies and Unworthies of this Age* (London, 1616), sig. A4.

[16]Thomas Middleton, *Blacke Booke*, sig. A3.

In all of these formulations satire is a social regulator that vividly displays exemplars of "low" or deviant modes that, by contrast, solidify the "high" or orthodox modes that are not present but are clearly invoked through a contradistinction; in the process it enacts a social stratification, a system in which "bad" is ascribed, "good" is implied, and order is achieved. It is helpful to think of the satiric mode as something similar to what Steven Mullaney has recently termed "a rehearsal of culture," in that these satires provide spaces in which the Renaissance culture could manipulate or "play" with its own self-constructed identity.[17] Satires provide a particularly effective stage for such rehearsals, for, in addition to their internal stratification of high and low, they situate themselves within such a hierarchy, clearly labeling themselves as "other" to the higher realms of order and orthodoxy; while satires label what *is* base, they also label themselves *as* base.[18] Brathwait claims that his poems are "portraide by a lesse art-ful fist" and further claims of every satirist that "th'lines he writes (if ought he writes at all) / Are drawne by inke that's mixed most with gall."[19] Marston, at various places, derides his poetry as "base ballad stuff," "serius iest, and iesting seriosnes" written in "rough-hew'd rimes," and "idle rimes" "in such shapeless formes, / That want of Art."[20] Established as the base, gross and low, satire in turn becomes a discursive arena in which the low can be constructed with no possibility whatsoever that this low will infiltrate the high.

The parallels between satire as a genre and Thersites as a character are obvious, and it is probably not too farfetched to label Thersites as a personification of satire. Thersites' penchant for lechery manages to replicate almost the entire inventory of standard satiric topics. Moreover, Thersites himself offers an

[17]Steven Mullaney, "Strange Things, Gross Terms, Curious Customs: The Rehearsal of Cultures in the Late Renaissance," *Representations* 3 (1983): 53–62.

[18]This structure is not original to the Renaissance. It dates at least as far back as Horace, who, in the *Satires* (I.4.39–39), derogates satire as being alien to the *mens divinior*. See C. O. Brink, *Horace on Poetry: Prolegomena to the Literary Epistle* (Cambridge, 1963), pp. 161–163.

[19]Brathwait, *Strappado*, pp. 2–3.

[20]Marston, *Scourge*, sigs. D8, F5, E4v–E5r.

explanation of his purpose that seems to imitate those of other satirists. As he says, "With too much blood and too little brain these two may run mad, but if with too much brain and too little blood they do, *I'll be the curer of madmen*" (V.i.47–49, my emphasis). Most important, while Thersites doggedly pursues the identification of the low, he himself also is devalued. Like the grotesque genre of satire, Thersites is a grotesque character, a bastard "scurrilous and deformed," a "vinewd'st leaven" and "whoreson cur" (II.i.14, 42), as Ajax calls him. The importance of Thersites' physical appearance is clarified by the words of another satirist, Philip Stubbes, who in *The Anatomie of Abuses* offers this formula, a commonplace in satires:

> If the least or meanest member of thy whole body be hurt, wounded, cicatrized, or brused, doeth not the heart, and every member of the body, feele the anguish and payne of the greeved parte, seeking and endevoring, by all meanes possible . . . , to repaire the same, and never ioying untill it be restored againe to his former integrity and perfection?[21]

The deformed outward shape is symbolic of an *entire* deformity. Like satirists, who cast their poems as devalued discourses, the play casts Thersites as a devalued speaker, a character whose very body imitates the decayed and bilious genre of the satire.

Thersites, then, is presented in discursive and generic terms designed specifically to draw attention to the sodomitical references that criticism has effaced. His affinity for the tropics of satiric sodomy is again reinforced by a recurrence of stories of Troy and of Troilus and Cressida as topics of satires during the Renaissance. Thomas Middleton's *Micro-cynicon* includes a lengthy satyre on "Ingling *Pyander*," a title that immediately states an affinity between the story of Troilus and Cressida and the language of sodomy.[22] Brathwait, too, engages the story. His satire of "The Conniborrowe" labels it as a "new *Troy*," which, like its namesake, is a place "where every female sinner / Resem-

[21]Philip Stubbes, *The Anatomie of Abuses* (London, 1585), p. 6.

[22]Thomas Middleton, *Micro-cynicon: Sixe Snarling Satyres* (London, 1599), sigs. C4v–C5r.

bles th'Moone, that has a man within her."[23] Although Brathwait's poem does not engage the topic of sodomy per se, it does clearly inscribe an association between stories of Troy and topics of sexual transgression within the Renaissance satiric tradition.

If the classificatory strategies of satire seem patently arbitrary and reductive, that is precisely the point, and it is precisely the point of the play's casting Thersites as a personification of satire. For there is nothing in the play to substantiate Thersites' bitter condemnations as more than mere possibilities. Especially in his construction of Patroclus these slurs seem fictitious. The action of the play does, indeed, demonstrate a certain bond between Patroclus and Achilles, but Patroclus himself transcends the base connotations of the labels applied to him. The course of the play most frequently presents Patroclus in the role of mediator, placating Thersites and arbitrating Ajax's headstrong combat with the railer (II.i). Moreover, when Patroclus dies, he dies in an almost epic catalogue of heroes presented by Agamemnon:

> The fierce Polydamas
> Hath beat down Menon; bastard Margarelon
> Hath Doreus prisoner,
> And stands colossus-wise, waving his beam,
> Upon the pashed corses of the kings
> Epistrophus and Cedius. Polixenes is slain;
> Amphimacus and Thoas deadly hurt;
> Patroclus ta'en or slain; and Palamedes
> Sore hurt and bruis'd.
>
> (V.v.6–14)

Nestor then orders the soldiers to "go bear Patroclus' body to Achilles" (V.v.17), and the image is complete: far from the minion depicted early in the play, Patroclus is now defined by a heroic idiom of war, blood, and death. The juxtaposition of Thersites' sodomitical Patroclus to this more heroic Patroclus begins to suggest a critique of satire and its strategies of social hierarchicalization. For if the image of a debased Patroclus is false, then the hierarchy of high and low achieved in Thersites'

[23]Brathwait, *Strappado*, pp. 151–152.

railing must also be false. This skepticism of stratification assumes an even more important level in the play than simply casting doubt on Thersites' commentary. Thersites constructs an image of Patroclus that is an absolute "other" to orthodox order—an otherness achieved through the construction of Patroclus as a sodomite—and the play itself in turn radically critiques this order by demonstrating that this image is not just a part of the low satiric idioms but also central to the high political machinations of the Greeks.

The intersection of Thersites' low discourse and the high orders of the Greek world occurs, significantly, in the most discursively ordered scene in the play, the famous Greek Council scene (I.iii). The scene begins with a speech by Agamemnon that echoes political primers of the Jacobean and Elizabethan eras:

> The ample proposition that hope makes
> In all designs begun on earth below
> Fails in the promis'd largeness: checks and disasters
> Grow in the veins of actions highest rear'd,
> As knots, by the conflux of meeting sap,
> Infects the sound pine and diverts his grain
> Tortive and errant from his course of growth.
>
> (I.iii.3–9)

In contrast to Thersites, who focuses specifically on deviations and affronts to order, Agamemnon speaks a language of absolute order, one in which seemingly gratuitous "checks and disasters" are, like knots in a pine, part of a divine design. Aberrations are puzzling only from the "earth below"; from a proper vantage point the hierarchy governing the world is a perfectly coherent text:

> Why then, you princes,
> Do you with cheeks abash'd behold our works,
> And call them shames which are indeed naught else
> But the protractive trials of great Jove
> To find persistive constancy in men,

The fineness of which metal is not found
In fortunes love?

(I.iii.17–23)

Agamemnon's speech has been compared to any number of possible sources—Elyot's *The Governour*, the homily *Of Obedience*, Aristotle's *Ethics*, Boethius's *De Consolatione Philosophiae*. Yet the specific source of the oration is not as important as its status as a reflection of a topos that permeated the Elizabethan and Jacobean ethos. Notably, the structure of the oration also presents the topos as a contradictory and inconsistent discourse. In describing the necessity of such "protractive trials," Agamemnon also unintentionally validates the possibility of a relationally (rather than absolutely) defined world:

For then the bold and coward,
The wise and fool, the artist and unread,
The hard and soft, seem all affin'd and kin;
But in the wind and tempest of her frown,
Distinction, with a broad and powerful fan
Puffing at all, winnows the light away,
And what hath mass or matter by itself
Lies rich in virtue and unmingled.

(I.iii.23–30)

The strong allegiance to order in Agamemnon's speech masks a recognition of its antithesis: the possibility that all is but chance; as Nestor phrases it, "In the reproof of chance / Lies the true proof of men" (I.iii.33–34). The end to this "tale of length" about degree is a startlingly relativistic formulation: "Troy in our weakness stands, not in her strength" (I.iii.137). Agamemnon's speech, so often taken as a one of the great Shakespearian statements of universal teleology, actually destabilizes the order it professes: there is the precept of order, the praxis of a war unwon, and no way to cohere these disparate themes.

This slippage in the rhetoric of order is also present in the most famous speech of the play, Ulysses' sixty-three-line *amplificatio* of Agamemnon's theme:

> The heavens themselves, the planets, and this centre
> Observe degree, priority, and place,
> Insisture, course, proportion, season, form,
> Office, and custom, in all line of order.
>
> (I.iii.85–88)

The teleology described here is responsible for virtually all worldly structures, and it is dependent on one dominant concept: degree.

> O, when degree is shak'd,
> Which is the ladder of all high designs,
> The enterprise is sick. How could communities,
> Degrees in schools, and brotherhoods in cities,
> Peaceful commerce from dividable shores,
> The primogenity and due of birth,
> Prerogative of age, crowns, sceptres, laurels,
> But by degree stand in authentic place?
> Take but degree away, untune that string,
> And hark what discord follows.
>
> (I.iii.101–110)

Again, Ulysses' rhetoric betrays a certain potentiality for slippage, for if degree is the necessary precondition for divine hierarchy, then men should be dependent on it, not it on men. Yet Ulysses's formulation seems to imply that order is a function of men's will to have it exist. As he says, "Degree being vizarded, / Th'unworthiest shows as fairly in the mask" (I.iii.83–84). Implicit in this statement is a hidden problem of agency: who does the vizarding? For if Jove controls degree, then it is never vizarded but only changed into a further "protractive trial"; but if Jove does not control degree, then not everything is ascribed a place in divine hierarchy, and the manifest validity of the hierarchy is negated. This question, indeed, is the simple but fatal indeterminacy underlying the entire scene; the question is, Does hierarchy inscribe men, or do men inscribe hierarchy—is order a matter of precept or of praxis? The philosophical problem beneath the rhetoric of the Greek council scene, then, is the anxious possibility that precept and praxis are not separate epistemological realms but, rather, are arbitrary divisions that randomly intermingle and exist coterminously.

The Greeks' strategy for redividing the tenets of their epistemology is, importantly, a recourse to the base idioms of Thersites' sodomitical discourse. The only solution offered to "the sickness found" (I.iii.140) is Ulysses' (re)construction of the catamitical Patroclus:

> The great Achilles, whom opinion crowns
> The sinew and the forehand of our host,
> Having his ear full of airy fame,
> Grows dainty of his worth, and in his tent
> Lies mocking our designs: with him Patroclus
> Upon a lazy bed the livelong day
> Breaks scurril jests,
> And with ridiculous and awkward action,
> Which, slanderer, he imitation calls,
> He pageants us.
>
> (I.iii.142–151)

This oration depicts Achilles as a debauched man entertaining a minion who basks on the couch and bitchily derides the Greek order. Like Thersites' construction of Patroclus, Ulysses' accusation clearly focuses on homoeroticism as an absolute base "other" to the world of order. His condemnation relies on images of imitation and pageantry, all theatrical in nature and hence suggesting a fake or artificial dimension. He continues:

> Sometime, great Agamemnon,
> Thy topless deputation he puts on,
> And like a strutting player, whose conceit
> Lies in his hamstring and doth think it rich
> To hear the wooden dialogue and sound
> 'Twixt his stretch'd footing and the scaffoldage,
> Such to-be-pitied and o'er-wrested seeming
> He acts thy greatness in; and when he speaks,

'Tis like a chime a-mending, with terms unsquar'd,
Which, from the tongue of roaring Typhon dropp'd,
Would seem hyperboles.

(I.iii.151–161)

The Patroclus constructed here is absolutely artificial and artificially bad. He struts like a player, sounds like a chime, and speaks in "terms unsquar'd" and hyperbole. Patroclus, claims Ulysses, specifically foregrounds the artificiality of theatrical presentation—something that cannot be tolerated in this world that is, after all, entirely theatrical:

And in this fashion
All our abilities, gifts, natures, shapes,
Severals and generals of grace exact,
Achievements, plots, orders, preventions,
Excitements to the field, or speech for truce,
Success or loss, what is or is not, serves
As stuff for these two to make paradoxes.

(I.iii.178–184)

Ulysses' recourse to theatrical metaphors fully inscribes his discourse within the low arenas of satiric sodomy, for throughout the Renaissance satirists intervalidated theatrical derogation and sodomitical stigmatism;[24] Edward Guilpin, to note but one ex-

[24]In addition to the associations with satire, Ulysses' theatrical metaphor would have carried particularly indecorous connotations in Renaissance minds, since Ulysses quite literally derides Patroclus for being a "boy actor," a problematic occupation that carried with it numerous sexual connotations. See Katherine Eisaman Maus, "Horns of Dilemma: Jealousy, Gender, and Spectatorship in English Renaissance Drama," *ELH* 54 (1987): 561–582; Lisa Jardine, *Still Harping on Daughters: Women and Drama in the Age of Shakespeare* (Brighton, 1983), pp. 9–33; and Orgel, "Nobody's Perfect," pp. 7–30. Linda Charnes provides an intelligent discussion of how this theatrical metaphor plays into a broader strategy "in which the play both posits and deconstructs an essentialist 'reading' of the characters" (Linda Charnes, "'So Unsecret to Ourselves': Notorious Identity and the Material Subject in Shakespeare's *Troilus and Cressida*," *Shakespeare Quarterly* 40, 4 [1989]: 432).

ample, derides the "fine fellow" "who is at every play, and every night / Sups with his *Ingles*. . . ."[25]

Ulysses' construction of Patroclus on one level replicates the intentions of Renaissance satire. Like, say, Marston or Brathwait, Ulysses is "mirroring" a "sickness found" in the hopes of isolating and expelling it. However, the play's careful correlation of Thersites' satiric railing and Ulysses' ordered oration also collapses the empowering division between high and low discursive arenas, and it further demonstrates that the sodomitical allusions within the play do not specify sexual difference so much as they open up a vast and complicated network of political meanings. This collapse and rupture is again apparent in the council scene. After Aeneas delivers the battle challenge from Hector, Ulysses begins to form his plan in a distinctly different rhetorical mode: "I have a young conception in my brain: / Be you my time to bring it to some shape" (I.iii.311–312). He is no longer delivering an oration about the shape of platonic order but is now attempting to order a shape for the exigencies of the present moment.[26] Moreover, like Thersites' construction of Patroclus, which ultimately is undercut by the action of the play, Ulysses' construction is also revealed to be at most false and at least misplaced:

> Blunt wedges rive hard knots; the seeded pride
> That hath to this maturity blown up
> In rank Achilles must or now be cropp'd,
> Or, shedding, breed a nursery of like evil
> To overbulk us all.
>
> (I.iii.315–319)

[25]Guilpin, *Skialethia*, sig. B1.

[26]Ulysses' actions at this point recall Greenblatt's formulation of improvisation as it relates to Iago: "the ability both to capitalize on the unforeseen and to transform given materials into one's own scenario" (Stephen Greenblatt, *Renaissance Self-Fashioning from More to Shakespeare* [Chicago, 1980], p. 227). Iago is more of a subaltern figure than Ulysses, and thus in the Greeks' world we see another dimension added to Greenblatt's formulation: the ability of an agent with access to centralized power to *create* the materials on which he will capitalize.

The problem is no longer, nor has it ever been, the sexual actions of Patroclus. The problem is Achilles' "pride"—at least according to Ulysses—and the foregrounding of Patroclus' catamitical possibilities has been merely a convenient "use" of sodomy designed to destroy Achilles.

The personal motive underlying, as well as the arbitrariness of, Ulysses' construction of Patroclus is continually foregrounded as Ulysses improvises his plan and the Greek council gradually abandons its original allegiance to divine order. Nestor recognizes that in the "sportful combat . . . much opinion dwells" (I.iii.335–336), and Ulysses knows that "the lustre of the better shall exceed / By showing the worse first" (I.ii.361–362). Degree is no longer a precept but a matter of praxis; in a remarkable tour-de-force of sophistry, Ulysses explains how the *mutability* of meaning can serve the Greeks in battle:

> What glory our Achilles shares from Hector,
> Were he not proud, we all should share with him;
> But he already is too insolent,
> And it were better parch in Afric sun
> Than in the pride and salt scorn of his eyes,
> Should he 'scape Hector fair. If he were foil'd,
> Why then we did our main opinion crush
> In taint of our best man. No, make a lott'ry,
> And by device let blockish Ajax draw
> The sort to fight with Hector. Among ourselves
> Give him allowance for the better man;
> For that will physic the great Myrmidon,
> Who broils in loud applause, and make him fall
> His crest that prouder than blue Iris bends.
> If the dull brainless Ajax come safe off,
> We'll dress him up in voices: if he fail,
> Yet go we under our opinion still
> That we have better men.
>
> (I.iii.367–384)

Again, this use of teleological slippage serves more of a purpose than merely saving face, for Ulysses ends his advice with his by now redundant theme: "Ajax employ'd plucks down Achilles' plumes" (I.iii.386). And the idea of a rigged lottery provides an ironically deflating embodiment of Nestor's earlier theoretical position that "in the reproof of chance / Lies true proof of men" (I.iii.33–34).

Ulysses' construction of Patroclus, then, leads the Greek world of precept into the mutable world of improvised praxis—the very world that the construction of Patroclus originally sought to efface. The point of Ulysses' "solution," then, is clear: behind the rhetoric of order rests a reliance on chaos; beyond the precept of politic theory is a praxis of mutability and individual difference. Precept and praxis conflate in the play's figure of homoeroticism, for Patroclus the catamite is at once what the Greek world does not want and what it can most fortuitously use. Sodomy and related areas of homoerotic meaning, then, do not just delineate the division between high and low—do not just make the stuff of satire; rather, they also demarcate the point at which high and low meet and may be transversed. There is an affinity between the representation of sodomy and the depiction of politic failure, for sodomy, a category that both creates and destroys a division between high and low, exists in the artificial but crucial space that teleological theory inserts between precept and praxis, between order and chaos, and between Man and men. The construction and (re)construction of Patroclus, then, begins to suggest the possible role that stigmatized sodomy might play in the construction of order, and, by extension, also suggests the place it might have in current critical practice. The structure of the play presents the discursive construction of order from two perspectives—the low idiom of satire and the high order of politic theory—and then deconstructs the assuredness of these perspectives by demonstrating how they intersect in their uses of sexual difference, an intersection marked vividly by the figure of sodomy. The construction of Patroclus demonstrates the simple but central principle that the articulation of order demands means of accounting for disorder, and these means frequently involve issues of sex, sexuality, and eroticism. Sexual difference functions as an epistemological space that can easily be contorted to account for discrepancies, and this variability of sexual significance is deflatingly exposed in Shakespeare's play.

Troilus and Cressida, then, might best be thought of as a critical primer: it teaches us to read the stigmatized sodomy of Renaissance ideology and, at the same time, teaches us to reread ideology through the figure of sodomy. And in the process it also empowers us to re*write*, to articulate the forces ordering Renaissance culture in their most fragmented and plural form, to create a hermeneutic that can demonstrate the margins within the centers, the lows within the highs, and the sodomy that helps make "history."

Writing Edward II

> Soone after was my fathers Corps inter'd
> Whilst Fate and Fortune did on me attend:
> And to the Royall Throne I was prefer'd.
> With *Ave Caesar* every knee did bend,
> But all these fickle ioyes, did fading end,
> *Peirce Gaveston*, to thee my love combinde:
> My friendship to thee scarce left me a friend,
> But made my Queene, Peeres, People, all unkind,
> I tortur'd, both in body and in mind
> Was vanquisht by the Scots a *Bannocks Bourne*:
> And I enforc't by flight some safety finde,
> Yet taken by my Wife at my returne,
>   A Red-hot spit my Bowels through did gore,
>   Such misery, no Slave endured more.[27]

John Taylor's sonnet on the life of Edward II from *A Briefe Remembrance of All The Englishe Monarchs* is one example from a large group of writings throughout the Renaissance about the infamous heir to Longshank's throne. Most famous of all are the several texts from the late Elizabethan era, Michael Drayton's *Mortimeriados*[28] and *Peirs Gaveston*, and Christopher Marlowe's *Edward II*, but Francis Hubert's 1628 verse chronicle is the long-

[27]John Taylor, *A Briefe Remembrance of All the Englishe Monarchs* (London, 1618), sig. B4.

[28]Drayton later rewrote the poem as *The Barons' War.* Hebel, in Drayton's *Works*, provides a good summary of the major changes in the rewriting.

est account of the king's reign. Ben Jonson's outline for a proposed tragedy about one of the king's peers, Mortimer, under the reign of Edward III, adds another Jacobean entry to the list, and continuing through the Restoration a number of anecdotal summaries of the king's life, all written between 1590 and 1650, were widely reprinted.

Taylor's sonnet is important for more than its choice of subject matter; its rhetoric also demonstrates a sort of ideological interchange that can be explicated by the reading lesson provided in *Troilus and Cressida*. Beginning with the king's rise to the throne, Taylor frames his narrative to stress that fate and fortune, the attendants of royal power, withdrew their favor when Edward "combinde" his love with Pierce Gaveston. After this star-crossed moment the poem suppresses moralizing. The turning of peers and people against the king is unquestioned. The wife's action of "taking" the husband, which directly contradicts typical tenets of domestic decorum, is never commented on. Even the barbarous murder offers few overt morals, as if to imply that the lessons are self-evident: a *contra naturam* love deserves an equally *contra naturam* death. The numerous affronts to "order" present in the incidents in the poems are all elided by the figure of homoerotic love, and the poem, in turn, becomes something like a Thersites or a Ulysses: it negotiates the space between politic order and sodomitical vice so as to efface the mutability of power and praxis that underpins the story.

Taylor's rhetorical strategy is doubtless effected by any number of cultural determinants, but it is also linked intertextually to a strong Elizabethan tradition. The strategy of redacting the political narrative of Edward's reign into an exemplum of sexual ethics is a recurring pattern in writings on the king's life, most notably in Drayton's poems but also as a literary inheritance in works like Taylor's sonnet and Hubert's chronicle.[29] This strat-

[29] Although I do not engage the issue in my analysis, these chronicles also obviously enact Hayden White's formulation of historical writings as "verbal structure[s] in the form of . . . narrative prose discourse[s] that [purport] to be a model, or icon, of past structures and processes in the interest of *explaining what they were by representing* them" (Hayden White, *Metahistory: The Historical Imagination in Nineteenth-Century Europe* [Baltimore, 1973], p. 2).

egy, which uses homoeroticism as a transition point between the realms of the politic (king) and the personal (sodomite), also can provide a transition point from the theatrical world of Shakespeare's Greeks to the historical world of Renaissance England, for the divisions negotiated in writings on Edward II are also the divisions that empowered Elizabethan England as its ordering principles shifted from political theology to political theory. Moreover, the strategy employed in these poems is then exposed to be a politically pragmatic maneuver in Marlowe's *Edward II*. The "writings" of Edward II in the aggregate, then, demonstrate the potentiality engendered in Renaissance figurations of homoeroticism both to construct order and then to mediate the exigencies of accounting for disruptions to order.

The Bod*ies* Politic

To speak of political theory during Elizabethan times is, at best, an anachronism. The Tudor system was more typically characterized by retrospective rationalizations than by prescriptive precepts, and the government was continually mediating between a past theocracy and a present autocracy.[30] The intermediary role of political discourse during the years between the death of Henry VIII and the coronation of James I resulted in several hybrid stratagems that both foreshadow the Jacobean hierarchical commonwealth and recall medieval structures of cosmic religious unification. The hybridization most central to an understanding of the representations of Edward II is the Elizabethan inheritance of the doctrine of the king's two bodies. When jurists in 1561 overturned Elizabeth's desire to rescind land grants made by Edward VI, they created a report that outlines the Elizabethan understanding of this doctrine:

[30] Brian O. Smith, *The Crown and the Commonwealth* (Philadelphia, 1977), focuses on the image of Elizabethan political doctrine as a holdover of medieval theology. I find Smith's study to be convincing, but here I am primarily using the phrase "theocracy" as a convenient way of distinguishing Elizabethan precepts from the prescriptive theoretical doctrine that emerged under James. J. W. Allen, *A History of Political Thought in the Sixteenth Century* (New York, 1928), provides an excellent survey of political philosophy during this period that complements my current interest.

> Altho' the natural Body of the King is subject to Infancy, yet when the Body politic is conjoind with it, and one Body is made of them both, the whole Body shall have all the Properties, Qualities and Degrees of the Body politic which is the greater and more worthy, and in which there is not nor can be any Infancy.[31]

The structure delineated here is one in which the temporal body of the monarch exists coterminously with a political body that is the seat of authority. Whereas temporal bodies decay, the body politic is eternal—and consequently monarchical decisions are also eternal. Elizabeth, the report claims, cannot change Edward VI's decision, for it is a decision for which *she* is responsible. In the terms derived from *Troilus and Cressida*, the *precept* of the politic body overpowers the *praxis* of the monarch's personal wishes; the primacy of the *Queen's* body politic remains unhindered by the wishes of the *woman's* temporal being.

As Marie Axton has noted, the doctrine of the two royal bodies "was never a *fact*, nor did it ever attain the status of orthodoxy"; it was, rather, "a legal metaphor defining the relationship between sovereign and perpetual state."[32] Most important, it was a metaphor that conveniently mutated according to the exigencies of the present moment. The jurists quoted by Plowden in the Duchy of Lancaster case vividly display the mutability of the concept in their ironic reaffirmation of the eternal power of monarchy as a means of refuting Elizabeth, the monarch. But Elizabeth herself also worked the metaphor to her own advantages. A skillful relay between temporal weakness and immortal power appears frequently in her public speakings. In 1561 she used her fleshly person to soften her audience for an impromptu Latin oration: "Although my feminine modesty deter me from making a speech and uttering these rude, off-hand remarks in so great an assemble of most learned men . . .";[33] in

[31]Edmund Plowden, *The Commentaries and Reports of Edmund Plowden* (London, 1779), p. 217.

[32]Marie Axton, *The Queen's Two Bodies: Drama and the Elizabethan Succession* (London, 1977), pp. x, 17–18.

[33]George P. Rice, ed., *The Public Speaking of Queen Elizabeth: Selections from the Official Addresses* (New York, 1951), pp. 71–72.

1601 she favored her divine immortality in order to gain popular favor: "And though God has raised me high, yet this I count the glory of my crown, that I have reigned with your loves";[34] and when addressing the troops at Tilbury in 1588 she highlighted the duality of her persona:

> I know I have the body but of a weak and feeble woman; but I have the heart and stomach of a king, and of a king of England too, and think foul scorn that Parma or Spain or any prince of Europe should dare to invade the borders of my realm; to which, rather than any dishonor should grow by me, I myself will take up arms; I myself will be your general, judge, and rewarder of every one of your virtues in the field.[35]

Present in all of these formulations is a recognition of a space between power and person that can be narrowed or widened depending on the circumstances. The theory of two bodies, then, was hardly a theory but was, rather, a regulator that could conveniently shift the terms of a debate almost instantaneously.

The dichotomy between politic body and temporal body is analogous to the dichotomy between precept and praxis that empowers the dramatic strategies of *Troilus and Cressida*'s presentation of the Greek world. This analogy in turn provides a point at which we may extend the hermeneutic found in Shakespeare's play into the historical dynamics of Elizabethan and Jacobean culture. This extension from the dramatic world to the historical world can be defended by the narratives of Edward's reign, for they are all informed by an interplay between temporal and divine bodies, and all of them use this interplay either to support or to critique the false division of precept and praxis that is central to Shakespeare's play. Initially, it is important to recognize that the "truth" of Edward's reign is far more complex than that proposed by Taylor's sonnet. As one historian of the Elizabethan period recounts Edward's reign, "There is a miserable level of political selfishness, that marks without exception every public man; there is no abundance of sincere deep feeling except in the

[34]Ibid., p. 106.
[35]Ibid., p. 96.

shape of hatred and revenge . . . and there is no great triumph of good or evil to add a moral or inspire sympathy."[36] Another anonymous chronicler says, "For want of good Government he lost the Realm of *Scotland*, and other Lands and Seigniories in *Gascoygne*, and elsewhere, which his Father had left him in Peace."[37] Stow's chronicle succinctly depicts the terrible material conditions under Edward: "Horse-flesh was counted great delicates; the poor stole fatte dogges to eate. Some, (as it was sayd), compelled through famine, in hidden places, did eate the flesh of their own children, and some stole others which they devoured."[38] Even in his youth as a prince Edward displayed imperfections. In 1305 Edward I exiled Gaveston after he and the young Edward broke into the grounds of the Bishop of Coventry. In short, Edward was not a perfect pattern of kingship, and the reasons for his downfall, though impossible to recover fully, were certainly more expansive than a homoerotic union.[39]

This praxis of political ineptness seldom surfaces in retellings of the king's life. Rather, narratives of the story typically shift the focus from political errors (the body politic) to fleshly homoeroticism (the temporal body). As in the speeches of Thersites and Ulysses, these narratives construct Gaveston as the catamite that destroys order. Drayton's *Peirs Gaveston* allows Gaveston himself to recount the societal view of his relationship with Edward:

> Some slaunderous tongues, in spightful manner sayd,
> That heer I liv'd in filthy sodomy,
> And that I was King *Edwards Ganemed*,
> And to this sinn hee was intic'd by mee.

[36]Quoted in Christopher Marlowe, *The Complete Plays*, ed. J. B. Steane (Harmondsworth, U.K., 1969), pp. 598–599.

[37]*A True Relation of the Life and Death of Edward II* (London, 1689), p. 3.

[38]Quoted in C. Hardwick, ed., *A Poem on the Times of Edward II* (London, 1849), p. iv.

[39]Sir Richard Baker's 1684 chronicle provides one of the best and most scathing accounts of the pragmatic problems with Edward's reign, especially in its accounts of Edward's troubles with Scotland and with the abysmal material conditions (Richard Baker, *A Chronicle of the Kings of England from the Time of the Romans Government unto the Death of King James* [London, 1684], pp. 111–118).

And more, (to wreck their spightful deadly teene,)
Report the same to *Isabel* the Queene.[40]

Gaveston suggests that the downfall of Edward resulted entirely from the realm's reaction toward the temporal realm of the king's sexual behavior. Hubert's chronicle substantiates this view:

This *Angel-Divell*, thus shrin'd in my heart:
This *Dragon* having got the golden Fruite;
My very Soule to him I did impart;
Nor was I ever deafe unto his suite,
He acted all, I [Edward] was a silent mute.
My being, seem'd to be in him alone,
Plantaginet was turn'd to *Gavestone*.

With such and many more, more wanton gloses,
Whereat thy virgin *Muse*, will blush for shame,
With unchast words, and Pander-like supposes,
This *Gavestone* so brought me out of frame,
That I neglected *Father, Friends,* and *Fame*:
And to those pleasures onely was respective,
That to my *Fancy* seemed most delective.[41]

Unlike the Duchy of Lancaster case, in which the body politic is invoked to thwart the temporal wishes of the monarch, these two chronicles efface the body politic of the king and present him as a pattern of fleshly vice. This inversion of bodies subverts the standard dominance of the atemporal body politic, but this temporary suspension ultimately solidifies monarchical right. For if the body politic of the king is eternal, then the ascription of a fault to it is also eternal and should result in a simultaneous weakening of all monarchs, past, present, and future. The strategy of isolating the reasons for revolt within the temporal body of the king forms the major trope in both Drayton's and Hubert's narratives. *Peirs Gaveston* removes the fall of Edward from the realm of politic theory by casting it in the genre of love poetry:

[40]Drayton, *Works*, 1, p. 194.
[41]Francis Hubert, *The Life of Edward II* (London, 1628), pp. 16, 23.

In pleasures there we spend the nights and dayes,
As with our revels entertaine the time,
With costly Banquets, Masks, and stately Playes,
Painting our loves in many a pleasing rime.
  With rarest Musick, and sweet-tuned voyces,
  (In which the soule of a man so much rejoyces.)[42]

These rhapsodic lines recall the cloistered passions of "The Passionate Shepherd" or "To His Coy Mistress," not the material realities of famine and revolt that characterized Edward's reign.

Hubert's chronicle presents a similar removal of the politic aspects of the narrative and thereby also becomes a tale of personal calamity, not kingly demise. Although Hubert's poem begins by invoking Fortune, an eternal force, it quickly shifts to temporal realms to account for the tale to follow: "Did I say *Fortune*? nay by *Folly* rather."[43] The shift moves the narrative from the eternal to the temporal and also moves Edward from king to subject. The removal of the narrative from the realm of the body politic is most clearly signaled in the chronicle's careful manipulation of progenital descent, which separates the temporal body of Edward from the bloodline of Longshank's body politic:

A *King* may leave his name unto his *Sonne*,
But to his *Sonne*, no *King* can leave his Nature:
In outward forme and shape, they may seeme one,
His Posture, Speech, both Countenance and Feature,
May make the *Son* be thought the selfe-same Creature,
I know in Face, *Sonnes* may be like the *Sires*,
But Faces like, have oft unlike desires.[44]

This analysis continues for another four stanzas, and includes practically every imaginable explanation of how a "bad" son can come from a "good" father:

[42]Drayton, *Works*, I, p. 190.
[43]Hubert, *Life*, p. 1.
[44]Ibid., p. 11.

> . . . as often times we read
> Of many griefes hereditary, taking
> First roote from Parents loynes, and not forsaking
> Their issues, untill many ages
> To wofull masters, most unwelcome Pages.[45]

This rumination on progenital descent further widens the space between the king's two bodies, for while the validity of the body politic passes from father to son, from king to prince, the temporal body of the son is heir to generations and generations of traits—some royal, some common, most unknown. In this schema Edward's homoeroticism is not only a temporal trait; it is also a trait that might well derive from any number of sources—except, of course, from Longshanks and the body politic.

The structure present in all of these narratives is similar to that present in the satires that empower the tradition embodied in Thersites. Homoeroticism is foregrounded as a temporal or fleshly weakness and thereby becomes the sign of stigma that can remove the story of Edward from the realm of the body politic to the realm of the temporal body. Homoeroticism is fully inscribed within a low discourse which by contradistinction empowers the high discourse that articulates it. Yet as we know from the reading lesson presented in *Troilus and Cressida*, such a structure also tacitly effaces a logical contradiction, for the originary signification of homoeroticism as low evolves from the high itself—and thus what is low is not an absolute other but, rather, finds its origin or counterpart in the high. This logical contradiction forms the primary dramatic action of Marlowe's engagement of the story. *Edward II* begins by invoking an image of homoerotic love that seems to imitate the divisions that motivate the narratives of Drayton and Hubert.[46] Gaveston enters the stage alone

[45]Ibid., p. 11.

[46]These lines have resulted in many readings of the play as a love story—a process that, ironically, enacts the containment strategies of other narratives on Marlowe's script. As my argument will demonstrate, I view such readings to be misreadings. For a representative example of this sort of reading, see Leonora Leet Brodwin, "*Edward II:* Marlowe's Culminating Treatment of Love," *ELH* 31 (1964): 139–155, which argues that love is "a

and offers a lengthy rhapsody on his imminent reunion with Edward:

> Sweet prince I come; these, these thy amorous lines
> Might have enforc'd me to have swum from France,
> And like Leander gasp'd upon the sand,
> So thou wouldst smile and take me in thy arms.
> The sight of London to my exil'd eyes
> Is as Elysium to a new-come soul.
> Not that I love the city or the men,
> But that it harbours him I hold so dear,
> The king, upon whose bosom let me die,
> And with the world be still at enmity.
> What need the arctic people love star-light
> To whom the sun shines both day and night?[47]

This classical dotage imitates the homoeroticism of a Virgilian eclogue or of Marlowe's own homoerotic epyllion, *Hero and Leander* (see chapter 3). Gaveston responds to "amorous" lines and craves to replace the material reality of London with the

---

saving value" in the play and that Edward voluntarily gives up the crown "because it has been the price of a dedication to love which he still affirms as the highest value of his existence." Though most critics stop short of this type of reading, few have deigned it appropriate to view the play as an overtly political one, preferring instead to view it as a play about "morality"; see, for example, Clifford Leech, "Marlowe's *Edward II:* Power and Suffering" *Critical Quarterly* 3 (1959), which claims that the play presents "ultimate suffering" as a means of attaining ultimate truths. Notable examples that do deal with the play in a historical and political framework include Irving Ribner, "Marlowe's *Edward II* and the Tudor History Play," *Journal of English Literary History* 22 (1955): 243–253, and Herbert Lindenberger, *Historical Drama: The Relation of Literature and Reality* (Chicago, 1975). Weill offers a morality reading of the play but also intermingles it with a reading of political types in the play. The result is a reading that is much more useful than most other criticism on the play (Judith Weill, *Marlowe: Merlin's Prophet* [Cambridge, 1977], pp. 143–169). One of the best political contextualizations of the play is Simon Shepherd, *Marlowe and the Politics of Elizabethan Theatre* (Brighton, 1986).

[47]Christopher Marlowe, *Christopher Marlowe: Complete Plays and Poems*, ed. E. D. Pendry and J. C. Maxwell (London, 1976), I.i.6–17. All subsequent citations will be to this edition.

erotically charged "Elysium," all for the chance to "die" on Edward's bosom—a dotage further inscribed within the private realm of temporal passion by the common Renaissance pun on death/orgasm. The speech seems to beg that the story to follow be read as a parable of fleshly impulse far removed from the politic realities of the "city or its men."

However, the image of temporality is contextualized in the play within a broader discourse of political ambition and power. Gaveston begins his speech with the seemingly innocent question, "What greater bliss can hap to Gaveston / Than live and be the favourite of a king?" (I.i.4–5), but his ending to the speech indicates that "favourite" is something other than a position of personal affection:

> Farewell base stooping to the lordly peers;
> My knee shall bow to none but to the king.
> As for the multitude, that are but sparks
> Rak'd up in embers of their poverty,
> *Tanti*! I'll fawn first on the wind,
> That glanceth at my lips and flieth away.
>
> (I.i.18–23)

For Gaveston, the prospect of a homoerotic reunion with Edward already intermingles the temporal and the politic, and the broad division of the king's two bodies in other tales here becomes a conscious conflation of them.[48] In a lengthy vision of his life with Edward, Gaveston delivers a passionate idyll of mythological love:

> Music and poetry is his delight:
> Therefore I'll have Italian masques by night,
> Sweet speeches, comedies, and pleasing shows;

[48]This argument has been somewhat anticipated by Claude Summers, who convincingly demonstrates that "the radicalism of *Edward II* resides in the play's intersection of sex and politics and in Marlowe's refusal to moralize either" (Claude J. Summers, "Sex, Politics, and Self-Realization in *Edward II*," in *"A Poet and a Filthy Play-Maker": New Essays on Christopher Marlowe*, ed. Kenneth Friedenreich, Roma Gill, and Constance B. Kuriyama, pp. 221–240 [New York, 1988], p. 222).

And in the day, when we shall walk abroad,
Like sylvan nymphs my pages shall be clad;
My men like satyrs grazing on the lawns
Shall with their goat-feet dance an antic hay;
Sometime a lovely boy in Dian's shape,
With hair that gilds the water as it glides,
Crownets of pearl about his naked arms,
And in his sportful hands an olive-tree,
To hide those parts which man delight to see,
Shall bathe him in a spring; and there hard by,
One like Actaeon peeping through the grove,
Shall by the angry goddess be transform'd,
And running in the likeness of an hart,
By yelping hounds pull'd down, and seem to die.
Such things as these best please his majesty.

(I.i.53–70)

But this lyric vision is again coterminous with a discourse of power, for Gaveston prefaces the speech:

I must have wanton poets, pleasant wits,
Musicians, that with the touching of a string
May draw the pliant king which way I please.

(I.i.50–52)

The rhetoric of homoerotic passion, which in other tales marks the place where politic concerns end and temporal ones begin, is, in this play, a *part* of the politic. Gaveston's homoeroticism, which is in other narratives the trait that removes the story from the politic, is here precisely the trait that makes him politically viable in Marlowe's play. There are not two bodies here but an amorphous one that mutates, stretches, and indeterminately transforms to fit the exigencies of power.

Marlowe's presentation of Gaveston, then, refuses to privilege the divisions of eternal power and temporal passion present in the king's two bodies and defended in the structure of other accounts of Edward's reign. But it is not enough to recognize that Marlowe's Gaveston collapses the division between passion and power, between vice-ridden temporality and the eternity of the politic. Marlowe's Gaveston demonstrates tacitly that, as in Ulysses' "remedy," the construction of the apolitical is always in and of itself political. Like Patroclus the catamite, Edward's homoeroticism is what these narratives in the aggregate always profess to shun, but always also stringently utilize. If we think of *Troilus and Cressida* as a lesson in reading, we can think of Marlowe's play as a lesson in *writing*, as an extended exposition (and hence a demystification and undercutting) of how to inscribe sexual difference onto the tabula rasa of amorphous power. Marlowe's Gaveston forces us to read the unmediated oneness of the temporal and politic, and the play as whole then vividly displays the process of mediating this oneness—a display achieved through its presentation of Mortimer.

Writing Edward II (2)

If we return to *Troilus and Cressida* for a moment, we might also draw a distinction between *how* and *why* sodomy is written. The process, as exemplified by the play's manipulation of the satiric Thersites and also as demonstrated in the chronicle presence of Gaveston, involves arbitrary stratification and the subsequent effacement of the human agency involved in the process under totalizing schema: in the Greek world, a theory of perfect divine teleology; in the narratives of Edward's life, the divisional epistemology of the monarch's two bodies. However, the hows of writing sodomy also efface the whys, for, as Ulysses' improvisational praxis demonstrates, the Greeks' motives for constructing Patroclus are always other than sexual: a lengthy, unsuccessful, and unjustifiable military engagement; the insolence of Achilles; internal dissent and the need to bolster morale. In this context homoeroticism is not only other within a system but is also the means of transferring dialogue to an entirely other debate. The Greeks' reason for constructing Patroclus is ideological in the purest sense, for the recourse to homoeroticism entirely obfuscates the power motivating the discourse and renders it inaccessible by channeling debate into discursive cul-de-sacs that are incapable of articulating the actual terms of power but that also make the offered solution seem universally beneficial. The construction of Patroclus enables the Greeks to articulate an affront to order, but it then also disables any articulation of the mutable power plays underpinning the construction.

This ideology of homoerotic construction is fully present in Marlowe's *Edward II*, for unlike other narratives, which typically begin after the originary decision of homoerotic construction, Marlowe's play also dramatizes the decision to write homoeroticism. In addition to presenting Gaveston as an undivided temporal/political character, the opening of the play also presents the actions of Edward's peers as they strike a decision to obfuscate motives of politic ambition with a rhetoric of temporal sexuality. The elder Mortimer initially presents the peers' opposition to Edward in a dichotomy that recalls the king's two bodies: "If you [Edward] love us, my lord, hate Gaveston" (I.i.79). The command recapitulates the binary oppositions empowering Renaissance political theory: "you"/"us" recalls "king"/"subject," and "love us"/"hate Gaveston" invokes the constructed rift between "public"/"private" and "politic"/"temporal." The younger Mortimer proceeds to offer a motive for this confrontation that supports the basic tenets of Elizabethan monarchical power:

> Mine uncle here, this earl, and I myself,
> Were sworn to your father at his death
> That he [Gaveston] should ne'er return into the realm;
> And know, my lord, ere I will break my oath,
> This sword of mine that should offend your foes
> Shall sleep within the scabbard at thy need,
> And underneath thy banners march who will,
> For Mortimer will hang his armour up.
>
> (I.i.81–88)

The problem here is analogous to that in the Duchy of Lancaster case, for the decision to banish Gaveston is one that Edward inherits as a part of the body politic; as such, Mortimer's affront to the king is actually an allegiance to the politic king. In a similarly explicable mode, Lancaster responds to Edward's query, "Beseems it thee to contradict thy king?" (I.i.91), with a recourse to the rhetoric of natural order:

My lord, why do you thus incense your peers
That naturally would love and honour you
But for that base and obscure Gaveston?

(I.i.98–100)

The problem is not, according to Lancaster, that subjects are rebelling against a king but that the king is rebelling against his own body politic.

However, the action prior to the construction of a homoerotically centered plan of action also demonstrates that the power motivating this rhetoric of order evades containment by the ideological dichotomy of politic/temporal. The second scene of the play, which dramatizes the peers' decision to force Gaveston's exile, demonstrates that their allegiance is with *neither* of the king's bodies.

ELDER MORTIMER: How now, why droops the Earl of Lancaster?
YOUNGER MORTIMER: Wherefore is Guy of Warwick discontent?
LANCASTER: That villain Gaveston is made an earl.
ELDER MORTIMER: An earl!
WARWICK: Ay, and besides, Lord Chamberlain of the realm,
And Secretary too, and Lord of Man.
ELDER MORTIMER: We may not nor we will not suffer this.
YOUNGER MORTIMER: Why post we not from hence to levy men?

(I.ii.9–16)

The focus here is neither on Edward nor on the threat of Gaveston's homoeroticism; the threat, rather, is from Gaveston's advancement—a fact rearticulated by both Lancaster and Warwick:

Thus arm in arm the king and he doth march—
Nay more, the guard upon his lordship waits,
And all the court begins to flatter him.

(I.ii.20–22)

Thus leaning on the shoulder of the king,
He nods, and scorns, and smiles at those that pass.

(I.ii.23–24)

The perceived threat here is not that Gaveston's homoeroticism subjugates the body politic to the temporal but that it allows Gaveston to traverse (or more properly, to act uninscribed by) the artificial division that keeps the two realms separate. Against this scenario of unmediated sexual/political/social power, the subsequent decision to write the fabula as a sexually temporal narrative (which is present in both Marlowe's peers and other narratives as a whole) is not an effort to *maintain* the empowering division between the politic and the temporal but, rather, an effort to *construct* it anew. The division of politic and temporal, then, can now be seen not as an a priori characteristic of power but as an ex post facto means of channeling power in such a way as to maintain systems of primogenital and political advancement that benefit the ruling class while effacing these very real concerns of power underpinning it.

The complicity of most narratives of the king's reign in this ideology of homoerotic construction shows forth most clearly in the figuration of the younger Mortimer (henceforth simply Mortimer), a character who throughout the Renaissance exercised an imaginative claim equal to that of Edward and Gaveston. Drayton devoted an entire poem to him, Jonson proposed to write a tragedy about him, and his role in other works (with the exception of Hubert's) is almost always nearly as large as, if not larger than, that of the king and his minion. One possible reason for the primacy of Mortimer within these narratives is that he, like Gaveston, also threatens the empowering rift between temporal and politic. For Mortimer's actions, regardless of how they are justified, are still the actions of a subject revolting against a king and gaining advancement as a result—a direct inversion of the expected course of gaining favor through service to the king. Hence, his actions always dangerously expose the pragmatics of power concealed by dichotomies of the politic and the temporal and the construction of homoeroticism.

The presence of this threatening power is ironically highlighted by its very absence in most narratives. Drayton, for example, casts *Mortimeriados* as a tragedy and takes as his subject "How *Mortimer* first rose, when *Edward* fell,"[49] a phrase that

[49]Drayton, *Works*, I, p. 368.

immediately ascribes Mortimer's rise to the weaknesses of the king. He calls Mortimer's entrance into the action "the ghastly Prologue to thys tragick act,"[50] a notion of the tale later adopted by Ben Jonson. Jonson's fragment, *Mortimer His Fall*, presents Mortimer as a character of classical tragic hubris; as the argument states,

> *The first Act comprehends* Mortimers *pride and securitie, raysed to the degree of an Earle, by the Queenes favour, and love.*
>
> Mortimers *securitie, scorne of the Nobilitie, too much familiaritie with the Queene, related by the* Chorus, *the report of the Kings surprizing him in his Mothers bed-chamber, a generall gladnesse, his being sent to execution.*[51]

The generic choice of tragedy provides a means of recasting Mortimer's political agency as an aspect of literary convention. Jonson's fragment suggests a play in which the actions of Mortimer are the manifestations of a Senecan pride and ambition, something stated strongly in Mortimer's first lines of the fragment:

> This Rise is made, yet! and we now stand, ranck'd,
> To view about us, all that were above us!
> Nought hinders now our prospect, all are even,
> We walke upon a Levell.[52]

The process of emblematically redacting Mortimer so as to negate the effects of his personal agency in the story is magnified in Drayton's poem, which conceives Mortimer as an innocent actor cast in his role by circumstances beyond his control; his rise begins from a quirk of the times. The civil war between the peers and the king is presented as a battle in which each side fights for the propriety of orthodox power—"Saint *George* the King, Saint

[50] Ibid., p. 312.

[51] Ben Jonson, *Ben Jonson: Works*, ed. C. H. Herford and Percy Simpson (Oxford, 1925–1952), 7, pp. 58–59.

[52] Ibid., p. 60.

George the Barrons cry"—and results in the decimation of England:

> Heer lyes a heap, half slaine, halfe chok'd, halfe drownd,
> Gasping for breth amongst the slymie seggs,
> And there a sort falne in a deadly swound,
> Scrawling in blood upon the muddy dreggs:
> Heere in the streame, swim bowels, armes and leggs.
> One kills his foe, his braine another cuts,
> Ones feet intangled in anothers guts.[53]

The slaughter resulting from *both* factions fighting for England creates an environment that chooses Mortimer as its champion:

> For *Mortimer* this wind yet rightly blewe,
> Darckning their eyes which else perhaps might see,
> Whilst *Isabell* who all advantage knewe,
> Is closely plotting his deliverie,
> Now fitly drawne by *Torltons* policie:
> Thus by a Queene, a Bishop, and a Knight,
> To check a King, in spight of all dispight.[54]

The terms of the final metaphor accurately depict Drayton's conception of Mortimer; lacking any degree of agency, he is reduced to a piece in a game with neither need nor capability to move himself.

Ironically, Mortimer, the opponent of the king, occupies a space in these chronicles analogous to that of Edward himself. For if Edward's relationship to cultural power is hidden beneath a rhetoric of politic order and temporal affront, Mortimer's relationship to it is equally obscured. This subsumption by cultural mythology is forcefully present in Drayton's construction of Isabella, who seems to be a conglomeration of all the female roles in *Macbeth*: brimming with ambition like Lady Macbeth, eerie and unnatural like the weird sisters.

[53]Drayton, *Works*, I, pp. 320–321.
[54]Ibid., 327.

A drowsie potion shee by skill hath made,
Whose secret working had such wonderous power,
As could the sence with heavie sleepe invade,
And mortifie the patient in one hower,
As though pale death the body did devower;
Nor for two dayes might opened be his eyes,
By all meanes Arte or Phisicke could devise.

Thus sits this great Enchauntresse in her Cell,
Invironed with spyrit-commaunding charmes,
Her body censed with most sacred smell,
With holy fiers her liquors now shee warmes,
Then her with sorcering instruments she armes,
And from her hearbs the powerfull juyce she wrong,
To make the poyson forcible and strong.

Reason might judge, doubts better might advise,
And as a woman, feare her hand have stayd,
Waying the strangenesse of the interprize,
The daunger well might have her sex dismayd,
Fortune, distrust, suspect, to be betrayd;
But when they leave of vertue to esteeme,
They greatly erre which thinke them as they seeme.[55]

This description ascribes Isabella a place within the terrible trio of "Sorcerers, Sodomers and Hereticks" that Coke brands as an unnatural affront to order. Like Edward, then, Mortimer becomes a character fully accounted for by the ideology of cultural stigmatism; once assigned to the *unworldly* specter of an evil woman, the actions of Mortimer need no longer be accounted for in the *world* picture. Drayton's description of Isabella is a particularly vivid example of a strategy that is almost de rigueur in the representation of Edward's reign. Jonson, as we have already seen, suggests that Mortimer rises "by the Queene's favour, and love";[56] Hubert, too, takes recourse to this demon-

[55]Ibid., p. 327.
[56]Jonson, *Works*, 7, p. 59.

ized rhetoric: "What Monstrous births from thy fowle wombe do spring, / So Grammar here is made to kill a king."[57] Textuality here becomes amazingly transparent precisely because of its opacity, for the inability of *any* vestiges of amorphous power to penetrate these cultural mythologies ironically bespeaks their presence through an anxious silence.

In all of these examples Mortimer is emblematically redacted into the inert material of cultural narration; like the problems of an unruly reign ideologically purified by the convenient rhetoric of a double body, he is accounted for by previously constructed rationalizations for treasonous behavior. What such rationalizations efface is startlingly exposed in Marlowe's presentation of Mortimer, a character who contains, but who is not contained by, these emblematizing discourses. The play's conception of Mortimer is most clearly presented in the long soliloquy on his advancement that he delivers near the play's end:

> The prince I rule, th'queen do I command,
> And with a lowly congé to the ground
> The proudest lords salute me as I pass.
> I seal, I cancel, I do what I will;
> Fear'd am I more than lov'd: let me be fear'd,
> And when I frown, make all the court look pale.
> I view the prince with Aristarchus' eyes,
> Whose looks were as a breeching to a boy.
> They thrust upon me the Protectorship,
> And sue to me for that that I desire:
> While at the council-table, grave enough
> And not unlike a bashful puritan,
> First I complain of imbecility,
> Saying it is *onus quam gravissimum*,
> Till being interrupted by my friends,
> *Suscepi* that *provinciam*, as they term it;
> And, to conclude, I am Protector now.
> Now all is sure: the queen and Mortimer

[57]Hubert, *Life*, p. 194.

Shall rule the realm, the king, and none rule us.
Mine enemies will I plague, my friends advance,
And what I list command who dare control?
Maior sum quam cui possit fortuna nocere.

(V.iv.48–69)

Mortimer here displays the same disregard for decorum of place that he used to justify Gaveston's condemnation. He is cast in the same rhetoric as will be Jonson's tragic Senecan version. And as a subject to these conventional rhetorics of containment, he also learns the conventional lesson reserved for unruly monarchical subjects:

Base Fortune, now I see, that in thy wheel
There is a point, to which when men aspire,
They tumble headlong down; that point I touch'd,
And seeing there was no place to mount up higher,
Why should I grieve at my declining fall?
Farewell, fair queen, weep not for Mortimer,
That scorns the world, and as a traveller
Goes to discover countries yet unknown.

(V.vi.59–66)

The final moments of the play show Edward III accepting Mortimer's severed head, and the closure is complete: the hubristic villain is reintegrated into a framework of fortune, fate, and order, and the validity of the body politic is reasserted in the person of a new king.

This redaction of Mortimer, however, encodes an alteriority that destabilizes the assuredness of the strategy. Rather than gaining renewed respect for fortune, Mortimer feels that he has no further use for it—that he has experienced it all, used it up, as it were. Indeed, this notion is succinctly presented in his own self-emblematization: *Major sum quam cui possit fortuna nocere* (I am too great for fortune). The idea here is of excess, of an overflowing or surpassing. There is inherent in Mortimer a notion of uncontainability, of existing as something that can only partially be captured by the discursive nets cast by the redactive ideologies present in other chronicles and in the play's partial mouthings of these same strategies. Mortimer, then, is a character defined by mythologies of closure but also defining of them; in his character we see both the how and the why of containing political agency, both the emblematic rhetoric of control and the amorphous power motivating it. Indeed, more than any other single character in the play, Mortimer espouses a theory that refuses to privilege the orthodox division empowering monarchical structure. He exposes a notion of the court as a system based on courtiers rather than kings (II.ii.173–177) and recognizes that kingly right is more a function of lucre than of divine right: "prodigal gifts bestow'd on Gaveston, / Have drawn thy treasure dry, and made thee weak" (II.ii.157–158). Similarly, he recognizes that power comes not from above but from the amorphous material relations of peers, parliament, and the people: "But as the realm and parliament shall please, / So shall your brother be disposed of" (IV.v.45–46). Unlike other chronicle versions, in this play it is Mortimer who aggressively woos the queen and subverts her natural inclination to pity Edward. Most important, Mortimer expresses a belief that the true power of this system lies elsewhere than with the titles:

> Think therefore, madam, that imports us much
> To erect your son with all the speed we may,
> And that I be Protector over him;
> For our behoof will bear the greater sway
> Whenas a king's name shall be underwrit.
>
> (V.ii.10–14)

If in other tales Mortimer becomes a redacted emblem supporting the rhetoric of politic order, in Marlowe's play he becomes a personification of the limits of that rhetoric, a character who continually juxtaposes before the audience both the words of order and the potentialities they seek to efface.

Significantly, this character who refuses to empower the obfuscatory aim of redactive mythologies is also the one who exhibits the keenest awareness of the relationship between the construction of homoeroticism and the pragmatics of power. Act one, scene four, presents the moment when Mortimer fully realizes both his own power and the power of homoeroticism, a realization precipitated by an aside from Isabella:

> MORTIMER: Fair queen, forbear to angle for the fish
> Which, being caught, strikes him that takes it dead—
> I mean that vile torpedo, Gaveston,
> That now, I hope, floats on the Irish seas.
> ISABELLA: Sweet Mortimer, sit down by me a while,
> And I will tell thee reasons of such weight
> As thou wilt soon subscribe to his repeal.
> MORTIMER: It is impossible; but speak your mind.
> ISABELLA: Then thus—but none shall hear it but ourselves.
> (I.iv.221–229)

In other chronicles the queen's role is highlighted and demonized; in Marlowe's play it is silenced and withdrawn from the audience. The attention rests solely on Mortimer's actions, which now change from avenging the un*just* actions of Edward to punishing the un*natural* role of Gaveston:

> My lords, that I abhor base Gaveston
> I hope your honours make no question;
> And therefore though I plead for his repeal,
> 'Tis not for his sake, but for our avail—
> Nay, for the realm's behoof, and for the king's.
> (I.iv.239–243)

Mortimer's action, he claims, is motivated by "a burning zeal / To mend the king and do our country good" (I.iv.256–257), but his fervor quickly surpasses the strictures of mere patriotism:

> But were he [Gaveston] here, detested as he is,
> How easily might some base slave be suborn'd
> To greet his lordship with a poniard;
> And none so much as blame for murderer,
> But rather praise him for that brave attempt,
> And in his chronicle enrol his name
> For purging of the realm of such a plague.
> (I.iv.264–270)

The purging of Gaveston is no longer a way to protect the politic order; it is now a means to both "praise" and a place in "the chronicle"; for Mortimer, the king's homoeroticism now provides a means of personal advancement and historical fame. The other peers sense the discrepancies in Mortimer's rhetoric, for, as Lancaster summarizes their reactions, "Such reasons make white black, and dark night day" (I.iv.247).

Mortimer as a character derives his power from a recognition that the king's homoeroticism does not just provide a means of maintaining politic order but also marks the point at which politic order and the power it seeks to contain meet and may be negotiated. This recognition shows most clearly in the difference between Mortimer's perception of the problem and that of the elder Mortimer. As the elder tries to instruct his nephew,

> Thou seest by nature he [Edward] is mild and calm,
> And seeing his mind so dotes on Gaveston,
> Let him without controlment have his will.
> The mightiest kings have had their minions:
> Great Alexander lov'd Hephaestion;
> The conquering Hercules for Hylas wept;
> And for Patroclus stern Achilles droop'd;
> And not kings only, but the wisest men.
> The Roman Tully lov'd Octavius;
> Grave Socrates, wild Alcibiades.
> Then let his grace, whose youth is flexible,
> And promiseth so much as we can wish,
> Freely enjoy that vain light-headed earl,
> For riper years will wean him from such toys.
> (I.iv.387–400)

For the uncle the reinstatement of politic decorum is the central issue, and as long as Edward acts in accordance with the strictures of the body politic, he can easily supply a catalogue of great homoerotic loves to justify the king's temporal actions. But for the nephew such an elision is impossible; rather, he tenaciously promotes Gaveston as the realm's scapegoat, continually refiguring him as the base cause of economic, social, military, and seditious rifts:

> His [Edward's] wanton humour grieves not me;
> But this I scorn, that one so basely born
> Should by his sovereign's favour grow so pert,
> And riot it with the treasure of the realm
> While soldiers mutiny for want of pay.
>
> (I.iv.401–405)

> Whiles other walk below, the king and he
> From out a window laugh at such as we,
> And flout our train, and jest at our attire.
>
> (I.iv.415–417)

> Thou [Gaveston] proud disturber of thy country's peace,
> Corrupter of thy king, cause of these broils,
> Base flatterer . . .
>
> (II.v.9–11)

All of these pronouncements indicate that Mortimer recognizes a falseness in the arbitrary theoretical division of the politic and the temporal, for each speech foregrounds the interrelatedness of fleshly action and material power. Moreover, Mortimer's course of action also demonstrates how his recognition of the role of homoeroticism in political construction enables him to efface his own agency. As Isabella notes in a moment of dissembling, Mortimer's actions provoke "unnatural wars, where subjects brave their king" (III.ii.86), but this treason is masked by Mortimer through a continued refocusing of attention on Edward's homoeroticism.

The pattern of using homoeroticism both to exercise and to conceal power that arises in Mortimer's dealings with Gaveston is drawn in even sharper terms in Mortimer's manipulations of the king's second set of minions, the Spensers. Whereas Gaveston casts himself in homoerotic terms as a means of gaining power—and thereby gives Mortimer an entry—the Spensers are presented in distinctly different terms that Mortimer nonetheless manipulates through accusations of unnatural behavior. After the exile of Gaveston, Edward emerges as a reborn king fully conscious of his body politic; speaking of himself in the third person, he says, "Edward this day hath crown'd him king anew"

(III.iii.76). The ritual of Edward's self-coronation is a rhetorical invocation of the eternal precepts of nature, order, and God. He kneels before Arundel and Spenser and vows that

> By earth, the common mother of us all,
> By heaven, and all the moving orbs thereof,
> By this right hand, and by my father's sword,
> And all the honours 'longing to my crown,
> I will have heads and lives for him, as many
> As I have manors, castles, towns, and towers.
>
> (III.ii.128–133)

The king who rises from this coronation speaks the language of monarchical power, not of temporal vice. He vows allegiance to his "royal standard" and "bloody colors" (III.ii.138–139) and "creates" Spenser "Earl of Gloucester and Lord Chamberlain" (III.ii.145–146). The resolve of Edward is bloody and vicious, to be sure, but it is also an operation of royal prerogative and a reestablishment of the body politic of a king that operates "despite of times, despite of enemies" (III.ii.147).

The creation of these new minions, then, is not an exchange of one love for another. It is, rather, a change from personal passion to politic power. Indeed, this change is reflected in the created Spenser. Spenser is, like Gaveston, a self-advancer and court parasite. But Spenser works through the channels of orthodox monarchical power, whereas Gaveston relies on sexual allure. His plan for advancement posits the king as the center of power—"But he that hath the favour of a king / May with one word advance us while we live" (II.i.8–9)—and he advises Baldock on the proper rules of court advancement.

> Then, Baldock, you must cast the scholar off,
> And learn to court it like a gentleman.
> 'Tis not a black coat and a little band,
> A velvet-cap'd cloak, fac'd before with serge,
> And smelling to a nosegay all the day,
> Or holding of a napkin in your hand,
> Or saying a long grace at a table's end,
> Or making low legs to a nobleman,

Or looking downward, with your eyelids close,
And saying 'truly, an't may please your honour',
Can get you any favour with great men.
You must be proud, bold, pleasant, resolute—
And now and then, stab as occassion serves.

(II.i.31–43)

As Baldock says, this advice is "mere hypocrisy" (II.ii.45). But even if the advice lampoons the conventions of the court, it also assigns a power to them—whereas Gaveston sees them as tricks to "draw the pliant king" (I.i.52) and Mortimer labels court rituals "idle triumphs, masques, lascivious shows" (II.ii.156). Moreover, when Spenser advises the king to withstand the peers' rebellion, he does so through an invocation of the king's lineage:

Were I King Edward, England's sovereign,
Son to lovely Eleanor of Spain,
Great Edward Longshanks' issue—would I bear
These braves, this rage, and suffer uncontroll'd
These barons thus to beard me in my land,
In mine own realm?

(III.ii.10–15)

Unlike Hubert's chronicle, which rewrites lineage to exclude Edward, Spenser fully privileges the tenets of primogenital descent.

If the change of minions presents a change from temporal passion to politic resolve, it serves primarily to highlight through contrast the stasis in Mortimer's course of action. Under the leadership of Mortimer, the peers continue to assail Edward as an "unnatural king [who] slaughter[s] noble men / And cherish[es] flatterers" (IV.i.8–9) and as a man with "a desperate and unnatural resolution" (III.iii.32). The foregrounding of Edward's temporal vice continues after its material cause has been removed, and the orthodox realm of the peers becomes, ironically, responsible for propagating the affront to order that it originally professed to want to contain. This idea is succinctly presented by Kent in a moment of contrition, when he notes that the actions of the peers under Mortimer are an "unnatural revolt" (IV.v.18);

later he moans, "O, miserable is that commonweal, / Where lords keep courts, and kings are lock'd in prison!" (V.iii.63–64).

The space between the original conception of homoeroticism as an affront to order and the new conception of it as a political tool shows most clearly in Mortimer himself. As his sense of dislocation from the rhetoric of royal order increases, it solidifies into this plan:

> The king must die, or Mortimer goes down. . . .
>
> . . . This letter, written by a friend of ours,
> Contains his death yet bids them save his life:
> '*Edwardum occidere nolite timere, bonum est*';
> Fear not to kill the king, 'tis good he die.
> But read it thus, and that's another sense:
> '*Edwardum occidere nolite, timere bonum est*'
> Kill not the king, 'tis good to fear the worst.
> Unpointed as it is, thus shall it go,
> That, being dead, if it chance to be found,
> Matrevis and the rest may bear the blame,
> And we be quit that caus'd it to be done.
>
> (V.iv.1–16)

The assignment of this plot to Mortimer is an entirely original invention in the play, and even Tarlton, the actual author of the letter, is reduced to the anonymous position of "a friend of ours." The speech also anatomizes the several disparate themes of power that converge in the character of Mortimer. He advocates a relational rather than an eternal definition of power—"The king must die, or Mortimer goes down"—and he professes a belief that there are spaces within the system than can be manipulated to gain advantage and avoid retribution. It is all the more fitting that Mortimer forges his plan from an ambiguity within language, for this has been precisely his stronghold throughout the play: that what is *said* to mean can always mean otherwise. What Mortimer as a character embodies is the simple but central principle that once sodomy is constructed as an affront to order, it then can be used to affront order. The precept of politic order and the praxis of other potential powers remain divided in these tales only by a constructed sexual rift and an ascription of arbitrary meaning. The artificiality of this process is continually reasserted in Mortimer, a character who both constructs homoeroticism and deconstructs the order enabling the construction.

The entire ending of *Edward II* punningly plays with this double bind of signification. The murder of Edward by raping him with a red-hot poker—quite literally branding him with sodomy—can be seen as an attempt to "write" onto him the homoeroticism constantly ascribed to him.[58] But more important, the ending of the play creates a bifurcated world in which the rhetoric of the kingly body politic exists simultaneously with a world that does not allow it to mean. This problem is humorously recognized by Baldock. When Edward yet again calls on his kingly resolve to fight the peers and commands "Give me my horse, and let's reinforce our troops, / And in this bed of honours die with fame" (IV.v.6–7), the pragmatic and scared Baldock gives Edward a proper perspective on the situation: "O, no, my lord! This princely resolution / Fits not the time: away!" (IV.v.8–9). Of course, Baldock is correct, for the bed reserved for Edward is not one of honor attended by fame but one of feathers

[58]This punning possibility is highlighted in the play by the removal of any practical reason for this choice of death. In Hubert's chronicle the death is related thusly:

> And then into my fundament they thrust,
> A little horne, as I did groveling lie.
> And that my violent death might shun mistrust,
> Through the same horne a red hot Spit, whereby,
> They made gutts and bowells for to frie,
> And so continu'd, till at last they found,
> That I was dead, yet seem'd to have no wound.
>
> (150)

In Marlowe's play these practical considerations are absent, and the choice of death is left up to Lightborn, an executioner who seems more perverted than practical (see the career summary he offers at V.iv.30–36). In an exceptionally intelligent argument, Karen Cunningham demonstrates how such removal of cause becomes a strategy of subversion in many of Marlowe's plays; see Karen Cunningham, "Renaissance Execution and Marlovian Elocution: The Drama of Death," *PMLA* 105, 2 (1990): 209–222.

attended by an executioner. This is, as Baldock realizes, no longer a world adequately inscribed by the precepts of royal political theory; it is now one that exposes such precepts as partial articulations of order attempting to mask an unstable world of amorphous power plays. The ending of *Edward II*, then, opens to view the strategies of containment present in other narratives of the king's reign. The character of Mortimer vividly displays the unmediated power existing as other to the ordered realms of politic theory. But more important, his manipulation of homoeroticism inverts the presumed relationship between sodomy and order. What begins in the play as an effort to *contain* chaos through sodomy quickly changes into an effort to *sustain* chaos through sodomy. Sodomy, a category that fluctuates through numerous discourses, is also a category that, when held in stasis, demonstrates most disturbingly how all other categories fluctuate around it. It is in this mode that Mortimer demonstrates to us both the hows and the whys of writing sodomy and, in the process, demonstrates a crucial point of the epistemology of Renaissance sodomy: sodomy does not create disorder; rather, disorder demands sodomy.

The Authority of Sodomy

> Numerous, strict prohibitions [on sexuality] exist. But they are part of a complex economy along with incitements, manifestations, and evaluations. We always stress the prohibitions. I would like to change the perspective somewhat, grasping in every case the entire complex of apparatuses.[59]

Foucault's desire to contextualize the language of prohibition within the apparatuses that motivate it in many ways forms a postmodern rearticulation of the function of homoeroticism in *Edward II* and *Troilus and Cressida*. To note this similarity is not to imply an ahistorical consciousness; it is, rather, to recognize a historic coincidence between modern discourses that, as Fou-

[59]Michel Foucault, *Politics, Philosophy, Culture: Interviews and Other Writings*, ed. Lawrence D. Kritzman (London, 1988), p. 111.

cault himself notes, are "amazed . . . that it [is] also possible to write the history of feelings, behavior and the body"[60] and late Elizabethan and early Jacobean discourses that were also learning such a lesson. I will claim that the pattern present in *Troilus and Cressida* and tales of Edward's reign is indicative of a broader pattern demanded by developing cultural theory of the time, a pattern that indicates that the articulation of cultural order always simultaneously creates—and relies on—the potentiality of its own destruction.

In order to do so, however, it is necessary to recognize that what has been presented in these various analyses is, in many ways, a false unity. Returning momentarily to *Troilus and Cressida*, we can see strikingly how the sustained association of sodomy and homoeroticism present in the tales of Edward II is an anomaly. Confronting Achilles for the first time about his sexual charges, Ulysses shifts his rhetoric in a way that is jarring to our modern notions of sexual determinacy:

> But 'gainst your privacy
> The reasons are more potent and heroical:
> 'Tis known, Achilles, that you are in love
> With one of Priam's daughters.
>
> (III.iii.191–194)

The moment seems out of place to modern readers primarily because all accusations up to this point have focused on Patroclus and have seemed, at least from an anachronistic perspective, homo*sexual*.

The significance of this accusation can be clarified through a brief comparison to Ben Jonson's *Sejanus*. Early in the action Arruntius derogates Sejanus, claiming, "I knew him, at Caius trencher, when for hyre, / He prostituted his abused body / To that great gourmond, fat Apicius; / And was the noted pathick of the time."[61] Later he returns to the theme and claims Sejanus to be "the ward / To his owne vassall, a stale *catamite*."[62] John

[60]Ibid., p. 112.
[61]Jonson, *Works*, 4, p. 362.
[62]Ibid., 432.

Gordon Sweeney, in *Jonson and the Psychology of Public Theater*, claims of these examples that "Jonson uses homosexuality as a charge against Sejanus. When Arruntius refers to him as Apicius' 'pathick' there is no doubt that this is a sign of Sejanus' degeneracy."[63] The analysis of the intention of the speeches is certainly correct, but what problematizes it is the use of the term *homosexual*. Arruntius's goal is best articulated in a different context by Sejanus himself: to "print [his] body full of iniuries."[64] The actual accusations play within the same catalogues of debauchery present in most of the satiric tradition, for, as Arruntius reminds us, Sejanus "hath his boyes, *and* beauteous girls tane vp." The issue is not what Sejanus is doing with whom but that he is doing it; Arruntius says as much: Sejanus is "an Emp'rour, only in his lusts."[65]

The sexual slurs in *Sejanus* return us clearly to the lengthy listings of deviance present in the satires of Brathwait, Marston, and Middleton. And they also remind us that homoeroticism during the period was not necessarily segregated as the contained, inscriptive discourse that has come to define the modern homosexual. Rather, homoeroticism in all of these texts is part of a fluid economy of power and meaning, one that refuses to sustain the deterministic principles of our own culture. This point is also obvious in *Troilus and Cressida*, when the discourse Ulysses employs to "pluck down Achilles' plumes" shifts almost instantaneously from a homoerotic condemnation of love for Patroclus to a heteroerotic indictment of passion for Polyxenes. The point here seems to be that when the body is politicized, bodily functions become political. This idea strikingly opens *Sejanus*; as Silius tells us, Sejanus's sycophants are "ready to praise / His lordship, if he spit, or but pisse faire, / Haue an indifferent stoole, or breake winde well."[66] Sodomy, therefore,

[63]John Gordon Sweeney III, *Jonson and the Psychology of Public Theater: To Coin the Spirit, Spend the Soul* (Princeton, 1985), p. 91. A much more subtle and important discussion of sexual transgression in the play can be found in Rebecca W. Bushnell, *Tragedies of Tyrants: Political Thought and Theater in the English Renaissance* (Ithaca, 1990), pp. 116–153.

[64]Jonson, *Works*, 4, p. 379.

[65]Ibid., p. 431. Emphasis mine.

[66]Ibid., p. 356.

is but one in a number of metaphoric schema that sought both to bridge and to manipulate the gap between transcendent precepts and the actuality of praxis.

The negotiation between precept and praxis visible within these texts' manipulations of sodomy, while showing most strongly in the figuration of the body, also can be seen in broader schema of politic order. Later in the Renaissance, the publication of Thomas Hobbes's *Leviathan* created an artifact that visually and verbally crystallizes the problems of teleological order exposed in the manipulations of homoeroticism in the plays of Shakespeare and Marlowe. The famous engraved title page of the original 1561 edition iconographically summarizes the contradiction inherent in the text. The bodies of infinite subjects form the shape of a king who towers above the landscape of a commonwealth. Beneath the landscape individual framed compartments hold symbols of the constituent forces of state ranked in degree and order: a church, a castled estate, a crown, a mitre, and a canon, to name a few. The subtitle of the work provides a fitting summary of the concerns of the illustration: "The Matter, Forme and Power of a Common-Wealth Ecclesiastical and Civill." However, the static nature of visual art complicates the image. The point may be that subjects are constrained by the form of a monarch, but it may also be that a monarch has no form without subjects. The individual symbols of state force may depict those things a strong king brings to a commonwealth, but they may also be those things that make a king strong. The engraving is very clearly a depiction of hierarchy, but it is a hierarchy with no specified direction; as such, it renders indistinct the equal possibilities that the base is constrained by the summit and that the summit is dependent on the base. What this engraving shows is that hierarchy in and of itself has no meaning, and it becomes the task of Hobbes's text to create a meaning that *seems* naturally linked to the structure shown on the title page.

The primary lesson to be learned from Hobbes's text is how the ascription of meaning to such a hierarchy affects the politicization of the gendered body. The choice of the human body as the central iconographic unit of the title page is replicated in Hobbes's text through a centralization and solidification of an image of Man. In the broadest sense this image enters the text through the famous analogy between the state and the body: "*Art* goes yet further, imitating that Rationall and most excellent worke of Nature, *Man*. For by Art is created that great *LEVIATHAN* called a *COMMON-WEALTH*, or *STATE* (in latine *CIVITAS*) which is but an Artificiall Man."[67] This trope becomes a structural principle that affects the entire tract. The opening segment, titled "Of Man," constructs an idealized scientific description of Man that validates the extrapolated political science that follows. The assumption is that the cross-validation will achieve a perceived "natural inevitability" in the notion of commonwealth equal to the "natural inevitability" of man himself.

However, lacking any inherent directionality (as the title page's icon demonstrates), the chiasm also opens the possibility of politicizing Man. And this potentiality is also fully operative within the text. Although Hobbes posits a divine Nature and God as rational frames for the world, a different locus of control emerges when he describes the motivation of men: "The Power *of a Man*, (to take it Universally,) is his present means, to obtain some future apparent Good. And is either *Originall*, or *Instrumentall*."[68] Unlike, say, the figure of Man in a morality play, which derives significance in the world through being an inert unit suspended between good and evil, Hobbes is now positing an interior source of power, a potential for felicity through individual movement toward a goal. This interior difference becomes a central premise of Hobbes's theory:

> Nor can a man any more live, whose Desires are at an end, than he, whose Senses and Imaginations are at a stand. Felicity is a continuall progresse of the desire. . . . So that in the first place, I put for a generall inclination of all mankind, a perpetuall and restlesse desire of Power and power, that ceaseth onely in Death.[69]

[67]Thomas Hobbes, *Leviathan*, ed. C. B. Macpherson (Harmondsworth, U.K., 1968), p. 81.

[68]Ibid., p. 150.

[69]Ibid., pp. 160–161.

The primary mark of Hobbes's Man is "desire," a movement outward from the subject but always valid only in relation to the subject.[70] The centrality of the desirous and defining subject is obvious in *Leviathan*, for Hobbes claims that the only two traits that differentiate Man from the animals are speech, a process of externalizing internal thoughts, and curiosity: "*Desire*, to know why, and how, CURIOSITY; such as is in no living creature but *Man*."[71]

Hobbes's political "science," then, is actually bartering between two types of Man: one a Man by precept, defined by his position within a predefined and defining rhetoric; one a Man by praxis, defined solely by those traits that differentiate him from the totalizing goals of that rhetoric. Ironically, *Leviathan* continually returns to the Man by praxis as a means of fortifying the precept of Man.

> For, (I believe) the most sober men, when they walk alone without care and employment of the mind, would be unwilling the vanity and Extravagance of their thoughts at that time should be publiquely seen: which is a confession, that Passions unguided, are for the most part meere Madnesse.[72]

> Ignorance of remote causes, disposeth men to attribute all events, to the causes . . . they perceive.[73]

Other examples can be given, but these suffice to prove the point. When the teleology of Hobbes's system fails, it is not a function of the system; it is, rather, a function of private passions or personal ignorance. It is never a problem *of* Man but always a problem *with* men.[74] Implicit in the structure of *Leviathan*, then,

[70]Cf. M. M. Goldsmith, *Hobbes's Science of Politics* (New York, 1966), pp. 60–65.

[71]Hobbes, *Leviathan*, p. 124.

[72]Ibid., p. 142.

[73]Ibid., p. 166.

[74]Hobbes's formulation of the individual is somewhat idiosyncratic. A contemporaneous text, Harrington's *Oceana*, formulates a market economy theory of politics that eschews this dependence on individual mutability. Its argument can be summarized: "Its major premiss [*sic*] was that political

is the structure made explicit in *Troilus and Cressida* and *Edward II* through the dramatization of the construction of homoeroticism. When *at play* within a political "science," subjected to, as Foucault would call them, the "apparatuses" that solidify power and efface discrepancies, the inconsistencies of the body politic fade. But when *displayed*—that is, both anatomized on the stage and torn from the social cables that moor it—the dependence of "logical" order on the "illogic" it seeks to contain becomes apparent.

Leviathan solidifies a strategy of gendered politicization that was prevalent throughout the late Elizabethan and Jacobean Renaissance. One of the primary examples of the gendering of Stuart theory comes from King James himself, who, in *The Trew Law of Free Monarchies*, praises monarchy as "which forme of government, as resembling the Divinitie, approacheth nearest to perfection, as all the learned and wise men from the beginning have agreed upon; Unitie being the perfection of all things."[75] The "Unitie" or teleology that James posits as the precondition of power is solidified in the tract by a recourse to gendered metaphors of masculine social structure:

---

power depends on military power which depends on economic power which depends on land-ownership, and its minor premiss was that, since the time of Henry VII, the ownership of land in England had become increasingly dispersed, a diminishing proportion being owned by the King and his natural allies, so that by 1640 the superstructure of royal political power had become top-heavy and ready to collapse" (J. W. N. Watkins, *Hobbes's System of Ideas* [London, 1965], p. 14.). However, the use of the individual in Hobbes's tract provides the best analogy to how homoeroticism was being used in traditional hierarchies of power and, hence, fits the purpose of this argument. My conceptualization of the "desiring individual" has been much influenced by C. B. Macpherson's important analysis of the function of "bourgeois man" in Hobbes's epistemology (C. B. Macpherson, *The Political Theory of Possessive Individualism, Hobbes to Locke* [Oxford, 1962]). Macpherson's thesis, however, has not been greeted with universal acceptance. For a broader perspective on Hobbes's thought, consult Samuel I. Mintz, *The Hunting of Leviathan* (Cambridge, U.K., 1962), which is particularly good at describing the history of anti-Hobbism; Goldsmith, *Hobbes's Science of Politics*; and Watkins, *Hobbes's System of Ideas*.

[75]James I, *Political Works*, 1, p. 53

> By the Law of nature the King Becomes a naturall Father to all his Lieges at his Coronation: And as the Father of his fatherly duty is bound to care for the nourishing, education, and vertuous government of his children; even as is the king bound to care for all his subjects. As all the toile and paine that the father can take for his children, will be thought light and well bestowed by him; so that the effect thereof redound to their profite and weale; so ought the Prince to doe towards his people.[76]

The "Unitie" validated by "Divinitie" transforms into a series of power relations validated by the actuality of gendered experience. Like *Leviathan*, which posits a Man but then relies on the differences of *men*, James's theory negotiates a space between the precept of a posited transcendent perfection and the praxis of a demonstrable realm of fleshly power.

The inherent problems of positing a theoretical position exclusively on the transcendent gendered paradigm of Man—which is, despite divergences, the implied goal of James and the explicit goal of Hobbes—are satirically anatomized in *Troilus and Cressida*. Near the beginning of the play Pandarus, while wooing Cressida on behalf of Troilus, offers an explication of Man that is meant to substantiate his persuasive rhetoric: "Do you know what a man is? Is not birth, beauty, good shape, discourse, manhood, learning, gentleness, virtue, youth, liberality and such like, the spice and salt that season a man?" (I.ii.256–60) And Alexander, likewise trying to teach Cressida the rhetoric of Man, offers a definition of "a very man *per se*" (I.ii.15), Ajax, who "stands alone" (I.ii.16):

> This man, lady, hath robbed many beasts of their particular additions. He is as valiant as the lion, churlish as the bear, slow as the elephant: a man into whom nature hath so crowded humours that his valour is crushed into folly, his folly sauced with discretion. There is no man hath a virtue that he hath not a glimpse of, nor any man an attaint but he carries some stain of it. He is melancholy without cause and merry against the

[76]Ibid., p. 55.

hair; he hath the joints of everything, but everything so out of joint that he is gouty Briareus, many hands and no use, or purblind Argus, all eyes and no sight. (I.ii.19–31)

In each case the rhetoric of Man, when pushed to its logical extreme, results in a lapse of meaning. Cressida, a character far more concerned with the actualities of her situation, can easily undermine these precepts; she labels Pandarus's speech as a recipe for "a minced man; and then to be baked with no date in the pie, for then the man's date is out" (I.ii.261–262), and when told that Alexander's "man *per se*" stands alone—that is, in singularity—she responds, "So do all men unless they are drunk, sick, or have no legs" (I.ii.17–18). When pushed to logical extremes, precept no longer accounts for praxis but, rather, appears to be disjointed, distanced, irrelevant. For is this not the point of Cressida's responses: that what she *knows* of Man does not correlate with what she is *told* of Man?[77]

Precept that is too internally consistent and circumscribed, then, risks becoming only self-referential; to say it in Jonson's terms, a body must be able to piss, shit, and break wind. The "flaws" in *Leviathan*—the points at which the "science" of Man lapses into a description of men—mark at once those points at which teleology fails and also those points at which it stakes a tenuous claim to the actualities of material society. They mark, in short, both failure and empowerment of gendered teleological theory. They also mark the exact position of homoeroticism in Renaissance epistemology. For, like Patroclus himself, homoeroticism is both what a system of Man does not want and what it can most fortuitously use. This interdependence shows clearly

[77]Many would disagree with my interpretation here, in that my argument can be perceived as attributing a degree of personal agency to Cressida (for the opposing argument, see Gayle Greene, "Shakespeare's Cressida: 'A Kinde of self'," in *The Woman's Part: Feminist Criticism of Shakespeare*, ed. Carolyn Ruth Swift Lenz, Gayle Greene, and Carol Thomas Neely [Urbana, 1983], pp. 133–149.). However, it is important to recognize that the "space of agency" here is being attributed not to some sort of humanist psyche or "real" self but, rather, to a space of hesitation opened up by the failure of teleologically inscriptive theory.

in *Edward II*, where Mortimer constructs homoeroticism as the margin of orthodoxy but then quickly accepts it as his center of attack. Hobbes himself provides an apt but unwitting analysis of this procedure. As he says,

> when [Man] cannot assure himselfe of the true causes of things, (for causes of good and evill fortune for the most part are invisible,) he supposes causes of them, either such as his own fancy suggesteth; or trusteth to the Authority of other men, such as he thinks to be his friends, and wiser than himselfe.[78]

Homoeroticism fills this space between event and cause and also serves to elide "true" causes that, if deciphered, would render impotent the voice of politic order. It is in this context that a commonwealth must depend not just on the "Authority of other men" but also on the authority of sodomy.

[78]Hobbes, *Leviathan*, p. 169.

CHAPTER 3

The End(s) of Sodomy

We maintain we have the right to exist after the fashion which nature made us. And if we cannot alter your laws, we shall go on breaking them. You may condemn us to infamy, exile, prison—as you formerly burned witches. You may degrade our emotional instincts and drive us into vice and misery. But you will not eradicate inverted sexuality.

—John Addington Symonds

If adjustment is necessary, it should be made primarily with regard to the position the homosexual occupies in present-day society, and society should more often be treated than the homosexual.

—Dr. Harry Benjamin

The Renaissance Metaphysics of Desire

I have suggested that the canon of writings about Edward II indicate that the supposedly monolithic inscription of the stigmatized sodomite masks a nebulous epistemological space useful precisely because of its ability to range, contort, and transmogrify. Moreover, I have also suggested that the "space" of sodomy is, in actuality, coterminous with a vast range of other terms of "difference" within the culture. I would like now to adopt an antithetical position and suggest that rigid codes that find power in the mutability of sodomy can, in turn, be seen to mutate in relation to sodomy. Whereas the legal rhetoric of sodomy branded it as an absolute anathema, other rhetorics, most notably those of domestic and erotic decorum, sought to contain it in a logical economy of desire. The place of homoerotic desire within such continua demonstrates even more strongly its destabilizing potentiality within the epistemology of Elizabethan erotics, and two poems appended to epyllia provide a starting point for my analysis.[1] In a poem attached to the 1589 edition of *Scillaes Meta-*

[1]The generic name for poems such as Marlowe's *Hero and Leander*, Shakespeare's *Venus and Adonis*, Drayton's *Endimion and Phoebe*, and the like has attracted disproportionate critical attention. Several terms have been suggested as proper, including epyllion (Paul W. Miller, "A Function of Myth in Marlowe's *Hero and Leander*," *SP* 50 [1953]: 158–167), brief epic

morphosis, "Beauties Lullabie," Thomas Lodge provides a telling rhetorical use of homoeroticism. In recounting the reasons why he should hope to win the beautiful woman he loves, the speaker pointedly refers to Ganymede after he has been chosen by Jove: "Admit but this, that *Ganimede* the cupp for *Iove* did chuse: / And if man might drink with Gods, would I the same might use." Removed from its erotic context, this allusion might seem equally at home in the typological tradition of Petrus Berchorius, who, in the fourteenth century, refigured Jupiter as a type of the Christian God and Ganymede as a symbol of the transcendent soul.[2] Yet this typological possibility is undermined by both the erotic context of the poem and the erotic meanings associated with Ganymede, who is, as Cooper defines him, "A boye used contrary to nature." The expectation of eroticism fostered by the genre of the love complaint forces a recognition of the erotic meanings of this allusion to famous male-male love, and yet this allusion also serves the "natural" purpose of celebrating hetero-erotic love. Contrastingly, in one of the "Certaine Satyres" appended to John Marston's epyllion, "The Metamorphosis of Pigmalions Image," Ganymede surfaces in a less flattering image:

> But ho, what *Ganimede* is that doth grace
> The gallants heeles. One *who for two daies space*
> *Is closely hyred*. Now who dares not call
> This *Aesops* crow, fond, mad, fantasticall?
> Why, so he is, his clothes doe sympathize,

(Elizabeth Story Donno, *Elizabethan Minor Epics* [London, 1963]), and Ovidian erotic narrative (William Keach, *Elizabethan Ovidian Erotic Narratives: Irony and Pathos in the Ovidian Poetry of Shakespeare, Marlowe, and Their Contemporaries* [New Brunswick, 1977]). I accept all of these terms as equally valid means of referring to the group of erotic poems produced in the late 1500s and early 1600s, all of roughly similar lengths and all dealing with mythological narratives involving issues of sex and sexuality.

[2]Berchorius devotes book 15, chapter 1, of *Reductium Morale* to a Christian typologization of Ovid entitled *Metamorphosis Ovidiana moraliter*; similar rewritings of Ovid include Cristoforo Landino's Christian glosses, which are discussed in Erwin Panofsky, *Studies in Iconology: Humanistic Themes in the Art of the Renaissance* (Oxford, 1939, pp. 179, 214), and William Golding's influential and common English translations.

And with his inward spirit humorize.
An open Asse, that is not yet so wise
As his derided fondnes to disguise.[3]

Appended to these two epyllia—almost inscribed in their margins—are two different homoeroticisms: one used as a neutral if not positive metaphor for successful sexual union, the other used as a scathing debasement of foppishness and fondness.

These two examples present the parameters of a *logical* economy of homoerotic meanings—logical, that is, in the sense of proceeding from the *logos*, supporting orthodox systems of sexual signification. In Lodge's poem the image of homoeroticism is rarefied to a metaphoric essence, and the particulars of male-male attraction are effaced by an overriding metaphoric concern with the image of consummated love, which in turn elaborates the heteroerotic topic of the poem. In Marston's satire the homoerotic image is used as a means of more sharply delineating the continuum of sexual meaning and of more precisely labeling those sectors that are unacceptable. Lodge metaphorically effaces the "homo" from his "eroticism," whereas Marston satirically sharpens it. There are two homoeroticisms here, one *contra naturam* and the other *supra naturam*. Yet despite the divergent modifiers, the object is always defined in terms of its relation to the totalizing schema of the "natural." If "nature" is a system of ordered meaning—the universal public manuscript of God, as Thomas Browne would call it—then both of these poetic examples support this system by constructing various eroticisms as discrete units of meaning that can easily be transported and juxtaposed to each other without losing their essential significations.[4]

[3]John Marston, *The Metamorphosis of Pigmalion's Image and Certaine Satyres* (London, 1598), p. 52.

[4]On this view of nature, see Bray, *Homosexuality in Renaissance England*, pp. 13–32, and Catherine Belsey, *The Subject of Tragedy: Identity and Difference in Renaissance Drama* (London, 1985), pp. 13–128. An extended analysis of "Nature" as an epistemological category can also be found in Carolyn Merchant, *The Death of Nature: Women, Ecology, and the Scientific Revolution* (San Francisco, 1980).

Despite the fact that these invocations of homoeroticism cross a line of taboo and speak that which "is not to be named among Christians," they do so in a very conservative way that uses homoerotic allusion as an ornament or flourish that elaborates a primarily heteroerotic field of meanings. This style of allusion, which might best be called *ornamental homoeroticism*, surfaces frequently in epyllia. One lengthy mythological digression in Thomas Heywood's *Oenone and Paris* employs an image of classical homoeroticism to prove that "love is in no lawe contained":

The Imperious boy made Hercules to stoope,
That tamed tyrants, and did master monsters,
And pent him up within a slender coope.
Ah lordly love, the minde of man misconsters,
  He makes Alcides put apart his glave,
  And to his tentes t'followe him like a slave.[5]

This allusion to Hylas is just one element of a larger catalogue of examples of love's might: "His force made Jove with Danaes to jest"; Jove's "scapes with fayre Europa shew loves might."[6] Ultimately this catalogue proves that "the wanton wagge [Cupid] he spareth not one nor other,"[7] and, as with Lodge's couplet, validates the emerging heteroerotic union in the poem.

In all of these examples homoeroticism is figured as a marginal desire. It is subordinate to primary heteroerotic concerns, but it is still a part of the same language of desire, something that, though at a remove or on the margin, is still comprehensible through the same basic terms. The concept of erotic desire tacitly expressed by these allusions replicates broad patterns of sexual epistemology current throughout the Elizabethan era. In 1589 Leonard Wright offered these words of advice to parents: "The occasions for youth to yeeld unto vices are many; their bloud doth naturally stirre them, their flesh doth provoke them, sensualitie doth allure them, the world doth blind them, and Sathan himselfe doth

[5]Thomas Heywood, *Oenone and Paris* (London, 1595), stanzas 111, 113.
[6]Ibid., stanzas 109, 110.
[7]Ibid., stanza 112.

tempt them."[8] This advice, grounded as it is within the pragmatic discourse of child rearing, seems to carry with it an inherent "common sense"; but the tract also depends on a tacit conception of desire similar to that present in the poetic examples. For Wright, desire is a natural entity, a force that acts on everyone from outside much as Satan would tempt Eve. Desire gives rise to action, but the meaning of this action—morality—is a secondary construct:

> As youth by law of nature, are bound to honour, reverence, and obey their ancients: whose steps, either in good or evill: they are most apt and ready to imitate: so are elders bound in dutie and conscience, by doctrine, counsell, and example of life, to traine up youth in vertue and honestie. The fattest soyle without husbandrie, is soone overgrowne with weedes: and the aptest wits without government soone corrupt with vice.[9]

The premises underpinning Wright's argument are succinctly encapsulated in the terms of his final metaphor, that of tilling the soil. Like plants, which all derive from the soil, sexual activities all derive from some type of assumed natural Ur-force. It is then the task of human "husbandrie" to subdivide between fields and plots, between weeds and crops, between bad and good.[10]

The "rarefied" example of mythological narratives and the "pragmatic" genre of progenital advice provide potent sites for anatomizing the fissures in the Renaissance epistemology of homoeroticism, for, as Nancy Armstrong and Leonard Tennenhouse have noted, "expressions of desire in fact constitute ideology in its most basic and powerful form, namely, one that culture designates as nature itself. . . . [They are] a form of power in their

[8]Leonard Wright, *A Display of dutie, dect with sage sayings, pythie sentences, and proper similes: Pleasant to reade, delightfull to heare, and profitable to practice* (London, 1589), p. 1.

[9]Ibid., p. 1.

[10]A similar view of desire is exposed in other advice epistles from the era; see, for example, Cecil, *Certain Precepts for the Well Ordering of a Man's Life* (Folger MS). For a discussion of the literary and social implications of advice epistles see Marianne Novy, *Love's Argument: Gender Relations in Shakespeare* (Chapter Hill, 1984), pp. 1–9.

own right."[11] But what concerns my argument is not so much the way that these examples encode power as the ways in which they engender a space within the encoding of power. For what Wright's tract and Marston's and Lodge's poems present is a *metaphysics of desire* that unintentionally works against the stability of the very system of signification that it seeks to support. In the most basic sense, what these formulations achieve is a rupture between desire and activity, between the "natural" Ur-force that is universally significant and the secondary constructs of "good" and "bad" that delineate the range of activities proceeding from that Ur-force. While such a system salvages desire as an entirely natural force, it also inserts a space of human agency between desire and sexual meaning. Hence, this rupture is, at best, two-handed, for although it solidifies desire by severing it from the secondary construct of meaning, it at the same time undermines the "natural" validity of sexual meaning by anchoring it in a realm of human agency removed from the very desire that should validate it.

Such a formulation ironically foreshadows postmodern theory in a very telling way.[12] Indeed, the most radical of contemporary sexual theorists, Guy Hocquenghem, has forged his argument in terms that seem little more than an effort to make explicit the implicit terms of these Elizabethan statements:

[11]Nancy Armstrong and Leonard Tennenhouse, eds., *The Ideology of Conduct* (London, 1987), p. 2.

[12]I am not alone in recognizing a historic coincidence between discourse in the Renaissance and discursive theory in the twentieth century. For eloquent defenses of the coincidence and its place within critical practice, see Patricia Parker, *Literary Fat Ladies: Rhetoric, Gender, Property* (London, 1987), pp. 1–7, and David Quint's introduction to *Literary Theory/ Renaissance Texts*, ed. Patricia Parker and David Quint (Baltimore, 1986), pp. 1–19. My argument here has been greatly influenced by Derek Attridge's application of Derridean metaphysics to Puttenham's poetic theory (Derek Attridge, "Puttenham's Perplexity: Nature, Art, and the Supplement in Renaissance Poetic Theory," in *Literary Theory/Renaissance Texts*, pp. 257–279) not so much for its content as for its conception and execution—both of which demonstrate some of the gains to be made by positing an analogy between the theory of the two periods.

> "Homosexual desire"—the expression is meaningless. There is no subdivision of desire into homosexuality and heterosexuality. Properly speaking, desire is no more homosexual than heterosexual. Desire emerges in a multiple form, whose components are only divisible *a posteriori*, according to how we manipulate it. Just like heterosexual desire, homosexual desire is an arbitrarily frozen frame in an unbroken and polyvocal flux.[13]

Hocquenghem's problematic is all the more appropriate for my argument because it specifically takes as its topic the epistemological problem of homoerotic desire. But it is also indicative of a broader program of sexual radicalism in contemporary theory. In literary theory the formula most recognized is that of Julia Kristeva, who has focused a similar argument about gender meanings; as she states, "the very dichotomy man/woman as an opposition between two rival entities may be understood as belonging to *metaphysics*."[14] For Kristeva, gender is metaphysical—that is, above the physical—because it is a system of meaning. And as the work of post-Saussurian linguistic philosophers has posited, meaning (*logos*) is a system of differentiation placed onto the physical; it is *meta*physical. In its broadest form, this idea of metaphysics has been used to posit a critique of the entire system of Western sexual meaning. As Félix Guattari summarizes it,

> Once desire is specified as sexuality, it enters into forms of particularized power, into the stratification of castes, of styles, of sexual classes. . . . Desire is everything that exists *before* the opposition between subject and object, *before* representation and production.[15]

[13]Guy Hocquenghem, *Homosexual Desire*, trans. Daniella Dangoor (London, 1978), pp. 35–36.

[14]Julia Kristeva, "Women's Time," *Signs* 7, 1 (1981): 13–35.

[15]Félix Guattari, "A Liberation of Desire: An Interview by George Stambolian," in *Homosexualities and French Literature: Cultural Contexts/Critical Texts*, ed. Elaine Marks and George Stambolian, pp. 56–69 (Ithaca,

Much can be said—and has been said—about all of these statements. What concerns my argument, however, is not the content of these theories but rather their status as sociopolitical events. As these statements suggest, current theories of sexual meaning, which in the aggregate constitute a sociopolitical event, devote themselves to destabilizing platonic or a priori conceptions of sexuality and gender and usually as a means of inciting revolutions within preconceptions of stability. They also demarcate a historical point at which radical skepticism of sexual meaning, combined with a recognition of the basic politicism of sexuality, has resulted in a system of theoretical taxonomy that recognizes pluralities of possibilities within the signifying practices of sexual meaning in Western culture. Suggesting that Wright, Lodge, or Marston demonstrate a similar *intentionality* might be irresponsible. However, they do indicate a similar *potentiality*, a similar destabilization that, though not yet radically vectored, exists as a part of the Elizabethan epistemology. In the allusions of Marston and Lodge, homoeroticism is a part of a metaphysics of desire, a unit that fluctuates within an economy of sexual potentialities—marks its margins—but never betrays the basically conservative decorum of the system. Margins, however, do not just mark the center of a system but also denote its edges, the aporia, the place where it stops making sense. If Marston and Lodge make homoeroticism signal the centrality of heteroeroticism, other poems of the time make it signal the end of the erotic, the places where schema of sexual meaning fall short of their own totalizing goals. For the argument at hand I would like to examine the critique of sexual metaphysics present in several diverse source texts from Elizabethan traditions of romance and mythological erotic narratives.

1979), p. 5. For a fuller development of this theory, see Gilles Deleuze and Félix Guattari, *L'anti-Oedipe: Capitalisme et Schizophrénie* (Paris, 1972). For an equally provocative and somewhat more accessible text dealing with similar ideas, see Jeffrey Weeks, Preface to *Homosexual Desire*, Guy Hocquenghem, pp. 9–34, and "Discourse, Desire, and Sexual Deviance: Some Problems in a History of Homosexuality," in *The Making of the Modern Homosexual*, ed. Kenneth Plummer, pp. 76–111 (London, 1981).

The Margins of Romance

Wright, the humanist, the educator in the tradition of Ascham and Elyot, would likely be shocked to find his tract used to signal an early Renaissance metaphysics of sexual meaning. But his literary contemporary Abraham Fraunce seems to revel in questioning the integrity of the decorum of sexuality. The opening of *The Countesse of Pembroke's Yvy-Church* recounts the tale of Amyntas's seduction of Phillis and a subsequent attempt by a Satyr to rape Phillis. In preparing for the rape episode, the narrator offers a skeptical assessment of the codes of sexual propriety:

> But sweete age of gold, for that this name of a noething,
> Idle name of nought, and dayly deceavable Idoll,
> Which fooles afterward, fine-fooles have made to be *Honnor*,
> Was nor nam'd, nor knowne, nor brought new lawes to the
>   countrey
> And poore countreymen, whose lives were onely directed
> By sweete Natures law, sweete Nature taught them a lesson,
> *If you will, you may*: and strait-lac't rules did abandon.[16]

As Wright's does in his tacit conception of desire, Fraunce posits a golden Ur-world in which "sweete Natures law"—desire—leads only to undifferentiated action: "*If you will, you may*." In no uncertain terms, the narrator declares that the demise of this undifferentiated sexual world resulted from an artificial process of division and mediation, a process of ascribing meaning where it did not exist:

> Honnor first cov'red wel-spring of lovely *Cupido*,
> Honnor pluckt water from scorched mouths of a Lover,
> Honnor taught fayre eyes theyr glittring beames to b[e]
>   hyding,
> And to darckned soul their light unkindly denying. . . .

[16]Abraham Fraunce, *The Countess of Pembroke's Yvy-Church* (London, 1591), sig. C2r.

. . . Honnor cal'd it a theft, which first was counted a free guift.
Honnor made it a cryme, which first was thought but a pastyme.[17]

Honor here is similar to the metaphysical constructs that figure so prominently in the work of Guattari, Hocquenghem, and Kristeva. It is an arbitrary system of differentiation that distinguishes between bad and good, vice and virtue, and transgression and decorum. Most important, honor is not an a priori characteristic of the golden Ur-world of desire but is rather an ex post facto construction of the brazen world of chastity, rape, and sexuality. And it is probably worth noting that the poet, Fraunce, was also one of the period's most noted rhetoricians—that is, a *linguistic philosopher*.

We might very well choose to be intentionally anachronistic and label Fraunce's text as a Kristevan romance, for what it presents is a very self-conscious foregrounding of the metaphysics of sexual meaning.[18] This structure is also present in the

[17]Ibid., sig. C2r.

[18]The metaphysical schema present in both Wright and Fraunce can be clarified and extended through an analogy to Derrida's conception of metaphor in "White Mythology" (Jacques Derrida, "White Mythology: Metaphor in the Text of Philosophy," in *Margins of Philosophy*, trans. Alan Bass, pp. 207–272 [Chicago, 1982]). Derrida posits two "metaphors": one that, like Aristotle's conception of it, is an act of ornamentation or transportation within language; another that is the originary loss of presence giving rise to and constructed by language (signification) in the first place. Wright overtly posits two "desires" that correspond to these two types of metaphor, and thereby Wright's text embodies an epistemological complication similar to that which Derrida deconstructs in the discourse of Western philosophy. Fraunce's structure is less overt, but it is still dealing with two "desires"—one that governs sexual meaning, the other that gives rise to the conditions of sexual meaning. Derrida's conception of this "double" metaphor is, I think, a model that can be used to clarify much in Elizabethan epistemology. Jonathan Dollimore, for example, recognizes a similar bifurcation in Renaissance uses of "chaos": "To the extent that it posits an underlying, primordial state of dislocation, the language of chaos mystifies social process. To the extent that it interrogates providentialist belief—robbing the absolute of *its* mystifying function—it foregrounds social process" (Jonathan Dollimore, *Radical Tragedy: Religion, Ideology, and Power in the Drama of Shake-*

most canonical of all Elizabethan romances, Philip Sidney's *The Countess of Pembroke's Arcadia*, but in a way that demonstrates the affinity between homoeroticism and the recognition of sexual metaphysics *as* metaphysics. Indeed, if Fraunce wrote Kristevan romance, Sidney wrote Hocquenghemian romance—a claim that I make because it is all the more shocking to yoke the gay radical of postmodern theory and the stalwart of Elizabethan courtly poetry in the same phrase.

Initially, it is helpful to look momentarily at the events that led to the composition of *The Old Arcadia*.[19] During the 1570s, when the issue of Elizabeth I's marital status reached a certain crisis owing, in part, to Sidney's own role in the development of a Protestant alliance with Germany and the Netherlands,[20] the poet drafted his famous and unsolicited letter of advice to the queen, saying,

> Often have I heard you with protestation say: 'No private pleasure nor self affection could lead you [to wed]'. . . . Nothing can it add unto you, but only the bliss of children: which, I confess, were a most unspeakable comfort, but yet no more appertaining to him, than to any other to whom the height of all good haps were allotted, to be your husband. And therefore I may assuredly affirm that what good soever can follow marriage is no more his, than anybody's.[21]

Sidney's letter reflects the frightful prospect of Elizabeth's union with the Duke of Alençon, a match that was associated in the communal psyche with both alien infiltration and Catholicism. On the broadest level, the letter exposes two contradictory no-

---

speare and His Contemporaries [Chicago, 1984], p. 44). This formulation, which, like Derrida's "metaphor," posits the possibility of thesis and antithesis within one concept, provides another apt analogy for the discursive strategies of Renaissance (homo)eroticism.

19For a fuller account of the issues I bring up here, see Richard C. McCoy, *Sir Philip Sidney: Rebellion in Arcadia* (New Brunswick, 1979), pp. 1–35.

20See ibid., p. 12.

21Philip Sidney, *Miscellaneous Prose of Sir Philip Sidney*, ed. Katherine Duncan-Jones and Jan Van Dorsten (Oxford, 1973), p. 51.

tions: the need to urge Elizabeth to wed to produce an heir and the need to restrain her right to wed to assure the sanctity of English national authority. This anxiety shows forth clearly in the very title of John Stubbes's pamphlet, *The discovery of a gaping Gulf wherein England is to be swallowed by another french marriage.* Yet the case of Stubbes, who ultimately had his right hand chopped off as punishment for his publication, also demonstrates that the scenario invokes another set of contradictions. The exercise of the patriarchal right of men to control the line of descent is, if only in an imaginary form, on the side of Sidney and Stubbes. And yet the exercise of such a right in this instance also demands that a subject presuppose authority over the monarch, in this case their *king*, Queen Elizabeth.[22] With the authoritative line of sexual decorum set at odds with the authoritative line of monarchical government, the premises of (male) power erode and vacillate.[23] And this erosion is directly responsible for *The Old Arcadia*, for Sidney's letter forced his retreat from the court into a temporary exile, during which he wrote the romance.[24]

Indeed, this particular text can be seen as complicit with a full-

[22]See Maureen Quilligan, "Sidney and His Queen," in *The Historical Renaissance: New Essays on Tudor and Stuart Literature and Culture*, ed. Heather Dubrow and Richard Strier, pp. 171–196 (Chicago, 1988), pp. 177–180.

[23]For a broader discussion of the Stubbs controversy, see J. E. Neale, *Queene Elizabeth I: A Biography* (New York, 1957), pp. 248–249, and Sidney, *Miscellaneous Prose*, p. 35.

[24]My argument here is indebted to Robert E. Stillman's brilliant analysis of the ways in which Sidney's text negotiates the cultural tensions at work in his era. See Robert E. Stillman, "The Politics of Sidney's Pastoral: Mystification and Mythology in *The Old Arcadia*," *ELH* 52, 4 (1986): 795–814. The exact relationship between Sidney's letter and his retreat from the court has been the subject of some debate. Richard Lanham has persuasively argued that the letter was not original with Sidney, but was motivated by Leicester and Walsingham; see Richard Lanham, "Sidney: The Ornament of His Age," *Southern Review* 2, 4 (1967): 327. Moreover, Katherine Duncan-Jones and Jan Van Dorsten have questioned both Elizabeth's ability and desire to effect the type of exile generally attributed to the scenario; see Sidney, *Miscellaneous Prose*, pp. 36–37. Since I suggest that the text reflects not the exact political circumstances but, rather, a set of anxieties underpinning the political scene, the question of direct causality is not directly relevant to my argument.

scale anxiety about the viability of male political power in general. The main narrative begins with a rupture in patrilineal power, a prophecy of kingly demise and domestic upheaval:

> Thy elder care shall from thy careful face
> By princely mean be stolen and yet not lost;
> Thy younger shall with nature's bliss embrace
> An uncouth love, which nature hateth most.
> Thou with thy wife adult'ry shalt commit,
> And in thy throne a foreign state shall sit.
> All this on thee this fatal year shall hit.[25]

Leonard Tennenhouse has persuasively argued that this scenario imitates the actualities of Elizabethan political anxieties; as he states, this passage mirrors the anxiety "that once embodied in the female, power can be transferred to an outsider, a foreign line perhaps, or a family not of aristocratic lineage at all"[26]—a problematic replicated in Elizabeth and her proposed union with the Duke of Alençon. This anxiety about the solidity of male power is also, I will claim, mirrored in a pattern of male homoerotic bonding presented in the Pyrocles and Musidorus subplot, an episode in which the concern over the maintenance of power "between men"[27] is metaphorically redacted and represented.

[25]Philip Sidney, *The Old Arcadia*, ed. Katherine Duncan-Jones (Oxford, 1985), p. 5.

[26]Leonard Tennenhouse, *Power on Display: The Politics of Shakespeare's Genres* (New York, 1986), p. 19. Further evidence of the intersection of the *Old Arcadia* and the political crisis of Elizabeth's marriage can be found in Philanax's advice to Basilius in the first book—"Let your subjects have you in their eyes, let them see the benefits of your justice daily more and more; and so must they needs rather like of present sureties than uncertain changes" (p. 7)—which directly parallels Sidney's letter to Elizabeth: "Against contempt at home, if there be any, which I will never believe, let your excellent virtues of piety, justice and liberality daily, if it be possible, more and more shine. Let some such particular actions be found out (which is easy, as I think, to be done) by which you may gratify all the hearts of your people" (Sidney, *Miscellaneous Prose*, pp. 56–57).

[27]Eve Kosofsky Sedgwick has noted that "homosocial" bonding, which is a means of solidifying power between men, depends on an intense "homophobia, fear and hatred of homosexuality" (Eve Kosofsky Sedg-

In Sidney's lengthy prose narrative about the fates of lovers and disrupted families, the major intrigue revolves around Pyrocles' desire for Philoclea.[28] This plot is introduced into the romance through a complicated interplay of rhetoric and homoeroticism.

> Till at length love, the refiner of invention, put in his head a way how to come to the sight of his Philoclea; for which he with great speed and secrecy prepared everything that was necessary for his purpose, but yet would not put it in execution till he had disclosed it to Musidorus, both to perform the true laws of friendship and withal to have his counsel and allowances.[29]

"Love, the refiner of invention" is duplicitous, for although its primary suggestion is that love motivates Pyrocles to greater action, the phrase also carries with it a distinctive image of artifice. No longer a "natural" course of "husbandrie," love is figured as a process of specifying ("refining") a human construct (an "invention"). Pyrocles himself figures his love as a process of limiting some preceding state of greater potentiality when he describes his first encounter with the image of Philoclea:

---

wick, *Between Men: English Literature and Male Homosocial Desire* (New York, 1985), p. 1, pp. 1–20 passim). Therefore, the breakdown of masculine power systems, as in both *The Old Arcadia* and the actual Elizabethan political arena, conversely might be expected to provide fissures that reveal these repressed dynamics. This is, in any event, the structure I am suggesting. I thank Stephen Orgel for pointing me to this idea.

[28]I am dealing with *The Old Arcadia* here primarily for its chronological coincidence with Fraunce's text and the other poems I discuss in the chapter. The significant changes between editions of the text do not affect the portions on which I base my argument. For a synopsis of the changes between editions see C. S. Lewis, *English Literature in the Sixteenth Century Excluding Drama* (Oxford, 1954), p. 332; for an exploration of the interpretive problems aroused by the multiple texts, see Annabel Patterson, "'Under . . . Pretty Tales': Intention in Sidney's *Arcadia*," *Studies in the Literary Imagination* 15, 1 (1982): 5–21. The most important and insightful study to date on the relationship between the several texts is Michael McCanles, *The Text of Sidney's Arcadian World* (Durham, N.C., 1989).

[29]Sidney, *Old Arcadia*, pp. 11–12.

> For since it was the fatal overthrow of all my liberty to see in the gallery of Mantinea the only Philoclea's picture, that beauty did pierce so through mine eyes to my heart that the impression of it doth not lie but live there, in such sort as the question is not now whether I shall love or no, but whether loving, I shall live or die.[30]

Pyrocles' explanation of his love expresses an economical system of desire similar to that in the allusions of Lodge and Marston. Although his original perception is a "fatal overthrow of all [his] liberty," this death results in the chance for a "greater" death, the chance for orgasm punningly encoded in the word "die." The initiation into love is a trade-off, a sort of risky business in which something is surrendered toward the hope of a greater future pleasure. Indeed, Pyrocles seems to be aware of the gamble he is taking. In response to Musidorus's admonitions that he should turn his attentions to his own mind's refinement, Pyrocles states:

> Condemn not, therefore, my mind to enjoy itself, nor blame not the taking of such times as serve most fit for it! . . . Doth not the pleasantness of this place carry in itself sufficient reward for any time lost in it, or for any such danger that might ensue? Do you not see how everything conspires together to make this place a heavenly dwelling. . . . Nor any less than a goddess could have made it so perfect a model of the heavenly dwelling.[31]

The loss of time, Pyrocles suggests, may be regrettable, but it may be offset by the pleasures to be had in some new gain. Significantly, this new gain is an encoding of the loss of originary presence, for the pleasurable land is "a model of the heavenly dwelling," not the heavenly dwelling itself. Pyrocles' love for Philoclea is continually figured as a loss of some original unity or presence, an idea that shows forth strongly in the fact that his loss

[30]Ibid., p. 16.
[31]Ibid., p. 14.

of liberty does not occur when he sees Philoclea but, rather, when he sees her painted image.

The romance in this romance continually returns to the notion that love is an artifice that replaces some preceding state but that such loss is compensated by, to borrow Derrida's phrase, "a dividend of pleasure."[32] Moreover, the romance is structured by a broad set of tropes that equate this derivative quest with heteroeroticism. Elizabethan medical theory metaphorized male sexuality in an equation of semen, orgasm, and death, with each orgasm shortening the life of a man—an idea that John Donne summarizes in "Farewell to Love": "since each such act, they say / Diminisheth the length of life a day"[33] Not only does Pyrocles' desire to decide whether "loving, [he] shall live or die" translate into a plea for orgasm, but the quarrel over dalliance—the wasting of time—translates into a debate on the effects of that orgasm. The entire opening of the romance, then, becomes something more than a tale of love. The quest for love is punningly associated with the tropics of heteroeroticism, and in the process the actions of Pyrocles become associated with a *decision* to enter heteroerotic meaning. Though not as blatant as Fraunce's diatribe on honor, the representation of Pyrocles' decision to pursue the love of Philoclea suggests a decision to enter a system of metaphysics, a system of meanings that appear all the more arbitrary

[32]Derrida, "White Mythology," p. 239. Although I am constructing my argument through a yoking of Renaissance and modern rhetorics, it is equally fascinating and valid to note an opposite historical directionality. The continual comparison of artifice and loss of presence in Sidney's text finds a strong analogue in Plato's parable of the table in *The Republic*, which figures mimesis as a break in unity with the creating mind (God); the state preceding the heteroerotic quest in the romance also figures favorably with Plato's *Symposium*, in which Pausanius describes the evolution of gender roles as a godly punishment and loss of an original polymorphism (or, rather, amorphism, since no roles have yet been created).

[33]John Donne, *John Donne: The Complete English Poems*, ed. A. J. Smith (Harmondsworth, U.K., 1971), p. 57. The exact etiology of this equation, as well as its relationship to Renaissance gynecological and reproductive sciences, has been explored by Thomas Lacqueur, "Orgasm, Generation, and the Politics of Reproductive Biology," *Representations* 14 (1986): 4–16, and Stephen Greenblatt, "Fiction and Friction," in *Reconstructing Individualism*, ed. Thomas C. Heller et al. (Stanford, 1986).

because implicit in the ability to decide is the ability to decide *otherwise*.

In Fraunce's narrative the metaphysical status of *all* sexual meaning is indicated by its juxtaposition to a metaphoric, golden Ur-world. In Sidney's text the juxtaposition is further specified and the metaphysics of heteroeroticism are signaled by an opposition between them and a bizarre set of partially sublimated homoerotic structures. Before Pyrocles can enact love's "refined invention," he must first bid farewell to this other system, "but yet [he] would not put it in execution till he had disclosed it to Musidorus, both to perform the true laws of friendship and withal to have his counsel and allowance."[34] The state preceding Pyrocles' loss of liberty is characterized by masculine friendship and male bonding—a system of interaction that, though not overtly sexual, defines itself in terms of same-sex exchanges. Pyrocles' quest for love, which appears to him to be an accrual of pleasurable dividends, appears in this Ur-world as a *loss* of pleasure. As Musidorus says,

> I do now beseech you, even for the love betwixt us (if this other love have left any in you towards me), and for the remembrance of your old careful father (if you can remember him, that forgets yourself), lastly, for Pyrocles' own sake (who is not upon the point of falling or rising), to purge your head of this vile infection. Otherwise, give me leave rather in absence to bewail your mishap than to bide the continual pang of seeing your danger with mine eyes.[35]

Pyrocles, Musidorus suggests, is not just falling into love but is falling between systems of meaning. What is a golden Ur-world of polymorphism for Fraunce becomes, for Sidney, a world of homoerotic masculinity. Polymorphism and homoeroticism become roughly analogous means of articulating what exists *before* the conception of sex and gender, before, to paraphrase Hocquenghem, the opposition between the subject of heterosexual discourse and that discourse itself.

[34]Sidney, *Old Arcadia*, p. 12.
[35]Ibid., p. 22.

The metaphysical aspect of heteroeroticism in the romance is increasingly foregrounded, for it is not only set in opposition to a homoerotic Ur-state but is also carefully correlated with high rhetorical modes that make it seem far removed from any "natural" significance. Indeed, Pyrocles' quest to find the presence of the painted image leads him into a widening spiral of art and artifice, for he chooses as his strategy the most unlikely plan of cross-dressing:

> I am resolved, because all direct ways are barred me of opening my suit to the duke, to take upon me the estate of an Amazon lady going about the world to practise feats of chivalry and to seek myself a worthy husband. I have already provided all furniture necessary for it; and my face, you see, will not easily discover me. And hereabout will I haunt till, by the help of her whose imprisonment darkens the world, that my own eyes may be witnesses to my heart it is great reason why he should be thus captived.[36]

With "all direct ways" barred, the only means to a "presence" of love is an ever-increasing complication of identities and genders. The structure here is one in which artifice and obfuscation are strategically bartered in the hopes that the "presence" of love achieved will be enough to outweigh the temporary obfuscation of signifying practices. It is also a process intrinsically interwoven with rhetoric and metaphor; as Pyrocles says, "As for my name, it shall be Cleophila, turning Philoclea to myself, as my mind is wholly turned and transformed into her."[37] His desire turns toward Philoclea, his mind turns into her, and his name turns into a turning of her name. His quest for heteroerotic romantic love always turns toward the tropics of turning, a Renaissance rhetorical strategy inherently linked with loss and gain, with invention and artifice:

> A Trope or turning is when a word is turned from his naturall signification, to some other, so convenientlie, as that it seeme

[36]Ibid., pp. 16–17.
[37]Ibid., p. 17.

rather willinglie ledd, than driven by force to that other signification. This was first invented of necessitie for want of words, but afterwards continued and frequented by reason of the delight and pleasant grace thereof.[38]

Pyrocles' plan might best be thought of as a troping of a trope, for if the romance begins by positing heteroerotic love as an ascriptive system, Pyrocles assumes an ability to reascribe it. But the text itself in turn tropes this troping: it reminds us that the strategy is a movement away from the originary presence it seeks by associating the plan with high rhetoric, not with "truth" or "presence."

As in the economies of Lodge and Marston, homoeroticism skulks at the margins of the "real" concern of this poem, the heteroerotic union of Pyrocles and Philoclea. But this homoeroticism is not the same sort of ornament or flourish. It is, rather, an indicator of everything that the romance's high artifice of heteroeroticism fails to capture. There is little point in trying to—or in wanting to—claim *The Old Arcadia* for some sort of homoerotic literary history. The love of Musidorus and Pyrocles occupies but a small section and is ultimately rewritten into the more "proper" couplings of Musidorus/Pamela and Pyrocles/ Philoclea (albeit only after some very messy permutations of couples and identities).[39] Musidorus, the spokesperson for the homo-

[38]Fraunce, *Arcadian Rhetoric*, p. 5.

[39]The "propriety" of the heteroerotic plot is, in itself, open to question. Alan Sinfield, for example, claims that "there are at least six ways in which the *Arcadia* manifests, in effect, a critique of absolutist tendencies" (Alan Sinfield, "Power and Ideology: An Outline Theory and Sidney's *Arcadia*," in *Essential Articles for the Study of Sir Philip Sidney*, ed Arthur F. Kinney [Hamden, Conn. 1986], p. 398). Sinfield also notes that the text "is primarily about the deeds of subaltern figures" (ibid., p. 398)—a point that interfaces well with my recuperation of a homoerotic component. The issue of female desire becomes especially problematized in the romance. Explaining the thoughts of Philoclea, who is enamoured of the cross-dressed Pyrocles and thinks him to be a woman, the narrator tells how "sometimes she would compare the love she bare to Cleophila with the natural goodwill she bare to her sister; but she perceived it had another kind of working. Sometimes she would wish Cleophila had been a man, and her brother; and yet, in truth, it was no brotherly love she desired of her" (p. 86). Implied

erotic Ur-world, becomes fully involved in a quest for romance that is every bit as artificial as that of Pyrocles. Indeed, it is even possible to imagine a level of compliment in the high artifice ascribed to heteroeroticism; for Sidney, after all, artifice was income—a way of wooing, if not for love, then certainly for lucre and advancement—and in the figure of Pyrocles we might see not critique but, rather, promotion of the poet's own social occupation.[40]

However, the point here is again one of potentiality, not one of intentionality. And the potential here is very clearly that homoeroticism can do more than signal where the center begins. In this case, it also becomes an index of the sort of male panic that resides beneath the surface of the entire text. For Sidney, faced with the prospects of a disastrous wedding, disfavor at court, exile, and disgrace, the very systems of masculine power that he courted so diligently must surely have seemed as disjointed and ephemeral as the homoerotic bond of Pyrocles and Musidorus—and the heterocentric dynamic of "courting" a queen must have seemed as loss-ridden and risky as the subsequent main narrative. Homoeroticism, then, can be perceived as something other than the margin of sexual meaning; it can also signal where the margins end and, in the process, indicate through implication the limited status of heteroerotic epistemology.

Epyllia and the End of the Erotic

The muted homoeroticism of Sidney's Hocquenghemian romance becomes, in the genre of the epyllion, harsh and brazen

---

here is a clear division between desire and its social expression, for Philoclea *desires*, and now attempts to find a socially recognized form through which to articulate it. We might also note how this desire is problematized by Basilius's lust for Cleophila (Pyrocles); for if we attempt to explain Philoclea's desire as "normal" by saying she is really attracted to the man beneath the costume, then Basilius's desire correspondingly becomes abnormal. I would like to thank my English 152 class at the University of California, Riverside, for bringing this analysis to my attention.

[40]These issues, especially as they relate to *Astrophil and Stella*, are all creatively discussed by Maureen Quilligan, "Sidney and His Queen," pp. 171–196.

declarations of a radically confrontational homoerotic potentiality. Whereas the appended poems of Marston and Lodge inscribe a conservative economy on the margins of epyllia, the more typical exploitation of homoeroticism within the genre is one of full-scale warfare on the intelligibility of heteroerotic systems. Michael Drayton, in *Endimion and Phoebe*, employs a series of hyperbolic mythical allusions to describe the sexual and aesthetic splendor of Endimion, and one that is distinctly homoerotic begins to suggest the ways in which the genre associates homoeroticism with a rupture in the economy of sexual meaning. "Endimion, the lovely Shepheardes boy," possessed such great allure that "fairies daunst the heydegies," "Satyrs . . . have been made tame by gazing in his face," and, most important,

> Jove oft-times bent to lascivious sport,
> And comming where Endimion did resort,
> Hath courted him, inflamed with desire,
> Thinking some Nymph was cloth'd in boyes attire.[41]

To a certain extent this catalogue of sexual appeal is necessitated by Drayton's earlier claim that "all the pleasures Nature could devise, / Within this plot [Mount Latmus] she did imparadize,"[42] and the homoerotic allusion becomes a means of inscribing the entire continuum of sexual meanings within the rhetorical landscape of the poem. However, this specific allusion also problematizes the continuum of sexual meanings, for it is difficult to discern exactly what Jove desires. Is this a simple recapitulation of the homoerotic myth of Jove and Ganymede, with Endimion tacitly cast as Ganymede? If that is the case, then why does the final line of the allusion add an element of travesty that complicates such a purely homoerotic pattern of desire? Indeed, the final line thoroughly obfuscates any possible reading of Jove's desire, for it is impossible to ascertain whether he desires a nymph he perceives beneath "boyes attire" or whether he desires the "boyes attire" he sees covering a nymph—and the impossibility is further sustained by the recurrence of Jove in both homoerotic and

[41]Michael Drayton, *Endimion and Phoebe. Ideas Latmus* (London, 1595), ll. 83–96.

[42]Ibid., ll. 19–20.

heteroerotic classical myths. On the one hand, the allusion is a means of rhetorically capturing *all* sexual meaning; on the other hand, it undercuts the possibility of *any* sexual meaning by rendering Jove's desire incomprehensible. The allusion, then, suggests something quite different from the economies of Lodge, Marston, and Heywood. It suggests that homoeroticism can exist not just as a type of sexual meaning but also as a critique of sexual meaning.

The anarchic potentiality encoded in Drayton's homoeroticism is fully exploited in Marlowe's *Hero and Leander*. Marlowe's text uses instances of highly specific homoerotic desire to foreground and display the discursive base of supposedly natural heteroerotic desire. The most accessible example of this strategy occurs in the lampooning of descriptive technique in the opening blazons of the poem. "Hero the fair" is mapped out in minute detail:

> The outside of her garments were of lawn,
> The lining purple silk, with gilt stars drawn;
> Her wide sleeves green, and bordered with a grove,
> Where Venus in her naked glory strove
> To please the careless and disdainful eyes
> Of proud Adonis that before her lies.[43]

"Her kirtle blue" (I.15), "myrtle wreath" (I.17), "veil [of] artificial leaves" (I.19), and "chains of pebble stone" (I.25) complete the outfit, and even such seemingly trivial particulars as "she ware no gloves, for neither sun nor wind / Would burn or parch her hands" (I.27–28) are carefully blazoned forth.

Hero's description participates in a strong literary tradition, but it is equally distinguished by its difference from the tradition. The female anatomical blazon derived from a French courtly tradition that, practically from its inception, was almost parodically overdetermined.[44] The most refined example of the

[43]Marlowe, *Complete Plays and Poems*, p. 401. All subsequent citations will be given by sestiad and line number.

[44]My discussion of the blazon is influenced heavily by Nancy J. Vickers's work on female descriptive technique (Nancy J. Vickers, "Diana Described:

genre, *S'ensuivent Les Blasons Anatomiques du Corps Feminin*, succinctly displays its traits even within its titles: "Blason de la joue," "Blason de la bouche," "Blason du sourcil," "Blason des cheveux." The logic underpinning the poetics here is very clearly one of divide and conquer; as Nancy Vickers has noted in her perceptive discussion of the genre, "bodies fetishized by a poetic voice logically do not have a voice of their own; the world of making words, of making texts, is not theirs."[45] But just as present in the poetic is an assumption about the transparency of language. For in order for the strategy to work, the poetry must be expressive—it must be able to give access to the subject it will in turn control. In such a formula language is part of a disappearing act, part of a strategy in which rhetoric is subservient to meaning, form subservient to content. Hero's description is, to be sure, meticulously placed within the confines of tradition. And yet this careful blazon also carefully undermines the validity of the genre. The dynamics of anatomizing female flesh that so typify the genre are rendered impotent. Hero has a head, but it seems to be little more than a support for her intricately described headgear. Her hand, though impervious to sun and wind, is pinioned and obscured by the weighty metaphoric phrases it must support. When her "bosom" and "naked neck" finally appear, they appear not in the flesh but in a moment of discursive conjecture about the mythological Cupid (I.37–44). Indeed,

---

Scattered Woman and Scattered Rhyme," in *Writing and Sexual Difference*, ed. Elizabeth Abel [Brighton, 1982]), as well as the pioneering work of Elizabeth Cropper, which also influenced Vickers (Elizabeth Cropper, "On Beautiful Women, Parmigiannio, *Petrarchismo*, and the Vernacular Style," *Art Bulletin* 58 [1976]: 374–394). Two other studies have also aided my work by demonstrating how the strains of female control that Vickers and Cropper find in the genre intersect with other systems of cultural power. Patricia Parker convincingly extends the genre into the realms of capitalism, mercantilism, and colonialism (Parker, *Literary Fat Ladies*, pp. 126–154). Jonathan Goldberg notes an intersection between the strategies of gendered power in the blazon and the systems of control implicit in the Renaissance pedagogy of writing and of forming the female hand (Jonathan Goldberg, *Writing Matter: From the Hands of the English Renaissance* [Stanford, 1990], pp. 137–155).

[45]Vickers, "Diana Described," p. 107.

compared to more typical examples of the genre, Hero's elaborate blazon barely manages to capture any of Hero, a comic impotency recognized by Thomas Edwards in his epyllion *Narcissus*:

> Welcome *Leander*, welcome, stand thou neer,
> Alacke poore youth, what hast thou for a pawne,
> What not a rag, where's *Heroes* vale of lawne?
> Her buskins all of Shels ysilvered ore,
> What hast thou noth? then pack yonder's the doore.[46]

Hero's blazon maintains the form and voids the content, but the exact implications of this maneuver are only visible in relation to the subsequent description of Leander. "Amorous Leander, beautiful and young" (I.51), has "dangling tresses that were never shorn" (I.55) and arms that "Fair Cynthia wish'd . . . might be her sphere" (I.59). His body appears unhindered by the clothing and obfuscating rhetoric of Hero's blazon:

> His body was as straight as Circes' wand;
> Jove might have sipp'd out nectar from his hand.
> Even as delicious meat is to the taste,
> So was his neck in touching, and surpass'd
> The white of Pelop's shoulder. I could tell ye
> How smooth his breast was, and how white his belly,
> And whose immortal fingers did imprint
> That heavenly path with many a curious dint
> That runs along his back.
>
> (I.61–69)

The "muse" continues to blaze poetically "Leander's eyes" and "those orient cheeks and lips" (I.72–73) and later presents his "pleasant smiling cheek, a speaking eye, / A brow for love to banquet royally" (I.85–86). Despite the poet's disclaimer that his "rude pen / Can hardly blazon forth the loves of men" (I.69–70), it is here that we see, in the masculine flesh of Leander, a true blazon and physical form. Hero is all clothing and words, but Leander is a *presence* to be dealt with:

[46]Thomas Edwards, *Narcissus* (London, 1595), stanza 26.

His presence made the rudest peasant melt,
That in the vast uplandish country dwelt.
The barbarous Thracian soldier, mov'd with nought,
Was mov'd with him, and for his favour sought.
Some swore he was a maid in man's attire,
For in his looks were all that men desire.

(I.79–84)

Leander is not, however, a maid in man's attire. He is, rather, a man in maid's attire: a masculine body anatomized and substantiated through the typically feminine rhetoric of the Renaissance blazon.

The structure of *Hero and Leander*'s opening undermines the assumed transparency of descriptive technique by refiguring the blazon as a sort of ready-made matrix that can be shifted between subjects regardless of the subjects' gender. Such a severing of form and content interrogates the techniques of gender control implicit in the genre.[47] There is, in other words, no discernible *logical* correlation between the blazon and the female gender in Marlowe's poem. However, the poem's critique of descriptive technique assumes an even more disruptive level in its manipulation of homoerotic desire. In turning the blazon technique to the masculine subject, the poem also turns male sexual desire onto the male subject and thereby suggests that the "natural" desire motivating metaphysical schema such as Wright's is not natural but rhetorical. Leander's blazon establishes him as "all that men

[47]The structure I am outlining here can be amplified by Bakhtin's helpful analysis of the blazon in *Rabelais and His World*. Using the example of Marot, Bakhtin describes how "the blazon preserved the duality of its tone in its appreciation; in other words, it could render praise ironical and flatter that which was usually not to be flattered. Blazons remained outside the official system of straight and strict evaluations. They were a free and ambiguous praise-abuse" (427). As with much of Bakhtin's work, I think there is an overestimation of transgressive potentiality here; there is nothing *inherent* in the genre that makes it radical. However, Bakhtin's central point—that the blazon activated a specific intersection of textuality and bodily strata that proved to be epistemologically troubling—seems irrefutable. This analysis also bolsters my own analysis of Marlowe's blazon technique, for it demonstrates how the genre itself occupied a space that could be easily contorted for *either* conservative or transgressive purposes.

desire" (I.84). Indeed, Leander is presented as the ultimate object of desire for men. He "would have allur'd the vent'rous youth of Greece" (I.57), and "Jove might have sipp'd out nectar from his hand" (I.62), an image that casts Leander as the irresistible Ganymede. His body is not just straight but "straight as Circes' wand" (I.61), as if to imply that he can enchant men like the great enchantress from *The Iliad*. His cheeks and lips exceed "his / That leapt into the water for a kiss / Of his own shadow" (I.73–75)—that is, he surpasses Narcissus, that youth so beautiful that he entranced even himself. "Rudest peasant" and "Thracian soldier" alike swoon for him, for, indeed, this description of Leander is "made for amorous play" (I.88). The catalogue of classical homoerotic allusions documents a desire that is fully homoerotic, as if to imply that the same technique of description that can fetishize a woman's body into an object of masculine desire can also do the same for a male body; the place of rhetoric in the route between object and desire is palpable, opaque; the blazon is revealed to be constitutive of desire, not expressive of it. In sum, the supposedly direct correlation between the world of words and the world of events that the blazon genre presupposes is displaced and inverted.

The descriptive technique of *Hero and Leander* in many ways replicates the dynamics of Sidney's text, for it manipulates the expression of homoerotic desire to demonstrate that systems of heterosexual significance are grounded in an opaque language, not in either "nature" or a language that can transparently express "nature." Of course, in the process homoerotic desire is also similarly exposed as a construct—but the dissymmetry of heteroeroticism as "natural" and homoeroticism as "unnatural" is now displaced in favor of a broader formulation of *desire* as unnatural. Words become, to borrow a phrase from Sir Richard Baker, "accidents without substances."[48] Such rarefied linguistic play is all too easy to ignore, devalue, or apoliticize. However, I would claim that the manipulation of homoeroticism in these

[48]Richard Baker, *Variegatus, or Catoes Morall Distichs: Translated and Paraphras'd, with Variations of Expressing, in English Verse* (London, 1636), p. 9.

texts demonstrates its broadest and most potent political potentiality. Peter Stallybrass and Allon White have noted that "control of the major sites of discourse is fundamental to political change."[49] When grounded in nature—validated solely for its relation to what it expresses—language appears monolithic, unassailable, outside the scope of human agency. But when, as in *Hero and Leander*, the expressive tie between word and content is severed, language becomes subject to change. It becomes something that can be redeployed to rearrange the assumed significances of various sights of discourse. Indeed, Marlowe's poem further demonstrates the full power implicit in its configuration of homoeroticism, and it does so by using homoerotic desire to interrogate the propriety of the domestic discourse that is the implicit topic of most epyllia.

Rhetoric to Deceive a Maid

In 1675 an anonymous letter to Parliament demanded legislation that adultery be made a crime punishable by death. Its logic specifically highlights the intersection of domesticity, sexuality, and political anxiety that, I will claim, is the topic of most, if not all, Elizabethan epyllia. The letter makes the demand but then respecifies it in terms of gender difference: "And they are more mischievous where the Woman breaks the Contract on her Part; for thereby a spurious Issue, that robs the Husband by Wholesale of his Estate, of all his own and his Ancestors Acquisitions, is brought into his Family."[50] This logic makes explicit several assumptions that underpin domestic polemics from throughout the Elizabethan and Jacobean Renaissance and into—as the date of the letter indicates—the Restoration. For in the letter female sexuality is specifically figured as the point of intersection between personal sexual behavior and patriarchal sociopolitical economic structure.

This letter in many ways signals a dynamic that can be read

[49]Stallybrass and White, *Politics and Poetics*, p. 202.

[50]*A Letter to a Member of Parliament: with two Discourses Inclosed in it* (London, 1675), pp. 91–92.

backwards through the history of domestic polemics. Once recognized, the intersection of "domesticall dutie," as William Gouge would call it, and the rhetoric of state order becomes apparent as the dominant trope informing the language of domestic propriety. *The Countess of Lincoln's Nursery*, for example, frames an impassioned plea for the nursing of children by their own mothers in a curious rhetoric of divine right and order:

> The Matter I mean, *Is the Duty of Nursing, due by Mothers to their own Children*. . . . In setting down whereof, I will, *first*, shew, that every Woman ought to nurse her own Child; and, *secondly*, I will endeavour to answer such Objections, as are used to be cast out against this Duty, to disgrace the same. . . . The *first* Point is easily performed, For it is the express Ordinance of God, that Mothers should nurse their own Children, and, being his Ordinance, they are bound to it in Conscience.[51]

The rhetoric here seems almost to plagiarize the language of James I in *The Trew Lawe of Free Monarchies*, who takes his task to be the delineation of those duties expressed by God that a prince is "bound in conscience never to forgive." The intersection of the domestic and the political is even more overt in Gouge's mammoth tome, *Of Domesticall Duties*: "The family is a seminary of the Church and common-wealth."[52] The chiasm of public power and private domain that informs these doctrines, as Catherine Belsey has noted, is not an aberration but, rather, is an articulation of the operative definition of the family throughout the Renaissance. "In the sixteenth and seventeenth centuries," she claims, "these two meanings of the family—as dynasty and as private realm of warmth and virtue—are both in play and indeed in contest."[53] I stress this problematic in the dynamic of the

[51]Elisabeth Lincoln, *The Countess of Lincoln's Nursery* (Oxford, 1622), p. 27.

[52]William Gouge, *The Workes of William Gouge in Two Volumes* (London, 1627), p. 10.

[53]Catherine Belsey, "Disrupting Sexual Difference: Meaning and Gender in the Comedies," in *Alternative Shakespeares*, ed. John Drakakis (London, 1985), p. 169. Besley's essay provides a cogent synopsis of the plethora

family—and especially as this dynamic relates to female sexual decorum—to provide a corrective to received notions of the epyllia. In current critical practice these poems are perceived to be, as Elizabeth Story Donno tells us, "mythmaking, sometimes

---

of reevaluations of the history of the family, some of which I will summarize here for readers unfamiliar with it. As Peter Laslett and the Cambridge Group for the History of Population and Social Structure have shown, the early modern English domus constituted a major but also unstable arena of political and social activity. In many ways, the domus of the Renaissance resembled that of the modern "nuclear family" and consisted of two generations—parents and children. The image of the extended clan on which Belsey focuses seems to have already diminished by the time of Elizabeth and continued to dwindle throughout the course of the Renaissance (Peter Laslett, *The World We Have Lost* [New York, 1965], and *Household and Family in Past Times* [Cambridge, U.K., 1972]). Yet despite these superficial resemblances, the Renaissance concept of the domus differs greatly from the modern one. The major difference is that the idea of "home" as an affective term was not the manifest mark that it is today. Although the tenets of filial obligation presented in the patriarchal formulations of, say, Filmer or James suggest an affective family structure, these families were equally, if not more so, economic units. Servants formed a major economic class, comprising up to 13.4 percent of the population in some preindustrial communities. For this class the domus was not an emotional base but a source of employment. Additionally, it was common practice for families to apprentice their children to other families where trades could be learned. Frequently this period of indenture was used to accrue a dowry, and the resulting delay in marriage accounted for a culture in which the average age for a man to marry and begin a family was in the early thirties (Laslett, *World We Have Lost*, p. 82). In short, "family life" was not necessarily the primary life-style for people during the Renaissance, but it was, in many ways, a second career after retirement from a first one of servitude. The economic base was not, however, the only motive for the family structure; the image of family life also served less tangible political purposes. Bacon points out, "Unmarried men are best friends, best masters, best servants; but not always best subjects, for they are light to run away" (Francis Bacon, *The Essays*, ed. John Pitcher [Harmondsworth, U.K., 1985], p. 81). On all of these points see also Lawrence Stone, *The Crisis of the Aristocracy, 1558–1641* (Oxford, 1965), pp. 269–302, and *The Family, Sex, and Marriage in England, 1500–1800* (London, 1977). Although the social-historical reevaluation of the family has led to radical revisionism in historical studies, it has also to some degree replicated the tendency I cite in the study of sodomy of seeking to establish one discursive arena—the domus—as a coherent and perfectly inscriptive site. Recent feminist and Marxist inquiry has, I think, produc-

lightly tossed off."[54] However, these poems also engage power at the most basic level present in the sociopolitical contestation of the family, namely the hymen and its associated discourses of chastity, fidelity, virginity, and seduction.

These poems are concerned not so much with erotic behavior as with the implications of power and social order underpinning it, a prominent concern in George Chapman's *Ovid's Banquet of Sence*. In the poem the heroine, Corynna, explicates the worth of her maidenhead:

> This glosse is common, as thy rudeness strange
> Not to forbeare these private times, (quoth she)
> Whose fixed Rites, none should presume to change
> Not where there is adjudg'd inchastitie;
> Our nakednes should be as much conceald
> As our accomplishments desire the eye;
> It is a secrete not to be revealde,
> But as Virginitie, and Nuptialls clothed,
> And to our honour all to be betrothed.
>
> It is a vault, where our aboundance lyes,
> Given a sole dowre t'enrich chast Hymens Bed,
> A perfect Image of our purities,
> And glasse by which our actions should be dressed,
> That tells us honor is as soone defild
> And should be kept as pure, and incompressed,
> But sight attaineth it: for Thought, Sights childe
> Begetteth sinne; and Nature bides defame,
> When light and lawles eyes bewray our shame.[55]

---

tively challenged this view and found the home to be an inconsistent site of authority containing multiple and conflicted positions of power, some of which provide authority for women in distinctly nonpatriarchal ways. On this latter viewpoint see Jacques Donzelot, *The Policing of Families*, trans. Robert Hurley (New York, 1979); Novy, *Love's Argument*; and Karen Newman, "Renaissance Family Politics and Shakespeare's *The Taming of the Shrew*" *ELR* 16, 1 (1986): 86–100.

[54]Elizabeth Story Donno, *Elizabethan Minor Epics* (London, 1963), p. 9.

[55]George Chapman, *Ovid's Banquet of Sence* (London, 1595), stanzas 77–78.

The speech presents an obfuscatory mythology of female sexuality but, at the same time, makes visible the terms of power beneath it. Corynna's modesty encodes a knowledge that her hymen is a "dowre," a "vault," a source of "aboundance." Implicit in the speech, then, is the same intersection of private action and public economics that empower the rhetoric of the letter to parliament.[56] However, the poem offers up the intersection ironically, for this is not the rhetoric of a man protecting patriarchy but the speech of a woman asserting her will against a man.

This disruption of domestic power motivates the dynamics of two epyllia in particular, John Weever's *Faunus and Melliflora* and Marlowe's *Hero and Leander*. In each poem, the politicization of the family structure is actively exposed and interrogated. Moreover, a comparison of the two poems also demonstrates clearly the bifurcated potentiality present in configurations of homo-

[56]The intersection of political power and "personal" passion present in the construction of female erotic value has been intelligently explored by several important studies in feminism and neo-Marxism. Following largely on the work of Claude Lévi-Strauss, who has described patriarchy as the male traffic in women (Claude Lévi-Strauss, *The Elementary Structures of Kinship Arrangements* [Boston, 1969]), Heidi Hartmann has finessed the suppression of and dependence on the female within masculine power; as she describes patriarchy, it is "relations between men, which have a material base, and which, though hierarchical, establish or create interdependence and solidarity among men that enable them to dominate women" (Heidi Hartmann, "The Unhappy Marriage of Marxism and Feminism: Toward a More Progressive Union," in *Women and Revolution: A Discussion of the Unhappy Marriage of Marxism and Feminism*, ed. Lydia Sargent [Boston, 1981], p. 14). Similarly, Gayle Rubin has noted that patriarchal power necessitates a suppression of all forms of sexuality incompatible with the dominant paradigm of male heterosexuality (i.e., male homosexuality, lesbianism, female sexual aggressivity, male sexual passivity) (Gayle Rubin, "The Traffic in Women: Notes on the 'Political Economy' of Sex," in *Toward an Anthropology of Women*, ed. Rayna Reiter [New York, 1975], p. 180). These initial inquiries have been forcefully extended by Eve Kosofsky Sedgwick, who has found within patriarchy an implicit "homosociality," a sort of triangulation of power in which men interact with men through a third position occupied by woman (Sedgwick, *Between Men*, pp. 1–20). Though not specifically mentioned in this argument, all of these formulations have informed my excavation of the political power present in the poetic representation of the maidenhead.

eroticism. Weever radically interrogates domestic politics while maintaining a logical economy of desire similar to those I have already elaborated; Marlowe's poem uses an intentional homoerotic disruption of desire to achieve its critique. I would like to examine the similarities and differences between the two poems at great length to demonstrate an implicit strategic essentialism at work in Marlowe's poem. As I have already suggested, homoeroticism functions as a free-floating epistemological unit in many discourses of Renaissance power, but *Hero and Leander* holds homoeroticism in stasis—momentarily freezes it—and thereby forces the discourse of domestic propriety to strain and fluctuate around it. The poem physicalizes homoerotic desire in order to force a recognition of the *meta*physicality of the discourses juxtaposed to it.

Both *Faunus and Melliflora* and *Hero and Leander* lay bare the intersecting discourses of domestic power much as does Chapman's poem. This process is most explicit in Weever's rhetorical manipulation of the language of the father. In lecturing his son on the responsibilities of marriage, Pycus delivers a stereotypical oration on filial decorum:

> Fond boy, quoth hee, and foolish cradle witted,
> To let base love with thy yong yeares be fitted:
> This upstart love, bewitcher of the wit,
> The scorne of vertue, vices parasite:
> The slave to weaknesse, friendships false bewrayer,
> Reasons rebell, Fortitudes betraier:
> The Church-mens scoffe, court, camp, and countrie's guiler,
> Arts infection, chaste thoughts and youth's defiler.[57]

And yet this mythology of chaste virtue and social order quickly lapses into a discourse of economic concern, for Pycus offers this alternative to his son's love for the nymph Melliflora:

> Thou art no souldier for Dianaes garison,
> Nor twixt her Nymphes and Faunus is comparison:
> Nymphes are like Poets, full of wit, but poore,

[57]John Weever, *Faunus and Melliflora* (London, 1595), ll. 521–528.

Unto thy kingdome, add a kingdome more
By marriage: let Pycus counsel thee,
Looke not (my boy) at wit, and Poetrie.[58]

Not only does Pycus equate marriage with wealth, but he also introduces a dichotomy between romantic love and dynastic advantage: "Remember love, and Pycus would the rather, / Forget his sonne he should forgoe his father."[59] The division here is clear and absolute; Faunus, like Romeo, must either deny romantic love and forget Melliflora or deny his father and forget his name. Love and marriage are antithetical, and the economic advantage of the latter erases any possible endorsements of the former.

The critique of the economics of domesticity implicit in this interchange is made explicit when Love enters the poem—quite literally and as a character. He offers a lengthy digression that brands such economic concerns as subversions of the "true" course of love. Explaining how, "fearing fathers ire, / Love is defeated of his chiefe desire," Love suggests that

This unkindnesse children yet must take,
Untill their parents price of them do make,
As in a market then what man wil crave them,
And give the most, shalbe to have them.[60]

In response to the subversion of love by patriarchal intrusion, Love explains, the Destinies decreed

That man for his unmanlike treacherie
Should be tormented with vile jealousie,
That maids from honest libertie restrained:
That twas some treasure from the which th'are tide,
Some Indian jewell which men us to hide,
Some strange conserve, sweete, deare, and pretious,
And women are by nature licorous. . . .

[58]Ibid., ll. 565–570.
[59]Ibid., ll. 585–586.
[60]Ibid., ll. 637–642.

That market marriages evermore should be:
Content the best, the worst to disagree.
The shrewdnesse should possesse the womans heart,
In stubbornesse the husband act his part:
Thus drawing opposite in one yoke, alive
Long might they live, but they should never thrive:
And since that time, all marriage enforced,
Never agree untill they be devorced.[61]

The punishment decreed is that women should be sexually constrained, that chastity should be commoditized, and that this commoditization should lead to covetousness; it is, in short, the status quo. The poem articulates the dynamics of domesticity, but in the context of godly punishment rather than inevitable truth, and thereby ironically highlights them as metaphysical constructs.

A similar critique of domestic meaning is found in a further commentary on blazon form in *Hero and Leander.* Halfway through the agonizingly long seduction of Hero, the narrator intercedes with a digression about the seduction of a country maid by Mercury. The tale begins with a structure that overtly mocks the earlier description of Hero:

[Her] careless hair, instead of pearl t'adorn it,
Glist'red with dew, as one that seem'd to scorn it.
Her breath as fragrant as the morning rose,
Her mind pure, and her tongue untaught to glose,
Yet proud she was (for lofty pride that dwells
In tow'red courts is oft in shepherds' cells),
And too too well the fair vermilion knew,
And silver tincture of her cheeks, that drew
The love of every swain.

(I.389–397)

The parenthetical aside forces a comparison with Hero's "tow'red court" and, more important, forces a recognition of the differ-

[61]Ibid., ll. 650–671.

ences between Hero and the maid.[62] Whereas Hero is blasoned as a pastiche of words, clothes, and feigned rites, the maid is fully involved in material sexuality. Like Chaucer's Alisoun, the maid is compared to and contains the same bountiful sexual ripeness that is found in nature. Neither clothes nor rites nor myths form her sexual allure—rather, her sexuality itself is alluring.

Stripping this female of the obfuscatory language that masks Hero also reveals the same contradictions of power present in Weever's poem. For the problem the maid faces is that her sex—her maidenhead—is not "natural" but economic. As the poem states, her "only dower was her chastity" (I.412). Although it is later claimed that "all women are ambitious *naturally*" (I.428, my emphasis), the ambition of this maid grows from a recognition of the economic value placed on her "parts which no eye should behold" (I.408). Knowing that her sexual activities are as much business transactions as anything else, and also knowing that she is dealing with a "rich buyer," a god, she demands "such a task / As he ought not perform" (I.429–430), to let her drink of the nectar of the gods. This overt economization of sexual practice becomes an interpretive lesson in the poem, for it both enables and forces us to recognize these same dynamics only barely concealed beneath the supposed "love" of Hero and Leander. Leander, we come to realize, equates Hero with "diamonds" (I.214), "golden strings" (I.229), "the richest mine" (I.232). He terms her maidenhead "this fair gem, sweet in loss alone" (I.247), a phrase that not only ascribes an economic value to Hero but also suggests that such value is only recognizable in an act of transaction. Indeed, the digression on the country maid provides

[62]Despite the attention devoted to this digression, no critic has studied it in relation to either Hero or the issue of chastity. Two of the more cogent analyses of it have been by Paul Cubeta, who analyzes it as the product of a monomaniacal narrator (Paul Cubeta, "Marlowe's Poet in *Hero and Leander*," *College English* 26 [1965]: 501), and Eugene B. Cantelupe, who questionably finds that "at its core lies as serious an intention and as moral a didacticism as a mythological morality by Lydgate" (Eugene B. Cantalupe, "*Hero and Leander*, Marlowe's Tragicomedy of Love," *College English* 24 [1962]: 296). Both critics read the digression as a narrative exemplum for Leander and ignore Hero.

terms that demonstrate that the romantic myth of Hero and Leander is every bit as much a "market marriage" as that presented by Weever; Leander further states, "Base bullion for the stamp's sake we allow, / Even so for men's impression do we you" (I. 265–266), and "Maids are nothing, then, / Without the sweet society of men" (I.255–256). This intermingling of transactional value and sexuality is succinctly embodied in one of the poem's most famous phrases, the description of Hero as "Venus' nun" (I.45). Renaissance iconography recognized two distinct Venus images: Venus Urania, the goddess of pure or neoplatonic love, and Venus Libitina, the goddess of lusty or prurient love.[63] Thus, to be "Venus' nun" could be to champion stoic purity, but at the same time it could also be to participate in the most sexually economic profession—to prostitute as a whore in Venus' "nunnery."[64] The poem's rhetoric of female sexuality, then, constantly grounds itself in concerns of wealth and dynasty—a grounding that severs the language from any "natural" significance and establishes it as a metaphysical, socially relative discourse.

Each of these poems, then, exposes the actual political terms of sexual power, and—important for the purpose of my argument—each poem also places homoeroticism in relation to this process of exposition. Moreover, the difference between how each poem places homoeroticism also replicates the split between homoeroticism as a part of an erotic economy, and homoeroticism as the end of the erotic. In *Faunus and Melliflora* the invocation of homoeroticism becomes a signal for recognizing a basically conservative epistemology beneath the poem's critique of market marriages. The poem begins with a lengthy digression recounting the lineage of Pycus designed to foreshadow Venus's

[63]Cf. S. Ann Collins, "Sundrie Shapes, Committing Headdie Ryots, Incest, Rapes: Functions of the Myth in Determining Narrative and Tone in Marlowe's *Hero and Leander*," *Mosaic* 4 (1970): 109; Keach, *Elizabethan Ovidian Erotic Narrative*, pp. 207–220.

[64]Cf. Martin T. Williams, "The Temptations in Marlowe's *Hero and Leander*," *Modern Language Quarterly* 16 (1955): 226–231.

punishment of changing him into an ugly bird (ll. 1007–1020) by establishing that "of al hee was most faire":[65]

> When Jove ambitious by his former sinnes,
> (From him al Muses, so my Muse begins)
> Deposde his Syre Saturnus from the throne,
> And so usurpt the Diadem Alone:
> Some higher power for aged Saturne strove,
> Gave him a gift, which angred lust-stung birth,
> Made poore the heav'ns to enrich the earth.[66]

Oddly enough, the genesis of the father is a moment of homoerotic intrigue among the gods, for the story recounted is that of Jove's introduction to Ganymede. This detail potentially suggests numerous levels of complication: presexual homoeroticism, as in *The Old Arcadia*; disrupted desire, as in *Hero and Leander*'s blazons; catalogues of sexual deviance, as in early satiric tropes. However, these meanings are never engaged in the poem. The allusion becomes merely another part of Pycus's considerable list of charms:

> His name was Pycus, yet surnam'd the Faire,
> Whome Circe chaunted in the scorne-gold haire,
> Whom Ladies lov'd, and loved of so many,
> The wood-Nymphes woo'd him, yet not won of any.[67]

The opening of homoerotic meaning is quickly closed within an inventory of heteroerotic desire, and the homoerotic allusion becomes a support for a most patriarchal and domestic conclusion: "Of fairest father, farre more faire a boy."[68]

Homoeroticism in this configuration is most obviously considered as an accessory or ornament, a notion that belies a deeper conservatism in the poem. For it is possible, in retrospect, to see a

[65]Weever, *Faunus and Melliflora*, l. 1012.
[66]Ibid., ll. 1–8.
[67]Ibid., ll. 17–20.
[68]Ibid., l. 26.

similar stability of sexual signification in the poem's critique of marriage. The poem initially conceives of love as a profoundly democratic force that undermines orthodox orders of propriety:

> Sometimes a King dotes on a countrie swaine,
> Sometimes a Lady loves a lad againe:
> Sometimes the meander with the greatest reject,
> No not a person Love will once respect.[69]

But this radicalism also plays into an economy of meaning similar to that in the poem's use of homoeroticism. The pitting of "love" against "market marriage" may critique part of the domestic system, but it ultimately validates the parameters of passion and patriarchy by conceiving of them as the only possible terms in the debate. Additionally, although the poem chastises Pycus's "market marriage," the alternative offered still results in an objectified female role:

> For maides were made to make such harmlesse plaies,
> Such honest sports, as daunce upon the laies:
> The hey-de-guise, and run the wild-goose chace,
> And trie the keeles, the Barlibreake, and base,
> But with a barly when the pastimes end,
> And maides must needes for milking homewards wend:
> As some depart, some are constrained to stay,
> For when they end, the Love begins to play.[70]

A maid's exit from paternal obligation is her entry into being an *object* of love; her debut in this role is as a social ornament, a debutante engaged in the social festivities of courtship associated with barlibreake. Even removed from the market, woman remains passive, inert, and defined by male-created roles. This idea is punningly encoded in the narrator's description of love's transformational power: love's "excellence / Is to transform the verie soule and essence / Of the lover, into the *thing* beloved."[71]

[69]Ibid., ll. 627–632.
[70]Ibid., ll. 613–620.
[71]Ibid., ll. 533–555. Emphasis mine.

Weever's conception of homoeroticism in the poem, then, is demonstrative of his conception of gender and sexual meaning in general. Categories such as "homoerotic," "maiden," or "woman" are repositories of meaning and act as "natural" signifying units. In this formulation, as in the allusions of Lodge, Marston, or Heywood, there is an a priori significance to certain sexual categories and actions, marriage being one of them. In these instances, "deviance" functions like an Aristotelian metaphor, a unit of meaning transported from its proper place in the continuum of meaning but never actually disrupting the ability of meaning to signify. The dynastic usurpation of marriage is, for Weever, just another *turning* of meaning, but it is a turning that obfuscates meaning rather than creates it. *Hero and Leander*'s critique of the same topic, however, suggests that there is no meaning *aside from* this unnatural turning of marriage—and it achieves this suggestion through an entirely different epistemology of homoeroticism.

The primary difference between *Faunus and Melliflora* and *Hero and Leander* is that whereas Weever's poem critiques the meaning of marriage—its content—Marlowe's poem critiques its ability *to mean*. Ironically, this strategy involves a sustained depiction in Marlowe's poem of the market motifs actively derogated by Weever. When the moment of consummation arrives for Hero and Leander, it is described through a mythological allusion that invokes a subtext of plundering and territoriality: "Leander now, like Theban Hercules, / Ent'red the orchard of th'Hesperides" (II.297–298). Moreover, the act of consummation fully reinscribes the characters within the traditional poetic rhetoric of dynastic sexuality. Hero is robbed of the rhetoric that exemplifies her opening description, and "she knew not how to frame her look, / Or speak to him who in a moment took / That which so long so charily she kept" (II.307–309). Hero's flesh, for the first time, fully enters the poem, as if to suggest that the inverted patterns of blasoned desire are now righted: "So Hero's ruddy cheek Hero betray'd, / And her all naked to his sight display'd" (II.323–324). Leander, too, fits perfectly within the discourse of dynastic union, and "his admiring eyes more pleasure took / Than Dis on heaps of gold fixing his look" (II.325–326). The fulfillment of their sexual union is also the fulfillment of a dynastic discourse, and Leander stands above his woman, surveying his wealth like a pirate inventorying his booty.[72]

Unlike Weever's poem, which exposes and then dismisses this conception of "market marriage," Marlowe's poem simply exposes it. However, this lack of censure is the basis of an even more devastating commentary, for despite the fact that the rhetoric of dynastic union remains intact in the poem, it is unable to enact its intentions. This impotency of the discourse is seen most clearly in Leander's rhetoric of seduction. Leander's rhetoric not only subtly encodes economics but also overtly overstates poetics. Indeed, the link between Leander's seduction and traditional rhetoric is stressed in the poem, for his orations are prefaced with the epithet "bold sharp sophister" (I.197), *sophister* being the Cambridge term for a second- or third-year under-

[72]Those who still believe that Marlowe's poem is unfinished may want to claim that my reading here is weakened by our inability to discern Marlowe's "ultimate intentions." I find such arguments about completeness singularly misleading. Due primarily to the assertion of George Chapman that the poem is incomplete, it carries the unfortunate literary label of *fragment*. However, as Clifford Leech has pointed out, Chapman's completion of the poem appeared in the same year as his translation of *The Iliad*, "and it seems likely that [Chapman] would be the one to decide that the poem of Sestos should have its Sestiades as Ilium had its Iliads" (Clifford Leech, *Marlowe* [Englewood Cliffs, 1965], p. 265). Moreover, as William Keach has noted, the poem "does not end at just any point in the story as Musaeus tells it, but at the crucial point where triumphant love turns into tragedy" (Keach, *Elizabethan Ovidian Erotic Narrative*, p. 86). Several important critics have also thoughtfully revealed how Chapman's continuation works against the purposes of Marlowe's poem, and therefore Chapman is, at best, a questionable authority (C. S. Lewis, "*Hero and Leander,*" *Proceedings of the British Academy* 38 (1952): 23–37.). As these critics indicate, there is a strong case to be made that the poem as it stands is complete, particularly given that the length of it as Marlowe wrote it is more or less in line with the general generic conventions of the tradition. In any event, for the purposes of my argument the question is irrelevant, for my topic is not what Marlowe intended but, rather, the social forces encoded in and encoding the text as it was produced in its own time. This entire critical debate, as well as its ramifications for interpretation, is cogently summarized in W. L. Godshalk, "*Hero and Leander*: The Sense of an Ending," in *"A Poet and a Filthy Play-Maker": New Essays on Christopher Marlowe*, ed. Kenneth Friedenreich, Roma Gill, and Constance B. Kuriyama (New York, 1988), pp. 293–314.

graduate.[73] Hero herself recognizes the specific genre of Leander's sophistry; she demands, "Who taught thee *rhetoric to deceive a maid*?" (I.338, my emphasis). As this query implies, Leander's language is part of a dynastic system designed to control the position of woman. It is a rhetorical enactment of the political demands made of Parliament in 1675. However, this language is also ironically impotent in the poem, for Leander is equally deceived by his own words. After his speech has succeeded and Hero is compliant, Leander finds himself unable to capitalize on the situation:

> [Hero] was afraid,
> In off'ring parley, to be counted light.
> So on she goes, and in her idle flight
> Her painted fan of curled plumes let fall,
> Thinking to train Leander therewithal.
> He being novice, knew not what she meant,
> But stay'd, and after her a letter sent.
>
> (II.8–14)

Leander understands only the rhetoric, not its intention; his words succeed, but he fails. He is a perfect counterpart to Shakespeare's Romeo, whose love, as Friar Laurence notes, "did read by rote that could not spell."[74] The traditional discourse of seduction, complete with economic subtext, is fully enacted in the text, but it is also fully unable to affect the actions at hand.

Hero and Leander, then, does not present the discourse of marriage as one whose content has been unnaturally turned, as does Weever's poem. Rather, it suggests that the discourse has no natural meaning of its own. This idea is fully incorporated in one of the poem's most famous similes, an effort by the narrator to describe Leander's response to seeing Hero in her tower:

> Like Aesop's cock, this jewel he enjoyed,
> And as a brother with his sister toyed,

[73]Leech, *Marlowe*, p. 256.

[74]William Shakespeare, *Romeo and Juliet*, ed. Brian Gibbons (London, 1980), II.iii.84.

Supposing nothing else was to be done,
Now he her favour and good will had won.

(II. 51–54)

The simile is immensely subtle and hides within it images of indecorous sex. References to cock and jewel invoke a bawdy subtext of intercourse, and the subsequent line suggests an image of incest. Yet primarily this simile is used to indicate that Leander's innate instincts toward Hero are not ones of sexual conquest. However, this "natural" naïveté is complicated by the social discourse of sexuality to which Leander has been exposed. The narrative continues:

But know you not that creatures wanting sense
By nature have a mutual appetence,
And wanting organs to advance a step,
Mov'd by love's force, unto each other leap?
Much more in subjects having intellect
Some hidden influence breeds like effect.
Albeit Leander, rude in love, and raw,
Long dallying with Hero, nothing saw
That might delight him more, yet he suspected
Some amorous rites or other were neglected.

(II. 55–64)

The reference to the natural state of animals recalls Leander's natural state: rude, raw, and satisfied to toy.[75] But whereas unregulated copulation is a natural function in animals, in creatures of "intellect / Some *hidden influence* breeds like effect." It is a compulsion to fulfill some "amorous rite," an image that recalls the contrived social and sexual rituals of wealthy Sestos that

[75]The use of animal behavior as a sexual exemplum is backed by a long tradition. Chaucer's use of animal imagery in *The Miller's Tale* is representative of the bestiary tradition of the Middle Ages (cf. T. H. White, *The Bestiary: A Book of Beasts, Being a Translation from a Latin Bestiary of the Twelfth Century* [New York, 1954]) and might be considered the precursor of the Renaissance tradition. Probably the most entertaining example during the Renaissance is found in Shakespeare's *All's Well That Ends Well* (ed. G. K. Hunter [London, 1967]), where Parolles uses a particularly bombastic version of it to console Helena (I.i.121ff.).

begin the poem (I.91–96). This hidden influence is something learned, something taught, something discursive; as the narrative states, "The more [Hero] strived, / The more a gentle pleasing heat revived, / Which *taught him all that elder lovers know*" (II.67–69, my emphasis). It is, in short, the social discourse of love: "Love always makes those eloquent that have it" (II.72).

The distinction to be drawn here is that while Weever's poetics seeks to rearrange the meaning of what can be seen to be a metaphysical system, Marlowe's strategy is to foreground the system *as* metaphysical. And this strategy opens a space in Marlowe's text for an entirely radical configuration of homoeroticism. When preparing to meet Hero for the third time, Leander "stripp'd him to the ivory skin, / And crying, 'Love, I come', leapt lively in" to the "narrow toiling Hellespont" surrounding Hero's tower (II.153–154, 150). Leander quickly encounters "Love," but not necessarily the one he anticipated:

> The sapphire-visaged god grew proud,
> And made his cap'ring Triton sound aloud,
> Imagining that Ganymede, displeas'd,
> Had left the heavens; therefore on him he seized.
>
> (II.155–158)

Neptune's passion quickly grows to be the most vivid sexual action in the poem.[76] "The lusty god embrac'd [Leander], call'd him love" (II.167), and

[76]The overt eroticism of this passage is typically extricated by criticism, and this repression only serves to verify ironically its sexual impact. The (in)famous example is from Rosemond Tuve, who believes that "remembering that the substitution of the physical ocean for Neptune was as natural as breathing to any Elizabethan, we can re-read the images as convincing and accurate description of the caressing flow of the water" (Rosemond Tuve, *Elizabethan and Metaphysical Imagery* [Chicago, 1947], p. 157). Granted, anything can be "re-read" to mean differently, yet even in this "re-reading" the scene retains sexual connotations—"the caressing flow." Other critics have attempted to allegorize the scene: "Contemporary interpretations of the *Aeneid*—those in the medieval tradition—held the sea's allegorical significance to be temptation to baseness which had to be dealt with in the search for wholeness and wisdom" (Williams, "Temptations in Marlowe's *Hero and Leander*," p. 227). Rebuttal against this strategy can come from the

He clapp'd his plump cheeks, with tresses play'd,
And smiling wantonly, his love bewray'd.
He watch'd his arms, and as they open'd wide
At every stroke, betwixt them would he slide
And steal a kiss, and then run out and dance,
And as he turn'd, cast many a lustful glance,
And throw him gaudy toys to please his eye,
And dive into the water, and there pry
Upon his breast, his thighs, and every limb,
And up again, and close beside him swim,
And talk of love.

(II.181–191)

Leander responds to Neptune's full physical eroticism bluntly and somewhat ridiculously: " 'You are deceiv'd, I am no woman, I' " (II.192). Leander demonstrates a monocular devotion to one system of sexual relations. Confronted with homoerotic physical passion, his immediate inclination is to label it a non sequitur. He is no woman, he is a man; as a subject to the traditional rhetoric of seduction that he uses in the poem, his seduction by Neptune quite literally can make no sense, for it is *outside* his range of discursive possibilities.

The limitations of Leander's comprehension are further demonstrated by Neptune's response. The god smiles and "then [tells] a tale" (II.193) that suggests an alternative world existing beyond the limits of Leander's narrow perspective:

How that a shepherd, sitting in a vale,
Play'd with a boy so fair and unkind
As for his love both earth and heaven pin'd;
That of the cooling river durst not drink,
Lest water-nymphs should pull him from the brink;
And when he sported in the fragrant lawns,

---

most unlikely of sources, C. S. Lewis, who reminds us that Marlowe is "our great master of *material* imagination" (Lewis, *English Literature in the Sixteenth Century*, p. 486, emphasis mine), and also from the fact that an equally strong tradition placed Neptune as a symbol of sensuality, as in book 3, canto 42, of *The Faerie Queene*.

Goat-footed satyrs and up-staring fauns
Would steal him thence.

(II.194–201)

Neptune never finishes, for Leander interrupts "ere half this tale was done" (II.201), but the fragment delivered reveals a rich traditional discourse. The central image is of Narcissus, who in Greek mythology is an image of ultimate desirability. This polymorphous myth, however, is incorporated in an even broader classical frame that specifies homoeroticism. The actual tale is of sexual play between a shepherd and a boy and immediately invokes Theocritus's *Idylls* and Virgil's *Eclogues*, both models recognized during the Renaissance as carrying homoerotic overtones.[77] The passion of Neptune is, to be certain, violent; it attacks Leander with a mace and almost drowns him. But it is also gentle, for it recalls the mace, "beat[s] down the bold waves," and "put[s] Helle's bracelet on his arm, / And [swears] the sea would never do him harm" (II.172, 179–180). It is also something that is viewed in the poem, to borrow one of its own phrases, as a "deep persuading oratory" (II.226), for before the digression ends, the narrator is careful to justify Leander's lack of rage at Neptune's advances by stating that

in gentle breasts
Relenting thoughts, remorse and pity rests,
And who have hard hearts and obdurate minds
But vicious, harebrain'd, and illit'rate hinds?

(II.215–218)

This statement appears almost to be a poetic paraphrase of a famous phrase attributed to Marlowe: "All they that love not tobacco and boys [are] fools."[78]

Obviously, Neptune's homoerotic world has little claim on the sensibilities of Leander. But just as obviously, it does have a

[77] I discuss the sexualization of the pastoral genre at length in Chapter 5.

[78] Richard Baines, "A Note containing the opinions of one Christopher Marly concerning his damnable judgement of religion and scorn of God's word," Brit. Mus. Harl. 6848: fol. 185.

claim on the task of interpretation encoded in the poem.[79] By positing an essential validity to the homoerotic meaning of Neptune's world—that is, an essential intelligibility outside of the social orthodoxies that construct it—the poem also clearly demonstrates the relativity of heteroeroticism. If in other poems homoeroticism is a trope that ornaments the language of heteroeroticism, then Marlowe's poem tropes this trope. By momentarily essentializing the language of homoeroticism, it turns the language of heteroeroticism into a figure—something that is a *part* of language, not *all* of it. Marlowe's poem, then, pushes homoeroticism to the logical breaking point of orthodox sexual epistemology. For whereas in the poems of Marston, Lodge, Heywood, and Weever homoeroticism is a part of the erotic, in Marlowe's poem—as in Sidney's and Drayton's—homoeroticism marks the end of the erotic, the places where orthodox metaphysics of sexual desire and decorum fall short of their own totalizing goals.

The End(s) of the Erotic

In his semiautobiographical work *Alienated Affections: Being Gay in America*, Seymour Kleinberg offers a definition of a recur-

[79]My reading at this point has been strongly influenced by Tzvetan Todorov, *The Fantastic: A Structural Approach to a Literary Genre*, trans. Richard Howard (Cleveland, 1973). In this famous study Todorov claims that the fantastic "implies an integration of the reader into the world of the characters; that world is defined by the reader's own ambiguous perception of the events narrated" (p. 31). This structure seems to me to be analogous to the sexual schema in Marlowe's poem in that the poem constructs for the reader a need to rectify the conflicting claims of propriety presented by the homoerotic and dynastic language systems. Even if this process results in a choice of dynastic belief, the manifest validity of that system is still undermined by having it now grounded in *choice* rather than *fact*. This structure is not uncommon in Marlowe's canon and, indeed, is found in his earliest play, *Dido, Queen of Carthage*. This play begins with a brief scene depicting the love of Jupiter and Ganymede, which seems unrelated to the Virgilian plot to follow but in reality opens an interpretive space that casts a satiric possibility on the ensuing tragedy. On this point see Eugene M. Waith, "Marlowe and the Jades of Asia," *Studies in English Literature* 5 (1964), and Jardine, *Still Harping on Daughters*, p. 22.

ringly problematic phrase, "gay sensibility": "Even if it is a phantom. . . . like the Protocols of the Elders of Zion, its mythic impact has been felt as if it were substantial. . . . Gay sensibility is truly subversive because it insists on the primacy of sexuality beneath the adoration of the civilized."[80] This formulation, while worthy of problematization in its own right, provides an apt metaphor for summarizing the disparate uses of homoeroticism in the romantic and erotic genres of the early Renaissance, especially in their more disruptive instances. These formulations do not delineate a logical range of homosexual definitions. Rather, they show how homoeroticism is typically associated with a space outside of logic (*logos*). It would, I think, be difficult to find an Elizabethan or Jacobean analogue to homoerotic sensibility, much less homosexual or gay sensibility (although some critics have argued otherwise). But there appears to be a concept of homoerotic *unsensibility*—a certain recognition that the ability of homoeroticism to step outside of heteroerotic metaphysics constitutes both a problem and a benefit. Hence, while homoeroticism sometimes intentionally solidifies social roles—as in the satires of Marston and the complaints of Lodge or, for that matter, in the chronicles of Edward's life or the Greeks' world in *Troilus and Cressida*—it also "asserts the primacy of sexuality" beneath social figures of order in other literary configurations. It functions as a part of gendered meaning, as in Weever's poem, and it also disrupts that meaning, as in Drayton's allusion. And often this unsensibility seems to be almost accidental or de facto, as in Sidney's romance—a text that ultimately reinscribes itself within the tropics of heterocentric union but that nonetheless figures homoeroticism as an analogue to liberated desire.

Such a formulation of unsensibility, particularly as I have argued it here, risks positing an essentialism in homoeroticism—ascribing it some sort of cosmic irreducibility that always emerges to attack the arbitrary tyrranies of heteroerotic epistemologies. Obviously, this is not the case. The ability of homoeroticism to speak in ways different than it was constructed in orthodox epistemology is, as I have suggested, just a more bla-

[80]Seymour Kleinberg, *Alienated Affections: Being Gay in America* (New York, 1980), p. 38.

tant exposition of the variability of significance of homoeroticism that orthodox power found useful. In other words, once homoeroticism is constructed as something that can mean otherwise, it then is *able* to mean otherwise. Moreover, the multiplicitous image of homoeroticism found in erotic poetry of the period is not unique but, rather, duplicates a similar instability in almost all gendered discourses of the period. If homoeroticism in these poems always speaks otherwise, this is simply a foregrounding of the strategies of power expressed in gender and sexuality in general. The pervasiveness of this power structure can be seen easily in *The Courtier*, an excellent book to make the point with because it is such a central text to Renaissance culture and also because it deals with such a central issue: the decorum of the male gender.

In his introduction to the volume, Castiglione (here adapted for the English by Thomas Hoby) admits that the courtier he is about to create is discursive and has no proper life outside the words in the volume:

> Others say, bicause it is so hard a matter and (in a maner) unpossible to finde out a man of such perfection, as I would have the Courtier to be, it is but superfluous to write it: for it is a vaine thing to teach that can not be learned. To these men I answere, I am content, to err with Plato, Xenophon, and M. Tullius, leaving apart the disputing of the intelligible world and of the Ideas or imagined fourmes: in which number, as (according to that opinion) the Idea or figure conceyved in imagination of a perfect commune weale, and of a perfect king, and of a perfect Oratour are conteined: so it is also of a perfect Courtier.[81]

The alliance with Plato is particularly telling. It is not enough for his courtier to be idealized; he must be ideal, residing side by side with Plato's forms in the world of which ours is only a shadow. Dwelling in this purely *metaphysical* realm, the courtier becomes uncontestable, unassailed by the political foibles, social battles,

[81]Balthazar Castiglione, *The Boke of the Courtier*, trans. Thomas Hoby (London, 1561), pp. 22–23.

fates and destinies that accost actual men and that question their superiority. The ideal courtier is also a subtle and effective political construct. When Sir Frederick Fregoso, who suggests the game of courtier construction, explains his reasons, they are more pointed than mere coterie amusement. As he says, "To disgrace therefore many untowardly asseheads, that through malepertnes thinke to purchase them the name of a good Courtyer, I would have suche a pastimes for this night."[82] In this context the courtier becomes not so much a construction of an ideal identity as an exclusion of deficient identities, a standard by which the court can exclude unworthies from its privileged world. The constructed courtier foreshadows Foucault's description of the "negative relation" of power and sex in the West, which

> never establishes any connection between power and sex that is not negative: rejection, exclusion, refusal, blockage, concealment, or mask. Where sex and pleasure are concerned, power can "do" nothing but say no to them; what it produces, if anything, is absences and gaps; it overlooks elements, introduces discontinuities, separates what is joined, and marks off boundaries. Its effects take the general form of limit and lack.[83]

The negative power of the courtier shows most clearly when the actual courtiers debate the gender identity of the ideal one. As Count Lewis strongly proposes, the ideal courtier cannot be "softe and womanishe as many procure to have" or "onely courle the hear, and picke the browes," for this would class them with "the most wanton and dishonest women in the worlde."[84] And he harshly derides such types: "These men, seing nature (as they seeme to have a desire to appeare and to bee) hath not made them women, but like common Harlottes to be banished, not onely out of prynces courtes, but also oute of the companye of Gentlemen."[85] Count Lewis indeed seems to have mastered the strategy

[82]Ibid., pp. 41–42.
[83]Foucault, *History of Sexuality*, p. 83.
[84]Castiglione, *Boke of the Courtier*, p. 52.
[85]Ibid., p. 52.

of this game, for even if his prescriptions do not yield an ideal courtier, they will also not allow "asseheades" into the court and will not let masculinity slip into the feminine. Indeed, Count Lewis not only formulates a perfect negative relation but also formulates the perfect means of maintaining it, *sprezzatura* (translated by Hoby as "Recklesness"): "And that is to eschew as much as a man may, and as a sharp and dangerous rock, Affectation of curiousity."[86] He continues to define the term: "to use in every thyng a certain Recklesness, to cover art withall, and seeme whatsoever he doth and sayeth to do it wythout pain, and (as it were) not myndyng."[87] Foucault realizes of power that "its success is proportional to its ability to hide its own mechanisms,"[88] and Count Lewis anticipates this insight by more than four hundred years. For, as he summarizes:

> Therefore that may be said to be a very art that appeereth not to be art, neither ought a man to put more diligence in any thing then in covering it: for in case it be open, it loseth credit cleane, and maketh a man little set by.[89]

Vectored toward the control of privileged society and hidden by its own art or "recklesness," *The Courtier* is more than a description of gender. It is an active and aggressive exertion of power—a power empowered precisely because of its metaphysical status, for if *The Courtier* is addressed to an ideal gender construct, it also, *always*, speaks otherwise.

Placed within the "trivial" or "esoteric" genres of erotic witticism and actively derogated both in its own time and in our own critical practice, Renaissance homoeroticism might seem, at best, marginal. But at the heart of the marginal play of this marginal sexuality is a foregrounding of the very conditions of power at work within the culture. Indeed, in terms of *conditions* of power (as opposed to the content or intention of power), the obvious antithesis between Castiglione's deification of the mas-

[86]Ibid., p. 59.
[87]Ibid., p. 59.
[88]Foucault, *History of Sexuality*, p. 86.
[89]Castiglione, *Boke of the Courtier*, p. 59.

culine, heteroerotic ideal and Marlowe's representation of the homoerotic alternative collapses. For if Castiglione constructs a gender in order to stigmatize the "asseheades" who should not have access to its power, Marlowe constructs a sexuality in order to stigmatize the "illiterate hinds" who do not admit its (potential) power. Renaissance homoeroticism, therefore, is more than a social governor or a scapegoating technique that solidifies orthodoxy. It is also, in the very terms of its social construction, something that defines what can be used to undo the system constructing it. Homoeroticism in all of these poems means only in relation to its placement in or against other languages—it has, in other words, no content of its own. But in this position it also becomes one of the most potent means of subverting the politics of gender and eroticism. For if the political power of eroticism is, to paraphrase Stallybrass and White, contingent on its ability to control sites of discourse (which is, after all, the hidden agenda of Castiglione's text), then homoeroticism, placed as it is on the ends of the erotic spectrum, becomes, in turn, a way of signaling the aporia of this spectrum. It is not just a part of the erotic but also the end of the erotic. And in this position it also exposes the very real, very central sociopolitical power that is—*always*—the end(s) of the erotic.

CHAPTER 4

Tradition and the Individual Sodomite

To be in love is merely to be in a state of perceptual anaesthesia—to mistake an ordinary young man for a Greek god or an ordinary young woman for a goddess.

—H. L. Mencken

Homosexuality is not all self-hate, or guilt feelings, or love, or domination or submission, or any one thing; it's a many-branching path, down which we are all walking.

—Samuel Steward (Phil Andros)

Declining Sodomy

Can we speak of the sodomite? The question is far more complex than it may appear. For if the language of sodomy demonstrates a complex multivalency in relation to its cultural placement, this complexity in turn only multiplies when we try to define how the language of sodomy defines a subject. Indeed, so polymorphous is the relationship between the language and its subject that the impulse is to decline to recognize the sodomite behind (or perhaps in front of) the sodomy and to label the discourse "subjectless." This is the approach Alan Bray finally adopts in *Homosexuality in Renaissance England*:

> It was not tolerance; it was rather a reluctance to recognize homosexual behaviour, a sluggishness in accepting that what was being seen was indeed the fearful sin of sodomy. It was this that made it possible for the individual to avoid the psychological problems of a homosexual relationship or a homosexual encounter, by keeping the experience merely casual and undefined: readily expressed and widely shared though the prevalent attitude to homosexuality was, it was kept at a distance from the great bulk of homosexual behaviour by an unwillingness to link the two.[1]

[1]Bray, *Homosexuality in Renaissance England*, p. 76.

Bray's analysis demonstrates a logic not unlike the economy of desire present in the poems of Lodge or Marston, in that regardless of what is happening on the material level, the epistemology of sexuality remains a constant and unperturbed stratum.[2] The rhetoric of the stigmatized sodomite is fully inscriptive, fully able to mark and identify the tabula rasa of the sexual subject, and, hence, every English subject necessarily thinks of male-male sexual behavior as the mark of subjective erasure, as a movement from the "rational" world of social subjectivity to the "irrational world" of the *contra naturam*. Bray's belief in the ability of sodomy to signify *in one way* in turn backs him into a corner, and he finds himself forced to define the subject of sodomy as a "subject on the run," an individual only able to maintain an identity by dodging the inscriptive abilities that he posits in the rhetoric of Renaissance sodomy. Subjectivity, then, becomes possible only in the rupture of the subjecting ability of language—a formulation that turns the sodomite (the person who thinks of him*self* as a being whose sexual meaning is marked by same-sex preferences) into a sort of freewheeling or sublinguistic subject who exists *despite* the society—and language—around him.

There are, of course, numerous factors problematizing Bray's formulation. As Bray himself notes, the desire to speak of the sodomite is possibly anachronistic,[3] for we cannot be sure of, to use an arbitrary example, when, historically speaking, the subject stopped thinking of himself as a farmer who sodomized and

[2]A similar critique of Bray has been set forth by Eve Kosofsky Sedgwick in an analysis of Bray's examination of molly houses in the restoration: "[Bray's] argument is, I think, circumscribed by an implicit assumption that male homosexuality and the European social order are incompatible in essence" (Sedgwick, *Between Men*, p. 84)—an observation that can easily be extended to the rift that Bray wants to engender between the discourse of sodomy and its subject. Sedgwick's argument has been taken to task—for all the wrong reasons, I think—by David Van Leer, "The Beast in the Closet: Homosociality and the Pathology of Manhood," *Critical Inquiry* 15 (1989): 587–605. In the subsequent debate that arose, Sedgwick outlined a defense that elaborated the merits of her position better than I can (Eve Kosofsky Sedgwick, "Tide and Trust," *Critical Inquiry* 15 [1989]: 745–757). See also Van Leer's rebuttal (David Van Leer, "Trust and Trade," *Critical Inquiry* 15 [1989]: 758–763.).

[3]Bray, *Homosexuality in Renaissance England*, p. 70.

started thinking of himself as a sodomite who farmed. Indeed, as much recent theory has told us, we cannot even be certain as to the exact historical emergence of the self, let alone the sexual self. And yet, as Bray's argument also indicates, the desire to find the sodomite is almost overwhelming. I would like to approach this problem as it is finessed in literature of the period. As I have already suggested, literary encodings seem to betray the totalizing goal of the rhetoric of sodomy and thereby suggest alternative forms of power. This process is also true of the relationship between sodomy and subjectivity, and by examining it I hope both to problematize our notion of how we can read the sodomite and to find a place for the sodomite within (rather than around, behind, or beneath) the linguistic practices of the culture.

An excellent place to start this argument is with Alain de Lille's *The Complaint of Nature*, which immediately suggests a way of declining the subject of sodomy totally different from that adopted by Bray. In the text, which exerts influence on literature from at least the time of Chaucer and was available in the Renaissance in reprinted editions,[4] male homoeroticism is figured in terms that both expand and reconfigure the Renaissance inscription of absolute stigmatism that was to follow:

> Such a great body of foul men roam and riot along the breadth of the whole earth, by whose seducing contact chastity herself is poisoned. Of such of these men as profess the grammar of love, some embrace only the masculine gender, some the feminine, others the common or indiscriminate. Some, as of heteroclite gender, are declined irregularly, through the winter in the feminine, through the summer in the masculine. Some, in the pursuit of the logic of love, establish in their conclusions the law of subject and the law of predicate in proper relation. Some, who have the place of the subject, have not learned how to form a predicate. Some only predicate, and will not wait the proper addition of the subject's end.[5]

[4]Cf. Lewis, *English Literature in the Sixteenth Century*, pp. 91, 115, 333.

[5]Alain De Lille, *The Complaint of Nature*, trans. Douglas M. Moffat (New York, 1908).

The "Man [who] is made woman," De Lille claims, "is both predicate and subject, he becomes likewise of two declensions, he pushes the laws of grammar too far."[6] De Lille's terminology overtly problematizes the language we would use to explain it: "subject" is ironically overdetermined by its participation in both grammatical and sexual fields, carrying as it does the connotations of "active" in contradistinction to the "passivity" of the predicate. But this intersection of the parts of grammar with the rhetoric of social and sexual subjectivity only serves to fortify the point: the sodomite here is a part of language, a being fully inscribed by it—he is "bad grammar." The rupture that Bray needs to empower his sodomite is seamed, and the sodomite returns to us as an effective, albeit shunned, subject position within De Lille's syntax of sexuality.[7]

Explicit in De Lille's text, then, is the assumption implicit in the epyllia I have analyzed; homoeroticism in this text is a determining difference *within* the grammar of sexual meaning, not just something that is defined by its otherness *to* meaning. Homoeroticism here is one of the determinants of the subject position the text posits—in other words, homoeroticism here does, indeed, make "sense," and the reader of the text must also make sense of it. Of course, the subject I have found is different from Bray's, for Bray is dealing with social subjectivity whereas De Lille is inscribing a textual subjectivity. The correlation between textual subjectivity and social subjectivity, if it exists at all, is far too complicated to explore in my argument. However, I will suggest that we can posit an analogy between the two, and to do so I will

[6]Ibid., p. 3.

[7]De Lille's text also situates other sexualities within the medieval ethos; as Maureen Quilligan notes, the text draws an analogy between "writing, agriculture, and human sexuality to reveal not only how each is analogous to the others, but how all three are part of the same creative service of God" (Maureeen Quilligan, *The Language of Allegory: Defining the Genre* [Ithaca, 1979], p. 159). Additionally, De Lille is not alone in his assumptions. John Boswell places De Lille's text within a relatively strong medieval sexual tradition (Boswell, *Christianity, Social Tolerance, and Homosexuality*, pp. 310–312). For the placement of De Lille's text in the tradition of literature leading to the Renaissance, see O. B. Hardison, Jr., et al., eds., *Medieval Literary Criticism* (New York, 1974), pp. 21, 51, 127.

need to outline a few terms. Traditionally the process of reading is thought of as identification or decoding. A reader *consumes* a text, unravels it and assimilates it, and, typically, achieves an empathy or identification with ideas expressed *in* the text. In this schema the reader is neutral, and the text acts as a contained unit transporting fixed ideas. However, contemporary Marxist criticism has foregrounded reading as a process in which a textual consumer is forced into a position of subjectivity posited by the text—a position from which the frequently disparate elements of a text achieve meaning or comprehensibility.[8] As Fredric Jameson has noted, interpretation is "an essentially allegorical act, which consists in rewriting a given text in terms of a particular interpretive master code."[9] The reader is not a consumer but, rather, a builder, and the act of reading consists of assuming a position of subjectivity that rectifies the determinants of meaning in the text with the determinants of meaning—the master codes—that constitute the reader as a social subject. Thus, meaning is neither in the text nor the reader but is instead in the new position achieved by the dialectical confrontation of text *and* reader.

Jameson's formulation is, of course, an amplification and a recasting of Althusser's famous formulation of literature as "ideological state apparatus"[10]—which is to say that literature from a specific culture creates structures that engage the basic

[8]The major texts that have paved the way for this formulation and that have influenced my own conception of the relationship between textual and social subjectivity are Louis Althusser, *For Marx*, trans. Ben Brewster (Harmondsworth, U.K., 1970), and *Lenin and Philosophy and Other Essays*, trans. Ben Brewster (London, 1977), and Terry Eagleton, *Criticism and Ideology* (London, 1976). Strong proponents of Althusser and Eagleton have argued that the subjective reformulation of Marxist textuality subordinates the materiality of "art" and exults the position of the Freudian psyche; I prefer, however, to recognize that a "work" is specifically designed as a consumer object and that therefore its "materiality" cannot be analyzed apart from its potentiality for "consumption." Catherine Belsey provides a cogent overview of the trends that are at play in the current debate on the neo-Marxist textual/social subject (Catherine Belsey, *Critical Practice* [London, 1980], pp. 56–102, 125–146).

[9]Fredric Jameson, *The Political Unconscious: Narrative as a Socially Symbolic Act* (Ithaca, 1981), p. 10.

[10]Althusser, *Lenin and Philosophy*, pp. 121–173.

assumptions or ideologies that empower the social formations of that culture. Jameson has not been alone in contesting the viability of Althusser's formulation; the point here, however, is not to engage the active debate on Marxist criticism but, rather, to recognize that in both formulations textual and social subjectivity, although not identical, are at least reciprocally interactive. In De Lille's text, homoeroticism is a *textual determinant*, a "quasi-material transmission point"[11] that aids in the reciprocal mediation of textual and social subjectivity. Crudely put, De Lille's readers must "read" sodomy, and hence sodomy becomes a part of who they are as readers. Obviously *The Complaint of Nature* is complicit with a process of sexual subjectivity that seeks to maintain an androcentric orthodoxy. But just as obviously the terms it uses ascribe a subjective potentiality to the rhetoric of homoeroticism. And although this potentiality happens in a literary milieu that is patently *not* the same as the material consideration of social subjectivity, if we accept, along with Althusser and Jameson, that textual subjectivity and social subjectivity are engaged with each other, then we can also assume that the presence of the sodomite in literature indicates the *possibility* of the sodomite in society. What we can find in literature, then, is not the *actual* sodomite but a delineation of the *conditions* for his existence. Recovering the material subject is, perhaps, impossible. By recovering historically specific textual subjectivities, however, we begin to sketch a spectrum of the possible determinants constituting the subject at a given historical moment. My topic here will be an examination of the *possibility* of the sodomite as it is expressed in the sonnet sequences of Barnfield and Shakespeare. Sonnets are a dynamic genre that consistently expose the conditions of sexual subjectivity by intersecting erotic expression, poetic subjectivity, and authorial self-fashioning. Moreover, the specific comparison of Barnfield's *Cynthia* (and its attendant publications) and Shakespeare's *Sonnets* additionally shows that the conditions that allowed "the sodomite" to be written also allowed sexual inscription in general to be unwritten and "the subject" to be empowered.

[11]Jameson, *Political Unconscious*, p. 154.

Folding Sodomy

Come live with me, and be my love,
And we will all the pleasures prove
That valleys, groves, hills and fields,
Woods, or steepy mountain yields.[12]

Christopher Marlowe's "shepherd" speaks these lines "to His Love" only with the assistance of a retrospective critical and textual process. The poem exists in a number of manuscript sources but only gains its title when included in *The Passionate Pilgrim*. Moreover, three printings must be consulted in order to find the entire poem: in *The Passionate Pilgrim* it is four stanzas long; in *Englands Helicon*, six; and a seventh stanza since expunged as corrupt appears in Izaak Walton's second edition of *The Compleat Angler*. The most important issue in this messy textual history is the insertion of the title, "The Passionate Shepherd to His Love." What is most obvious about Marlowe's brief lyric is that it is a seduction song, an invitation to love. And yet without the title an RSVP is next to impossible. Is this the voice of a man seducing a woman, the voice of a woman seducing a man, or something else altogether? Even with the title, which specifies the voice as male, the poem is still contingent on a reader's choice and can be read in at least three specific ways: as a homoerotic plea from man to man; as a heteroerotic plea from man to woman; as a platonic abstraction, such as Drayton might write, that directly addresses an *idea* of love. It is easy to overlook the gendered decisions that must be brought to a reading of this poem, for it is precisely such choices of gender that processes of socialization efface by positing them as "natural" or "inevitable" a priori facts. But neither gender nor sexuality is attached to Marlowe's words. Rather, gendered meaning must be ascribed as a subsequent process of interpretation.

The genre of the pastoral love complaint, of which Marlowe's poem is exemplary, is rife with such problems. One example that provides a telling contrast to Marlowe's lyric is the first eclogue of Barnfield's *The Affectionate Shepheard Sicke for Love*. Daphnis,

[12]Marlowe, *Christopher Marlowe*, p. 485.

the male singer of the eclogue, articulates his plea in the familiar rhetoric of pastoral seduction:

> If thou wilt come and dwell with me at home;
> My sheep-cote shall be strowd with new greene rushes:
> Weele haunt the trembling Prickets as they rome
> About the fields, along the hauthorne bushes
> I have a pie-bald Curre to hunt the Hare:
> So we will liue with daintie forrest fare.[13]

Daphnis's plea, however, is preceded by a dramatic contextualization that supplies the voice missing in Marlowe's song. As Daphnis describes it,

> Scarce had the morning Starre hid from the light
> Heauens crimson Canopie with stars bespangled,
> But I began to rue th'vnhappy sight
> Of that faire Boy that had my hart intangled;
> Cursing the Time, the Place, the sense, the sin;
> I came, I saw, I viewd, I slipped in.
>
> If it be sinne to loue a sweet-fac'd Boy,
> (Whose amber locks trust vp in golden tramels
> Dangle adowne his louely cheekes with ioy,
> When pearle and flowers his faire haire enamels)
> If it be sinne to loue a louely Lad;
> Oh then sinne I, for whom my soule is sad.[14]

The problematics of voice are eradicated here as surely as if Marlowe's lyric were to be retitled "The Passionate Sodomite to His Boy": this is a homoerotic plea from man to boy, with intimations of sodomy encoded in the punning Caesarian allusion "I came, I saw, I viewd, I slipped in."

The establishment of a homoerotic voice is clear and purposeful in Barnfield's poem. Not only does the continued stress on

[13]Richard Barnfield, *The Affectionate Shepheard. Containing the Complaint of Daphnis for the loue of Ganimede* (London, 1594), p. 11.
[14]Ibid., p. 6.

"sinne" align the speaker's voice with the common Renaissance legal rhetoric of homoeroticism, but the narrative of the eclogue also undermines the lucidity of heteroerotic meaning. The erotic complication in the poem is that Daphnis loves Ganimede but Ganimede loves the nymph queen, Guendolen. Guendolen, however, is enamored of a dead youth and pursued by an old man. In describing how this chain of diverted passions formed, Daphnis recounts that

> Death and *Cupid* met
> Upon a time at swilling *Bacchus* house,
> Where daintie cates vpon the Board were set,
> And Goblets full of wine to drinke carouse:
> Where Loue and Death did loue the licor so
> That out they fall and to the fray they goe.[15]

In the drunken revelry Death and Cupid confuse their arrows and bring death to the boy meant to love Guendolen and love to the old man meant to die. The passion of Daphnis may be *contra naturam*, but it certainly makes more sense than the heteroerotic love in the poem, which is explained in terms of slapstick mishaps, deathly misfires, and divine mistakes. If we are tempted, perhaps, to disclaim the problematic of Marlowe's poem—to say that it "naturally" makes heteroerotic sense—then just as certainly we must recognize the *difference* of Barnfield's poem and admit that it makes homoerotic sense.[16]

[15]Ibid., p. 6.

[16]The homoeroticism of Barnfield's poems has, ironically, been fully inscribed within the homophobia of modern critical practice. The best—and thereby worst—example of this is from C. S. Lewis: "His sonnets, like the *Affectionate Shepherd*, are pederastic, whether because Barnfield suffered in fact from the most uninteresting of all misfortunes or in a sheer humanist frenzy of imitation" (Lewis, *English Literature in the Sixteenth Century*, p. 497). Frenzied or boring: the polarities that govern pederasty for Lewis are probably more of a comment on his own psyche than on the "value" of Barnfield's poetry. In a contrasting manner, these poems have been adopted by gay literary historians to empower a tradition of gay male writing. Extracts from them are present in Byrne R. S. Fone, ed., *Hidden Heritage: History and the Gay Imagination: An Anthology* (New York, 1980), and the very important Penguin anthology (Stephen Coote, ed., *The Penguin Book*

Barnfield's poem is particularly important for examining the implied social subjectivity behind textual subjectivity, for the subsequent publication of *Cynthia. With certain Sonnets, and the Legend of Cassandra* indicates, first, that the reading audience of the time recognized the potentiality of the sodomite within Barnfield's eclogues and, second, that homoerotic subjectivity was something that could be both expressed and controlled textually. In the epistle to the volume, Barnfield alludes to a controversy that intersects the textual and social precisely at the point of "the sodomite":

> Some there were, that did interpret *The affectionate Shepheard*, otherwise then (in truth) I meant, touching the subiect thereof, to wit, the loue of a Shepheard to a boy; a fault, the which I will not excuse, because I neuer made. Onely this, I will vnshaddow my conceit: being nothing else, but an imitation of *Virgill*, in the second Eglogue of *Alexis*.[17]

Barnfield's defense succinctly encapsulates many of the problems of speaking of the sodomite. On the one hand, it indicates that his reading public recognized themselves as subjects to a homoerotic discourse. They were forced to make sense of homoeroticism and were displeased. But, on the other hand, it also demonstrates how Barnfield could disengage his authorial subjectivity from his text through a simple act of disavowal: I may have *said* it, but I did not *mean* it. Exactly what we can read from this text, then, is up for grabs. But what is not up for grabs is the fact that, as Barnfield acknowledges, one thing that could (and can) be read is the sodomite. And the possibly coy disavowal also indicates that at least some of Barnfield's reading public interpolated a link between the textual subject of sodomy and Barnfield's own social subjectivity.

While this exposure of a transaction between the textual and

of Homosexual Verse [Harmondsworth, U.K., 1983]). Of course, I am here taking the position that both of these appropriations—for the homophobes and for the homophiles—are misplaced efforts.

[17]Richard Barnfield, *Cynthia. With certain Sonnets, and the Legend of Cassandra* (London, 1595), p. 4.

the social is in and of itself interesting, the volume is even more fascinating because of the tacit belief presented in it that the sodomite (that is, the potentiality for homoerotic subjectivity) can be both expressed and controlled. The twenty "certain Sonnets" included in the volume ironically reinvoke the homoeroticism that the epistle has disavowed:

Sporting at fancie, setting light by loue,
  There came a theefe, and stole away my heart,
  (And therefore robd me of my chiefest part)
Yet cannot Reason him a felon proue.
For why his beauty (me hearts thiefe) affirmeth,
  Piercing no skin (the bodies sensiue wall)
  And hauing leaue, and free consent withall,
Himselfe not guilty, from loue guilty tearmeth,
Conscience the Iudge, twelue Reasons are the Iurie,
  They finde mine eies the beutie t'haue let in,
  And on this verdict giuen, agreed they bin,
Wherefore, because his beauty did allure yee,
  Your Doome is this: in teares still to be drowned,
  When his faire forehead with disdain is frowned.

(I.1–14)

Like Daphnis's pastoral lament, this sonnet includes gendered textual determinants—determinants that *constitute* a homoerotic discourse. The poem genders the "theefe" as "him" (4) and "Himselfe" (8) and mentions *his* physical allure three times (5, 12, 14). Moreover, although the poem does not determine the gender of the speaker—the "I"—the volume as a whole has already twice gendered the "I" as male, once in the male speaker of "Cynthia" and once in the "I" of the epistle, Barnfield himself.

The homoerotic subjectivity of the sequence is further entrenched both intertextually and vernacularly through the sustained use of the name Ganymede. Sonnet 4 introduces the term by stating "Two stars there are in one faire firmament, / (Of some entitled *Ganymedes* sweet face." (1–2). The use of the name establishes a web of connections between the sequence and, on the one hand, the social rhetoric of sodomy, and, on the other, Barnfield's own canon. Not only does the term carry with it vernacular associations of sodomy, but the possible Neoplatonic or "desexualizing" traditions sometimes ascribed to the term are removed from the sequence by sonnet 3, an extended rumination on philosophical traditions that claims that "the Stoicks thinke . . . / That vertue is the chiefest good of all, / The Academicks on *Idea* call" (1–3).[18] These traditions, which might construe "Ganymede" as a typological emblem, are contradistinctive to the poetry at hand, for, as the couplet says, "My chiefest good, my chiefe felicity, / Is to be gazing on my loues faire eie" (13–14). Moreover, the sequence frequently exploits the conflation of mythological and vernacular meanings. Sonnet 10 begins with "Thus was my loue, thus was my *Ganymed*" (1), which seems to draw on the vernacular analogy of male lover and Ganymede, but then also imports the myth of Venus, creating "faire *Ganymede*" from "pure blood in whitest snow yshed" (4–7). Sonnet 15 likewise begins with the personal/sexual address "Ah fairest *Ganymede*," but then reinscribes this address within the pastoral tradition from whence it derives by stating, "Though silly Sheepeheard I, presume to loue thee, . . . / Yet to thy beauty is my loue no blot" (1–4). The recourse to pastoral also completes an intertextual loop, returning us to the pastorals of *The Affectionate Shepheard* and a recognition that Ganymede is also the name of Daphnis's love in that condemned eclogue cycle. Unlike the epistle, then, which distances "the sodomite" from the pastorals and Barnfield from sodomy, this sequence shatters these established distances of decorum and places the sodomite in the volume.

Untitled and curiously placed after a chivalrous romantic poem—"Cynthia"—these twenty sonnets pose a textual dilemma; indeed, they would seem more at home as a conclusive coda to Barnfield's pastoral volume than they do in this volume, which, after all, disavows homoerotic intentionality. However, the purpose of the sequence becomes apparent in relation to the structure of the volume as a whole. Immediately after the se-

[18]The allusion to "Idea" obviously encodes an attack on Drayton, whose sonnet cycle, "Idea's Mirrour," would have been in circulation by the time Barnfield composed his (see Louise Hutchings Westling, *The Evolution of Michael Drayton's Idea* [Salzburg, 1974]).

quence comes an ode, titled, simply, "Ode," that is another speech by Daphnis, the central speaker of *The Affectionate Shepheard*. But the poem reverses the plot of the eclogues, for it recounts how

> Love I did faire *Ganymed*;
> (*Venus* darling, beauties bed:)
> Him I thought the fairest creature;
> Him the quintessence of Nature:
> But yet (alas) I was deceiu'd,
> (Love of reason is dereau'd)
> For since then I saw a Lasse
> (Lasse) that did in beauty passe,
> (Passe) faire *Ganymede* as farre
> As *Phoebus* doth the smallest starre.
>
> (ll. 51–60)

The ode fully rewrites the lament of Daphnis as a conventional lament for an unobtainable woman, complete with a frustrated epithalamion:

> Her it is, for whom I mourne;
> Her, for whom my life I scorne;
> Her, for whom I weepe all day;
> Her, for whom I sigh, and say,
> Either She, or else no creature,
> Shall enjoy my Loue: whose feature
> Though I neuer can obtaine,
> Yet shall my true loue remaine:
> Till (my body turn'd to clay)
> My poore soule must passe away,
> To the heauens.
>
> (ll. 73–83)

Read as the conclusion to the sonnet sequence, the ode serves to make the volume a mimetic enactment of Barnfield's epistle. If *The Affectionate Shepheard* confronted readers with the sodomite, then the sonnets reinvoke this position and the ode subsequently separates Barnfield from it by casting the sodomite as one distinct subject position that is disavowed in favor of "normal" heteroerotic subjectivity.

The process of disavowing homoerotic subjectivity is further stressed in the ode by a manipulation of poetic voice. Whereas the eclogues and sonnets speak in the first person, the ode prefaces Daphnis's speech with a lengthy narrative introduction that establishes a distinctive difference between the poet and the shepherd. The "I" of the poem wanders through a pastoral glade where "nights were short, and daies were long" (l. 1) and sees

> By a well of Marble-stone
> A Shepheard lying all alone.
> Weepe he did; and his weeping
> Made the fading flowers spring.
> *Daphnis* was his name (I weene)
> Youngest Swaine of Summers Queene.
>
> (ll. 11–16)

The conflation of author/"I"/Daphnis present in the eclogues and sonnets is replaced by a clear division between author/"I" and Daphnis. And although the ode's Daphnis is troubled by a conflict between Love's command to love the Lasse and Fancy's command to "not remoue / My affection from" Ganymede (61–63), the author/"I" sees nothing in the scene but a clear dictate to adopt the heteroerotic norm—a norm made all the more normative by the invocation of the traditional tribute to "Eliza":

> Scarce had he [Daphnis] these last words spoken,
> But me thought his heart was broken;
> With great griefe that did abound,
> (Cares and griefe the heart confound)
> In whose heart (thus riu'd in three)
> Eliza written I might see:
> In caracters of crimson blood,
> (Whose meaning well I vnderstood.)
> Which, for my heart might not behold,
> I hyed me home my sheep to folde.
>
> (ll. 87–96)

With this return to the fold, the poem is folded back into the preface.[19] The homoerotic subject constructed in the sonnets reconstructs the subject of the eclogues, but this entire subject is then relabeled as the "fancy" of a fictional shepherd; the "I" of the ode becomes a distanced spectator fully concordant with the orthodox author of the volume's preface. The strategy was evidently successful, for the preface to Barnfield's next volume, *The Encomium of Lady Pecunia: or The Praise of Money*, recalls the favorable acceptance of *Cynthia*: "Gentlemen, being incouraged through your gentle acceptance of my *Cynthia*, I have once more aduentured on your Curtesies: hoping to finde you (as I haue done heretofore) friendly."[20]

Regardless of how it is adjudicated, homoeroticism in all of these poems is recognized as a specific nexus of intersecting meanings that, in the aggregate, make "sense." And, hence, sodomy is more than a universal sign of unintelligibility; sodomy, here, *is* the sodomite. The demonized sodomite of ortho-

[19]The use of the ode as a closure or rewriting of the sonnets is not entirely atypical; Carol Thomas Neely examines several examples of sequences that "diffuse . . . the conflicts into other poetic modes" (Carol Thomas Neely, "The Structure of English Renaissance Sonnet Sequences," *ELH* 45 [1978]: 360). Neely's essay is the most encompassing study of the generic qualities of the Elizabethan sonnet cycle. I differ with it, however, on several points, the key one being that Neely claims that "most of the English sequences conclude unresolved, but all make gestures toward closure" (p. 360). This claim results from Neely's dependence on thematic and narrative analyses. I claim that the project of the sequences is to clear a subjective space for the poet, and the unresolved plots are actually fully operative strategies within this greater project. Aside from Neely's essay, the primary generic studies that have contributed to my thought are Janet Scott, *Les Sonnets Elizabethains* (Paris, 1929), and J. W. Lever, *The Elizabethan Love Sonnet* (London, 1956). Two important articles on individual sequences also demonstrate both the benefits and problems of structural analyses of sequences and have informed my analysis: Northrop Frye, "How True a Twain," in *The Riddle of Shakespeare's Sonnets*, ed. Edward Hubler (New York, 1962), and Louis Martz, "The *Amoretti*: Mostly Good Temperament," in *Form and Construction in the Poetry of Edmund Spenser* (New York, 1962).

[20]Richard Barnfield, *The Encomium of Lady Pecunia: or The Praise of Money* (London, 1598), p. 83.

dox ideology—the "anti-subject" existing only in an implied space outside of meaning—here becomes a character *within* the language of subjective possibility. Barnfield's canon as a whole begins to suggest some of the myriad issues we must keep in mind when discussing any subjectivity during the period, for it indicates the ways in which *the* subject fractures into *many* subjects. My discussion has not stressed the point, but I have been dealing with several different subjects: the subject *in* Barnfield's text—the position designated as intelligible for various characters by the codes of meaning within the poetry; the subject *of* Barnfield's texts—the position a reader finds herself or himself in when reading the text; the narrating subject—the position of the speaking voice determined by the intersection of systems of meaning it is bringing to its topic, as well as its nebulous relation to the author; the writing subject, or author—a seemingly monolithic concept that immediately disintegrates when we realize the difference between how Barnfield was interpreted by his reading audience and how he constructs his own intentions. There are, of course, deciding differences between all of these subjects. However, as Jameson suggests and as Barnfield's epistle bears out, these subjects, though all different, are neither mutually exclusive nor unrelated. But what is of central importance to my argument is the fact that all of these positions in relation to Barnfield's texts are contingent on a *subjective* comprehension of homoeroticism. If, in the world of the text, sodomy can make a sodomite, should we believe it is *necessarily* different in the "real" world?

The sodomite within Barnfield's texts derives from neither an anomaly nor a mistake. Rather, the ability of the text to dictate the sodomite is concordant with the basically conservative views of language present in Barnfield's poems and implicit in the very tradition of the sonnet. In the dedication to the Earl of Darby that prefaces *Cynthia*, Barnfield outlines an androcentric project that typifies the sonnet genre:

> Small is the gift, but great is my good-will; the which, by how much lesse I am able to expresse it, by so much the more it is infinite. Liue long: and inherit your Predecessors vertues, as

> you doe their dignitie and estate. This is my wish: the which your honorable excellent giftes doe promise me to obtaine: and whereof these few rude and unpollished lines, are a true (though an undeserving) testimony. If my ability were better, the signes should be greater; but being as it is, your honour must take me as I am, not as I should be.[21]

The dedication is obviously informed by certain proprieties of patronage, but it also indicates the extent to which poetry and patrilinearity intersect: Barnfield's poems are a "testimony" to the progenital conformity of the earl's masculine lineage. Although the preface is, perhaps, as much a convention as it is anything else, it also intersects with the basic assumptions underpinning sonneteering in general. Giles Fletcher, who provides one of the most sophisticated manifestos about sonneteering in his preface to *Licia*, succinctly outlines the dynastic (and patriotic) assumptions carried with the task of the sonneteer:

> Peruse but the writings of former times, and you shall see not onely in other countreyes, as *Italie* and *France*, men of learning, and great parts to have written Poems and Sonnets of Love; but even amongst us, men of best nobilitie, and chiefest families, to be the greatest Scholler and most renowned in this kind.[22]

For Fletcher, this patrilineal heritage is intricately linked with the propriety of language, for he takes as the task of his sequence the purification of English:

> If aniething be odious amongst us, it is the exile of our olde maners: and some base-borne phrases stuft up with such newe tearmes as a man may sooner feele us to flatter by our incrouching eloquence than suspect from the eare.[23]

The critical assumption of both Fletcher and Barnfield is clear:

[21]Barnfield, *Cynthia*, p. 43.
[22]Giles Fletcher, *Licia* (London, n.d.), p. 4.
[23]Ibid., p. 8.

great men write sonnets in a language that, in turn, expresses the greatness of men.[24] The ability of Barnfield to express the sodomite, then, becomes part of the "natural" ability of poetry to express, delineate, and control meaning in general—an ability tacit within and necessary to the continuance of the patrilineal power manifest within his culture and implicit within language itself. Hence, the sodomite is fully returned to us not as the exception but as a part of the very conditions of meaning within the Renaissance culture.

Unfolding Sodomy

The ability to find "the sodomite" within the subjective rhetoric of Barnfield's canon also, ironically, problematizes our ability to read *any* subjects. For while Barnfield's texts are an effort to construct the sodomite, they are also equally an effort to construct Barnfield. And in this latter subjective effort a space opens up that confounds the subjecting ability of language: Barnfield creates himself only by creating what he is not. There is, therefore, an implicit exceeding of language, an idea that Barnfield him*self* exists in some sort of de facto sense and that his poetic self-representation is simply an effort to toss aside the chaff of opinion. There is here, to borrow Stephen Greenblatt's famous formulation, a very strong idea that "there [are] both selves and a sense that they [can] be fashioned."[25] But this "self"—what we might think of in heterocentric terms as the "real" self—ironically comes to occupy a space analogous to Bray's sodomite, for it is a self that Barnfield fashions only from a rupture in signification, from an ability to place his "self" in the negatively con-

[24]The assumed conductivity of language present here also has literary roots deep within the sonnet tradition. The transparency of language forms the basis of most Western cultures ("in the beginning was the Word, and the Word was God" [John 1:1]) and also strongly informs Petrarch's early and influential work in the sonnet genre (see John Freccero, "The Fig Tree and the Laurel: Petrarch's Poetics," in *Literary Theory/Renaissance Texts*, ed. Patricia Parker and David Quint [Baltimore, 1986], pp. 20–32.)

[25]Greenblatt, *Renaissance Self-Fashioning*, p. 1.

tingent space implied by the subjective constitution of his sodomite. The sodomite becomes a determining other, for what Barnfield's canon as a whole says is, This is what *it* is, and I am that which *it* is *not*.

This subjective difference, which at first might seem minor, can be clarified and foregrounded through a brief examination of Sir Philip Sidney's *Apology for Poetry*. In the tract, Sidney draws a distinction between the subjecting ability of poetry and that of other social discourses. "There is no art delivered to mankind," he claims, "that hath not the works of nature for his principal object, without which they could not consist, and on which they so depend, as they become actors and players, as it were, of what nature will have set forth."[26] Sidney explicates his argument through a set of concrete examples:

> So doth the astronomer look upon the stars, and, by that he seeth, setteth down what order nature hath taken therein. So do the geometrician and arithmetician in their diverse sorts of quantities. So doth the musician in times tell you which by nature agree, which not. The natural philosopher thereon hath his name, and the moral philosopher standeth upon the natural virtues, vices, and passions of man. . . . The lawyer saith what men have determined; the historian what men have done. The grammarian speaketh only of the rules of speech; and the rhetorician and logician, considering what in nature will soonest prove and persuade, thereon give artificial rules, which still are compassed within the circle of a question according to the proposed matter. . . . And the metaphysic, though it be in the second and abstract notions, and therefore be counted supernatural, yet doth he indeed build upon the depth of nature.[27]

For Sidney, these disciplines are stigmatized by a self-containment and preordination. The deductive strategy involved, in Sidney's view, renders them impotent: by looking *for* stars, one never finds anything *but* stars. Hence, the topic governs the

[26]Philip Sidney, *An Apology for Poetry*, in *Critical Theory since Plato*, ed. Hazard Adams (New York, 1971), p. 157.

[27]Ibid., p. 157.

science—the cart leads the horse—in a way that renders these disciplines secondary to poetry:[28]

> Only the poet, disdaining to be tied to any such subjection, lifted up with the vigor of his own invention, doth grow in effect another nature, in making things either better than nature bringeth forth, or, quite anew, forms such as never were in nature, as the Heroes, Demigods, Cyclopes, Chimeras, Furies, and such like: so as he goeth hand in hand with nature, not enclosed within the narrow warrant of her gifts, but freely ranging only within the zodiac of his own wit.[29]

Unsubjected by the a priori strictures of the sciences, the poet is free in turn to be the subjector, to create anew the conditions of meaning and, by extension, the conditions of being.[30]

Already we can feel resonances between Sidney's placement of the poet and Barnfield's placement of both the sodomite and himself. However, the plank of Sidney's argument most necessary for delineating the conditions of poetic subjectivity that empower Barnfield's self-(re)presentation rests in the apology's broader notion of epistemology and specifically in its revaluation of classical epistemology. Later in the apology Sidney returns to his condemnation of self-contained sciences and relates them to the concept of *architectonike*:

[28]Sidney's distinction between and hierarchicalization of discourse and content is likely informed by Aristotle's *Rhetoric*, which claims that "rhetoric is not bound up with a single definite class of subjects" (Aristotle, *Rhetorica*, ed. W. Rhys Roberts [London, 1971], 1355b7).

[29]Sidney, *Apology for Poetry*, p. 157.

[30]Although Sidney's tract is literary theory, its participation within broader modes of cultural power has been well documented. Alan Sinfield, for example, finds that "the diverse constituents of the *Defence* reveal an intersection at a particular political juncture, aimed at appropriating literature to earnest protestant activism through a negotiation of the divergent codes of pagan literature and protestantism" (Alan Sinfield, "The Cultural Politics of the *Defence of Poetry*," in *Sir Philip Sidney and the Interpretation of Renaissance Culture: The Poet in His Time and in Ours: A Collection of Critical and Scholarly Essays*, ed. Gary F. Waller and Michael D. Moore [London, 1984], p. 124). The influence of the *Apology* as both a literary and social artifact during its own time is discussed fluently in Richard Helgerson, *The Elizabethan Prodigals* (Berkeley, 1976), pp. 125–127.

> But when by the balance of experience it was found that the astronomer looking to the stars might fall into a ditch, that the inquiring philosopher might be blind in himself, and the mathematician might draw forth a straight line with a crooked heart, then, lo, did proof, the overruler of opinions, make manifest that all these are but serving sciences, which, as they have each a private end in themselves, so yet are they all directed to the highest end of the mistress-knowledge, by the Greeks called *architectonike*, which stands (as I think) in the knowledge of a man's self, in the ethic and politic consideration, with the end of well doing and not of well knowing only—even as the saddler's next end is to make a good saddle, but his farther end to serve a nobler faculty, which is horsemanship; so the horseman's to soldiery, and the soldier not only to have skill, but to perform the practice of a soldier.[31]

Architectonike—that science which has no content in and of itself but that orders all other sciences—is most closely related to our modern term *epistemology*. It is not something with meaning, but it is the condition of all other meanings. Sidney's recasting of the term sets up a number of important concepts. First, all modes of knowledge, whether as rarefied as astronomy or as pragmatic as saddlery, are set into a sort of referential drift. The art of making a saddle is a self-contained practice, but its purpose always lies *elsewhere*. Additionally, this drift is, as in the patrilineal assumptions of Fletcher's manifesto on sonnets, refigured in terms of social stability. And finally, these principles are solidified under the banner of the subject—for what makes "sense" of Sidney's epistemology is knowledge of the "self."[32] Sidney's apology,

[31]Sidney, *Apology for Poetry*, p. 159.

[32]In her essay on Sidney, Margaret W. Ferguson perceptively notes that "a defense, whether a legal, military, or psychical phenomenon, always responds to preexisting charges, attacks, or threats" (Margaret W. Ferguson, *Trials of Desire: Renaissance Defenses of Poetry* [New Haven, 1983], p. 138); therefore, the genre is always implicitly an assertion of the "self." Ferguson contextualizes her analysis within the matrix of Freudian analysis, but the structure here is also closely related to Lacan's "I" (Jacques Lacan, *Ecrits: A Selection*, trans. Alan Sheridan [New York, 1977], pp. 1–7), especially since the Lacanian "I" is produced and producing of a discursive web not unlike the implicit discursive restraints of the apology genre—which is

then, sets up a system of power that almost too obviously presages our current understandings of material practice and ideological control: practice serves the state, but this servitude is in turn obfuscated by the ideological construction of the subject, for in Sidney's terms the service to the state is the very mark of the subject's autonomy.

The *Apology* extends the implicit assumptions of Barnfield's textual self-creation to abstract theory and thereby stresses to us the importance of reading the sodomite in Renaissance culture. For Barnfield, constituting the sodomite becomes a means of reconstituting his own subjectivity; for Sidney, *any* constitutive discourse—*but only in a negatively contingent manner*—constitutes the self. There is a bifurcated understanding of the subject at work here, one in which *a* subject can be expressed and controlled but in which the *real* or *true* (or, we might say, *important*) subject is always simply implied by this act of control. There is, then, a different sense of subjectivity here, one that might best be thought of as sub*junct*ivity. Indeed, this notion is clearly presented in Sidney's equation of the self and *architectonike*. For, like that Greek science that gains meaning only in its position of otherness to other discourses, Sidney's "real" subject exists only in the contingent and undefined space implied by the juncture and collision of other subjecting discourses. This is exactly the structure of Barnfield's sodomite, for homoeroticism in his canon creates a subjectivity, but only for the purpose of implying a different space of sub*junct*ivity for Barnfield. Barnfield's poems return the sodomite to the fold, but only for the purpose of unfolding Barnfield himself.

Barnfield's sodomite, then, which at first might seem radically

---

not to contradict Ferguson but simply to note the far-reaching implications of her reading. We might note, however, and only partially facetiously, that since psychoanalysis begins with the assumption of the subject and then attempts to explain it, it falls into those categories of sciences derided by Sidney as "putting the cart before the horse." But this is a topic for another essay. Ferguson also exquisitely contextualizes the *Apology* within Sidney's life and canon and within the industry of Sidney criticism; I refer readers to this fine book for such histories. Here I primarily relate my analysis to recent trends in material culturalism that are outside the scope of Ferguson's analysis.

affrontive to the mores of his society, actually is a manifestation of the configuration of power present in sonnets in their most traditional forms. For there is always in the genre a sense that the highly subjective rhetoric of the poems is preceded and validated by—and that it thereby validates—the Ur-subject, the figure of the poet himself. Indeed, Sidney's own sequence, *Astrophil and Stella*, begins with an extended rumination on language and expression that exposes this structure:

Loving in truth, and faine in verse my love to show,
That she (deare she) might take some pleasure of my paine:
Pleasure might cause her reade, reading might make her know,
Knowledge might pitie win, and pitie grace obtaine,
I sought for words to paint the blackest face of woe,
Studying inventions fine, her wits to entertaine:
Oft turning other leaves, to see if thence would flow
Some fresh and fruitfull showers upon my sunne-burn'd
braine.
But words came halting forth, wanting Inventions stay,
Invention, Natures child, fled step-dame Studies blowes,
And others feete still seem'd but strangers in my way.
Thus great with child to speake, and helplesse in my throwes,
Biting my trewant pen, beating my selfe for spite,
Foole, said my Muse to me, looke to thy heart and write.
(I. 1–14)[33]

This passage compares favorably with similar opening lines from Spenser's *Amoretti*:

And happy lines, on which with starry light,
those lamping eyes will deigne sometimes to look
and reade the sorrowes of my dying spright,
written with teare in harts close bleeding book.
(I. 5–8)[34]

[33]Philip Sidney, *The Poems of Sir Philip Sidney*, ed. William A. Ringler, Jr. (Oxford, 1962).

[34]Edmund Spenser, *Poetical Works*, ed. Edward De Selincourt (Oxford, 1912).

The central image in each invocation is that of the speaker exceeding language. Sidney's speaker fails in his quest to find "fit words" and "inventions fine," but just as much the failure is that of the words, which are unable to express the "heart" of the speaker. Hence, we are returned to the *Apology* in this almost exact poetic recapitulation of the condemnation of the "rhetorician and logician," who, "considering what in nature will soonest prove and persuade,"[35] banish themselves from the "truth" of the (architectonic) self to which the privileged poet is led by the muse. Similarly, the worth of Spenser's verse is in its ability to efface the tangibility of words and instead to convey a direct sense of "teares in harts close bleeding book." The central concern is that of subjective excess, of positing through feigned incoherence something greater than the language on the page.[36] The subject of the speaker is not expressed through these words, but the space in which he exists is *subjunctively* implied by a clear delineation of that which he is not. The speaker becomes fully described and inscribed by a void, a space of nonmeaning that by default becomes greater than language itself, and language becomes a negotiated path leading toward, but stopping just short of, the "truth" that is the speaker's mind.

Although this sub*junct*ivity appears to betray the totalizing logocentrism of sub*ject*ivity, it is, of course, true that it actually exposes an even more insistently inscriptive definition of "the subject." The two-fold inscription of the subject—by defining what he is not and by empowering this negative space—first assumes an inherent ability in language to signify what is other and then assumes that the a priori significance of the poetic subject manifests some sort of "inevitable" or "natural" meaning that need not be articulated but will be fully understood in contradistinction. I have not, therefore, rescued the sodomite

[35]Sidney, *Apology for Poetry*, p. 157.

[36]This "poetic excess" compares favorably with a similar structure Fineman finds in Shakespeare's *Rape of Lucrece*. As he states, the poem is profoundly concerned with "the phenomenology of the spurt" (Joel Fineman, "Shakespeare's *Will*: The Temporality of Rape," *Representations* 7 [1987]: 59)—a structure that implies poetic/sexual excess, overflowing, uncontainability, etc.

from the logocentrism of Bray's formulation. However, the dynamic present here opens a larger space for the sodomite than that permitted by the legal rhetoric of the Renaissance. For if the Adamic link between poetic language and the subject of the poet is fragmented and tangential in sonnet sequences, we can posit, perhaps, a similar potentiality within the socially subjecting language of Renaissance sodomy. Although it may be true that the legal rhetoric of sodomy inscribed a monolithic subject, it may also be true that there was a multiplicity of ways to assume subjective meaning in relation to this inscription. *The* legal sodomite, therefore, opens the space for *many* sodomites. This recognition of a tangential rather than linear relationship between inscription and subjectivity, while it recuperates a greater subjective space for the sodomite, also complicates our ability to read *any* subject—and the parameters of this problematic are the overt topic of Shakespeare's *Sonnets*.

The Shakespearian Sodomite

The history of commentary on Shakespeare's sonnets is also the history of how to read humanistically.[37] Questions of the identity of the dark lady, the rival poet, the boy;[38] debates on the identity of W. H.;[39] biographical arguments over what is sexual, what is platonic, and what was Shakespeare's sexual preference:[40] these questions, which form the bulk of criticism about the sonnets, all presuppose that the importance of the text is in its ability to act as a conduit of atemporal human emotions—the sort

[37]For an excellent overview of Shakespearian criticism and the question of humanism, though not specifically on the sonnets, see John Drakakis, ed., *Alternative Shakespeares* (London, 1985), pp. 1–25.

[38]This trend, which began primarily with Wordsworth and the Schlegel brothers, reaches its most refined and least productive level in Leslie Hotson, *Shakespeare's Sonnets Dated, and Other Essays* (Oxford, 1949).

[39]This problem has been masterfully put to rest by Donald W. Foster, "Master W. H., R.I.P.," *PMLA* 1 (1987): 42–54, which convincingly argues that W. H. is a misprint for W. Sh., i.e., William Shakespeare.

[40]All of the critical issues mentioned here are objectively anatomized in appendix 1 (pp. 543–549) of Booth's edition, and rather than accumulate a lengthy bibliographic note I refer readers to this excellent resource.

of basic drives that, in a humanist criticism, transcend time and become the key to all mythologies.[41] Even very recent criticism tends to adopt hybrid forms of this strategy. Joseph Pequigney, in *Such Is My Love: A Study of Shakespeare's Sonnets*, takes as his aim "a searching and persuasive exposition of Shakespeare's Sonnets, one elucidative of their aesthetic coherence, their moral values, and their psychological depths."[42] The presupposition is that the sonnets necessarily function as expressions of an authorial psyche—or, in a more simplistic manner of speaking, of Shakespeare himself—and that the purpose of reading them is to explicate the *man* behind them and expressed through them.[43]

Such a program of reading inherently betrays the epistemology of sonnets, for, as we have seen, the subjectivity within sequences typically is designed to fall short of and thereby only imply the assumed subjunctive space occupied by the poet. A more appropriate program of reading has been proposed by Joel Fineman, who finds in the sonnets "the internally divided, post-idealist subject of a 'perjur'd eye'."[44] Through the "using up" of

[41]Cf. Belsey, *Critical Practice*, pp. 1–36.

[42]Pequigney, *Such Is My Love*, pp. 4–5.

[43]The role of this "Authentic Shakespeare," as Stephen Orgel would call him—the assumed figure of authority validating our interpretive practice—has been explored inventively in relation to debates of authorship of the plays in Marjorie Garber, "Shakespeare's Ghost Writers," in *Cannibals, Witches, and Divorce: Estranging the Renaissance*, ed. Marjorie Garber, pp. 122–146 (Baltimore, 1987), and in relation to performance and editing problems in Stephen Orgel, "The Authentic Shakespeare," *Representations* 21 (1988): 1–26. Garber has also wittily extended her analysis through a psychoanalytic matrix, drawing an analogy between the "Authentic Shakespeare" and the "phallic mother" of Freudian fetishism (Marjorie Garber, "Shakespeare as Fetish," *SQ* 41, 2 (1990): 242–250.). Terence Hawkes provides perhaps the most wide-ranging examination of the topic, interrogating the institutionalization of British humanism through an extended deconstruction of the "Authentic Shakespeare" (Terence Hawkes, *That Shakespeherian Rag: Essays on a Critical Process* [London, 1986]). A reactionary defense of the "Authentic Shakespeare," which I mention only for the sake of thoroughness, can be found in Richard Levin, "The Poetics and Politics of Bardicide," *PMLA* 105, 3 (1990): 491–504.

[44]Joel Fineman, *Shakespeare's Perjur'd Eye: The Invention of Poetic Subjectivity in the Sonnets* (Berkeley, 1986), p. 29.

epideictic conventions, Fineman claims, the sequence severs poetics from the poet and establishes a space of true poetic subjectivity for the authorial figure. Ironically, while Fineman's argument short-circuits the humanist assumptions underpinning criticism of the poems, it also accepts without question the sexual subjectivity of them; that is, Fineman accepts, in accordance with tradition, that the first one hundred and twenty-six sonnets are an erotic address to a boy by a man and that this pattern of desire is then reconfigured into heteroerotic lust for the fabled "dark lady." I would like to put into play the variable of sexual difference that Fineman takes as a given and argue that Fineman's formulation of the "divided subject" is betrayed by his "belief" in erotic language. The purpose of the "boy sonnets," as they have come to be known, is not erotic but linguistic. Indeed, these poems, which are among the few canonized examples of "the sodomite," actually take as their project the task of frustrating the ability to read erotic meaning in general. If Barnfield's sodomite is a means of achieving subjectivity through the control of sexual meaning, the Shakespearian sodomite procures the poet's subjectivity at the expense of sexual meaning.

The difference of the sequence can be quickly sketched out by examining the Shakespearian parallel to the invocatory sonnets of Sidney and Spenser.

> So is it not with me as with that Muse,
> Stird by a painted beauty to his verse,
> Who heauen it selfe for ornament doth vse,
> And euery faire with his faire doth reherse,
> Making a coopelment of proud compare
> With Sunne and Moone, with earth and seas rich gems:
> With Aprills first borne flowers and all things rare,
> That heauens ayre in this huge rondure hems,
> O let me true in loue but truly write,
> And then beleeue me, my loue is as faire,
> As any mothers childe, though not so bright
> As those gould candells fixt in heauence ayer:
> Let them say that like of heare-say well,
> I will not prayse that purpose not to sell.
>
> (21.1–14)

Although the convention of deriding language to establish poetic autonomy seems fully operative here, the analogue between this and the other poetic invocations is complicated by an addition of metageneric punning. The distinction the speaker draws between "me" and "Muse" may be a stock method of exceeding language, but it just as strongly establishes the speaker as a spectator of poetic practice, "Muse" being a traditional metonymy for poet. Moreover, the puns in the sonnet continually question the image of the speaker as the Ur-subject or "truth" behind the poetic language. The cognate pun of air/heir establishes a stress between the possibilities of all and nothing.[45] The "heauens ayre" of line eight is a means both of saying "everything" and of specifying heavens's possessor, God, as the *only* thing. Similarly, "those gould candells fixt in heauens ayer" ironically undercuts the power of poetic idiomatics by suggesting that they are too contrived to describe true love, but it also suggests that there is an absolute source of truth, the transcendent light of heaven's heir. The dichotomy of possibilities is perfectly encoded in the most famous line of the sonnet, "O let me true in loue but truly write." The cognate pun of write/right allows for two possibilities: the possibility that, as with Sidney's speaker, this speaker wants simply to look to his love and "write," and the possibility that there is something truly "right," some platonic or atemporal origin like heaven's heir. For Sidney and Spenser, poetic language signifies the other that establishes the poet, but in the Shakespearian sequence this otherness is made even more profound. The continually irreducible punningness of the poem makes poetry itself an other to fixed meaning. The economy of self and other metaphorically created by Sidney's and Spenser's construction of a poet/poetry opposition becomes meaningless: where does the poet begin if we cannot find where the poem ends?

The difference of the Shakespearian invocation is also stressed by its placement, for, unlike a traditional invocation, which leads off a sequence, sonnet 21 is offset from the opening by twenty intervening poems. Fineman claims this invocation as the culmination of a sub-sequence that "equates the true poetry and true

[45]Shakespeare, *Shakespeare's Sonnets*, p. 169.

love that goes with the young man."[46] However, just as the "truth" of poetry in this poem dissolves into the grayness of pun, the "love" that precedes it diffuses along an axial of polysemous ambiguity. The beginning sonnets of the 1609 quarto are generally accepted as a self-contained unit, one that "give[s] expression to one compelling case, that of saving from time and wrack the rare and ravishing beauty of the youth addressed."[47] The boy who is so prominent in these readings seems to me to be much more difficult to find in the poems themselves. The familiar opening of the first sonnet outlines the difficulty:

> From fairest creatures we desire increase,
> That thereby beauties *Rose* might never die,
> But as the riper should by time decease,
> His tender heire might beare his memory.
>
> (1.1–4)

The need to read gender into this poetry replicates the complication implicit in Marlowe's "Passionate Shepherd." The thematic insistence on *husband*ry might imply that the receiver of this advice is male. However, in *All's Well That Ends Well*, Parolles offers advice to a female, Helena, claiming that "loss of virginity is rational increase, and there was never virgin got till virginity was first lost" (I.i.125–127).[48] This biological exhortation, then, is not inherently gendered as a male-male language. The gendering of this quatrain fully inscribes itself within the punning multiplicity of sonnet 21. As Stephen Booth has noted, the coordinating conjunction "but" carries the possible meanings of "and" and "except."[49] Hence, the "decease" of the "riper" imports the momentary possibility of undermining the immortality of "beauties Rose." Moreover, line 4 incorporates two cognate puns that recall the dichotomous puns of 21, "heir"/"air" and "bear"/"bare": the heir of a father who carries on the memory of

[46]Fineman, *Shakespeare's Perjur'd Eye*, p. 75.

[47]Pequigney, *Such Is My Love*, p. 7.

[48]William Shakespeare, *All's Well That Ends Well*, ed. G. K. Hunter (London, 1967).

[49]Shakespeare, *Shakespeare's Sonnets*, p. 135.

patrilineal lineage is also at the same time something vaporous that strips away that memory.

Nothing in this sonnet conveys a single meaning, let alone a single gender or sexuality. The narcissistic person "contracted" or tithed to "thine owne bright eyes" (1.5) is also potentially a person "contracted" or reduced to "bright eyes." In the first case the person is belligerently irreverent; in the second the person is stereotypically inscribed in the language of the sonnet and blazon genres. And when this person (as yet not specified as male or female) is said to "within thine owne bud buriest thy content" (1.11), the derision may be toward either masturbation or monogamy, since "owne" and "one" are Renaissance cognates. We could be confronting here a man who masturbates, a woman who masturbates, or a man who satisfies himself with only one vagina. Moreover, the sexual charges here are fully complicated by Renaissance idiomatics: "buriest" foreshadows the "graue" of the final couplet and implies death and the demise of "beauties Rose"; death, however, also implies orgasm and "increase"; and the image of a flower also recalls the Renaissance euphemism for menstruation. What is happening here is hard to tell—and this, more than likely, is not the problem but the point.

The strategy involved in this sonnet can be clarified if we again return to the idea of the first twenty-one sonnets as a sub-sequence. The unity of these sonnets is frequently taken to be an effect of Shakespeare's extended use as a source of Erasmus's "Epistle to Persuade a Young Gentleman to Marriage" as reprinted in Thomas Wilson's *The Arte of Rhetorique*. This argument, which has been scrupulously analyzed by Katherine M. Wilson,[50] usually accepts Wilson's example of Erasmus as a *thematic* inspiration for Shakespeare's poems. However, if we consider the epistle's context, a more interesting set of possibilities arise. Erasmus's epistle is included in the *Rhetorique* as an example of persuasive oration, and in many ways it can be viewed as an exemplum that works within the specific textual dynamics of Marlowe's pastoral lyric. Persuasion, like seduction, is a highly

[50]Katherine M. Wilson, *Shakespeare's Sugared Sonnets* (New York, 1974), pp. 146–167. Cf. Thomas Wilson, *The Arte of Rhetorique*, ed. G. H. Mair (Oxford, 1909).

motivated discourse that seeks specific ends. Wilson's use of Erasmus, then, in the simplest form, can be thought of as an example of how to make language *work*. The first sonnet of the Shakespearian sequence, in contrast, is an example of how to *stop* language from working. And it achieves this end by the same means I have discussed in relation to Marlowe's poem: it simply erases the gendered determinants present in the title of Erasmus's epistle. What is in Wilson's *Rhetorique* a conservative effort to assure the continuance of the patrilineal line becomes, in the Shakespearian poetic, a way to stop making sense. Hence, the link between the text and the source, although involving thematic issues, might best be formulated on the theoretical level: both the *Rhetorique* and the *Sonnets* are extended ruminations on the significatory propriety of language.

To a certain extent the multiplicity of the first sonnet might be dismissed as the effect of the inherent polysemy of any language and particularly of the unregularized English of the Renaissance. However, this slipperiness of sexual meaning is consistently exploited throughout the first twenty sonnets in a way that indicates more than accidental multivalence. Each sonnet in this sequence constructs a pattern that demands a gendered reading, but each poem also frustrates attempts to find the determinants that would make such a reading possible. The second sonnet, for example, begins with traditional imagery of warfare:

> When fortie Winters shall besеige thy brow,
> And digge deep trenches in thy beauties field,
> Thy youthes proud liuery so gaz'd on now,
> Wil be a totter'd weed of smal worth held.
>
> (2.1–4)

But this imagery, usually associated with the female, is only a further complication of the man-to-son expectations brought to bear on the text by its relation to Erasmus's epistle. Furthermore, the poem can be read in (at least) two entirely independent ways. In the Erasmian tradition it works coherently as an exhortation to a young man to breed. In the tradition of Parolles it might be a demand to a woman to surrender her virginity. The two possibilities exist coterminously because there is no convenient "Stella" in the title to gender the sequence; there is only "Shake-speares Sonnets Neuer before Imprinted."

The process of interpretation demanded by these opening sonnets is metaphorically redacted in sonnet 8, when music is used to describe that "speechlesse song being many, seeming one" (8.13). Like a concord sounded in unison, third, fifth, and sixth, these poems, which appear as one sequence, continually break into constituent parts. But unlike a chord that achieves a "mutuall ordering" (8.10), the poems create a disordering of the assumptions that must precede the meaningfulness of gendered language. This interpretive frustration can be traced throughout the first eighteen sonnets. The couplet of sonnet 13 seems to imply that the receiver is male, for it suggests, "You had a Father, let your Son say so" (13.14), but then we realize that this patrilineal order affords two positions between grandfather and grandson: son and daughter. Sonnet 9 seems to specify a similar gendering, for the couplet claims, "No loue toward others in that bosome sits / That on himselfe such murdrous shame commits" (9.13–14). But a backward glance reveals that this sentiment refers not to the receiver of the sonnets but to a hypothetical "vnthrift" (9.9); the gender of the receiver remains a mystery. The ambiguity of these sonnets shows forth especially in comparison to Barnfield's; if Barnfield's demonstrate how to "make" a sodomite, Shakespeare's encode the *possibility* of the sodomite, but only as one of many that, in the aggregate, *un*make the possibility of any *one* coherent subject. All of which, of course, can be seen as a means of creating a greater sub*junc*tive space for the poet. The poet in Barnfield's sequence is he who orders our experience of and differs from the sodomite; the poet in Shakespeare's is he who unorders all gendered experience, and hence is he who differs from all the (poetically) conventional strategies of making gendered sense.

We can therefore extend Fineman's analysis of the *Sonnets*' use of poetic tradition to their use of sexuality, and specifically to their use of the sodomite. For, as with the instance of epideictic tradition, these sonnets "use up" sexual rhetoric—expend its subjecting ability through an "embarrassment of riches" and excessive meanings. The importance of the Shakesperian sodomite within this hermeneutic becomes apparent in sonnet 19, when the sustained neutrality of gender is pointedly suspended. The speaker implores time to

> . . . carve not with thy howers my loues faire brow,
> Nor draw noe lines there with thine antique pen,
> Him in thy course vntainted doe allow,
> For beauties patterne to succeding men.
>
> (19.9–12)

There is no possible referent for "Him" other than "my loue." The effect of this specificity genders the sequence retroactively and makes us aware that what we have been reading is, indeed, "the sodomite." However, the delay in this specification is as important as its arrival, for the solidification of gender makes us also aware of its indeterminacy in the preceding poems. We become aware, in short, that we have not been dealing in textual truths but, rather, have been importing our own assumptions—hetero-, homo-, or otherwise erotic. And in the process it also stresses the inability of conventionalized language to restrict the expression of desire.

That the critique of language and not the construction of the sodomite is the topic of these poems seems certain, for the sequence follows the specification of gender with a poem that is a tour-de-force and condensation of the obfuscational strategies deployed throughout the preceding poems. Although sonnet 20 is one of the most famous of the cycle, its centrality to the sequence—and my argument—makes it worth presenting in toto.

> A Womans face with natures owne hand painted,
> Haste thou the Master Mistris of my passion,
> A womans gentle hart but not acquainted
> With shifting change as is false womens fashion,
> An eye more bright then theirs, lesse false in rowling:
> Gilding the object where-vpon it gazeth,
> A man in hew all *Hews* in his controwling,
> Which steales mens eyes and womens soules amaseth,
> And for a woman wert thou first created,
> Till nature as she wrought thee fell a dotinge,

And by addition me of thee defeated,
By adding one thing to my purpose nothing.
  But since she prickt thee out for womens pleasure,
  Mine be thy loue and thy loues vse their treasure.

The poem creates a perfectly androgynous—or, perhaps more appropriately, hermaphroditic—reading experience, for it is equally gendered as both male and female.[51] This perfect duplicity is amply displayed in the famous crux of the poem, the coinage of "Master Mistris": is this a man (master) who is used as a mistress would be or a mistress who holds a primary (master) position in the speaker's mind?[52] The overt hermaphroditism of this phrase is punningly and subtly sustained throughout the entire sonnet. The first explication of the "Master Mistris" seems to gender the receiver of the poems as female (3–6), but this possibility is juxtaposed to the equal possibility that the receiver is male (6–8). As in many of the sonnets there is almost an infinity of meanings here, two of which are particularly telling. One possibility is that the speaker is addressing a woman who surpasses the "fashion" of other women and, through her chaste gentility,

[51]Phyllis Rackin, "Androgyny, Mimesis, and the Marriage of the Boy Heroine on the English Renaissance Stage," *PMLA* 102, 1 (1987): 29–41, provides a perceptive discussion of the epistemological differences between the androgyne and the hermaphrodite in the Renaissance, as well as an application of them to the Renaissance stage with special attention to Shakespeare's comedies. The etiology of the term *hermaphrodite* has been historically analyzed in Steve Brown, "'. . . and his ingle at home': Notes on Gender in Jonson's *Epicoene*," Renaissance Society of America, Philadelphia, 21 March 1986.

[52]Few critics have actually recognized this famous phrase as one that in and of itself indicates androgyny. Most begin with the assumption that the phrase is masculine (cf. James Winny, *The Master-Mistresse: A Study of Shakespeare's Sonnets* [New York, 1969], and Neely, "Structure of English Renaissance Sonnet Sequences," pp. 366–367). This tendency is also demonstrated in Fineman's work. He sees sonnet 20 as "the *locus classicus*" in a debate that presupposes homoerotic rhetorical intents: "Given the poet's love for the young man, and the young man sonnets surely give it frequently enough, the question that remains is just what it is the young man's poet wants" (Fineman, *Shakespeare's Perjur'd Eye*, p. 272). Such statements, I think, insert a critical determinism into Fineman's argument that betrays its overall destabilizing intentions.

"gilds" (i.e., renders worthy or priceless) the man on whom she "gazeth" ("A man . . ." in this case being an appositive for "object"). Yet there is also the possibility that the speaker addresses a man and that "a womans gentle hart" is a metaphor for the unique beauty of the male. As Stephen Booth has noted, "acquainted" carries with it a pun on the noun *quaint*, a slang term for the vulva.[53] With this meaning in place, an apt paraphrase of the lines (3–8) might be "a woman emotionally, but not physically, a man capable of entrancing both men and women." And in either case the symmetrical placement of masculine and feminine metaphoric referents frustrates attempts to decide between them.

The overabundance of possible meanings continues throughout the poem as a nemesis to interpretation. The sonnet maintains, "And for a woman wert thou first created," a seemingly straightforward line that, nonetheless, fragments into varied possibilities: "you were first created *as* a woman"; "you were first created for sexual pleasure with women (but now shall have it with men)"; "you were first created for your mother (but now should take a wife)." And when the sonnet "sexualizes" the rhetoric with the famous phrase "nature . . . me of thee defeated, / By adding one thing to my purpose nothing," the gendering is still not stabilized. The juxtaposition of "one thing" and "nothing" visually captures on the page a yoking of phallic and vaginal imagery. But the "one thing," which is so frequently taken to be the penis, might just as easily refer to the problematic self-entrancement that keeps the receiver from marrying. There is, in short, no possible way to determine the meaning, for these lines all mean *too much*. Indeed, this conflation (and, hence, nullification) of meanings is perfectly demonstrated in the couplet "But since she prickt thee out for womens pleasure, / Mine be thy loue and thy loues vse their treasure." Here the speaker says, "Since you were created with a penis to pleasure women, I will love you platonically and women will use you sexually." But he also says, "Since you were created to be used as a woman (i.e., penetrated), I will be your lover, and others (presumably women) will have to

[53]Shakespeare, *Shakespeare's Sonnets*, p. 163.

masturbate ("use of treasure" playing within the metaphors of usury associated with onanism)."

Like Erasmus's epistle, this sonnet is also an exemplum of persuasive rhetoric, but what we are persuaded of is that this is a poet unfettered by the strictures of gendered and sexualized rhetoric that are generically indicative of his medium. Sonnet 20, then, becomes the alter ego of the invocation in 21 and severs the poet from sexual linguistic constraint as surely as 21 severs him from poetics itself. Every effort to read these poems continually reminds us that here is a poet who has created a text that constantly recoils when we touch it. When we find one meaning, it is only at the expense of the many. The importance of the punning play within sonnet 20 cannot be overstated, for the sonnet also sets up a system of obfuscation that implicates the entire cycle. The speaker's description of "a Womans face with natures owne hand painted" (1) incorporates the cognate pun of "one"/"own" already seen in the first sonnet and thereby immediately establishes the poem as a Janus-like statement.[54] If painted by nature's "own" hand, the receiver's allure is validated as natural. But if painted by nature's "one" hand, it remains that nature's *other* hand may soon grab a brush and paint again. In the first instance sexual allure is naturally or platonically absolute; in the second it is part of a continual flux of possibilities. This latter instability implicates the entire sequence, for it is indeed true that nature's other hand surfaces:

> For since each hand hath put on Natures power,
> Fairing the foule with Arts faulse borrow'd face,
> Sweet beauty hath no name no holy bourse,
> But is prophan'd, if not liues in disgrace.
>
> (127.5–8)

[54]The cognate pun of "one"/"owne" was originally brought to my attention in an informal presentation by Randall McLeod, part of a seminar on the history of Shakespearian editorial practices convened by Margreta DeGrazia at the University of Pennsylvania in 1987. Although McLeod presented some of the implications of the pun in sonnet 21, he did not mention its use as a broader structural trope and its relationship to sonnet 127.

One hundred and six sonnets separate nature's own/one hand from this other that surfaces in the first of the so-called dark lady sonnets. But the resurfacing of the hands of nature collapses the linearity of the cycle and draws us back to the "master mistris" even as it pushes us ahead to the "mistress." Although "each hand" is, in the poem's own syntax, a metonymy for the work of other poets, it is also a macro-device within the sequence that, as the poems turn from homo- to heteroerotics, also returns us to the hermaphroditism of sonnet 20. The rhetorical point is clear: nature does not dictate *one* course of desire; desire is, rather, multifaceted and is always subject to repainting by the strokes of a powerful but deferred other hand.

The ordering of the 1609 quarto does much to support such a polymorphously perverse interpretation.[55] Sonnet 126, which

[55]Scholarship has generally come to a point where it accepts the 1609 ordering (Pequigney, *Such Is my Love*; Shakespeare, *Shakespeare's Sonnets*). The most important point in the argument is that alternative orderings are always, at best, as unauthorized as that of the 1609 quarto. For example, Brents Sterling's massive effort at recollating the poems on the basis of thematic links ultimately becomes nothing more than assertion of how Stirling thinks the sonnets should read (Brents Sterling, *The Shakespeare Sonnet Order: Poems and Groups* [Berkeley, 1968]). The sonnets are, indeed, in a received order, one that is certainly the same as the order they were in when buyers in 1609 purchased their copies. The 1609 order thus most assuredly supplies to us the same process of reading and the same status of textual authority as was present during the Renaissance. Authenticity, then, becomes a problem only when the sonnets are viewed as an example of Shakespeare's mind rather than as a Renaissance printed text.

Carol Thomas Neely makes a point that is central to this argument. Using the examples of the *Canzoniere* manuscripts and the several revised editions of Drayton's *Idea*, she claims, "An examination of its development shows that Drayton's sequence, like Petrarch's, was a structured yet elastic work which could expand, contract, and regenerate itself without altering its fundamental characteristics" (Neely, "Structure of English Renaissance Sonnet Sequences," p. 362). This point is important, for it suggests that the structure of sequences in general does not rely on linear narration but, rather, is a retrospective process that puts the poems into an almost iconic form designed to convey a total "sense" or "experience." This idea is paramount for Shakespeare poems and my reading of them, for I am suggesting that the overall sense of the poems is designed to frustrate the decoding of meaning and, therefore, they would fulfill this purpose with or

can be considered the envoy to "my louely Boy" (126.1), ends with a missing couplet, as if to imply that the passion of the first one hundred and twenty-six sonnets never ends but, rather, exists coterminously with the passion presented in the "dark lady" poems. Yet even without the questionable support of textual order, one thing remains certain: these poems punningly intermingle virtually all sexual subjectivities, and to the end of demonstrating what they cannot contain—namely, the poet himself. Stephen Booth, who has done more than any other critic to open up the polysemantics that I see as central to the sequence, has also provided one of the wittiest and most succinct summaries of the sexual problematic of reading the poems: "William Shakespeare was almost certainly homosexual, bisexual, or heterosexual. The sonnets provide no evidence on the matter."[56] And, indeed, Booth is correct, for the sonnets do not *constitute* any sexual meaning but, rather, *disrupt* all sexual meanings. There is, then, a decided distinction between Barnfield's sodomite and that of Shakespeare. For Barnfield the sodomite enters language as a means of delineating subjectivity and implying the different space of the poet within the language of sexual possibility. For Shakespeare the sodomite destroys or uses up language and thereby establishes a space different from language for the poet. Barnfield's poems fold both the poet and the sodomite into the economy of orthodox meaning; Shakespeare's poems unfold this economy and mark its edges and impotencies. For by continually intermingling the tropics of hetero- and homoerotic desire, the sequence creates an experience wherein we are continually able to read the sodomite but are never quite sure if we should. The Shakespearian sodomite, then, might best be thought of in the poet's own words: it is "one thing" but, to the poet's purpose, "no thing."

---

without rearrangement. Moreover, the suggestion of cycles as a form of retrospective ordering also implies that whoever decided on the order of the 1609 quarto did so from the perspective of a Renaissance subject creating iconic sense from the individual poems; thus, the 1609 order, regardless of its "authority," becomes the "valid" order.

[56]Shakespeare, *Shakespeare's Sonnets*, p. 548.

Tradition and the Individual Sodomite

When I was otherwise than now I am,
  I loved more, but skilled not so much;
Fair words and smiles could have contented then,
  My simple age and ignorance was such.
But at the length experience made me wonder
That hearts and tongues did lodge so far asunder.[57]

The sexually, socially, and generically conservative lyrics from William Byrd's 1598 volume, *Songs of Sundry Natures*, seem, perhaps, a world away from the sodomitical machinations of the sonnets of Barnfield and Shakespeare. However, these words also sketch out the problematic of the subject in such a way as to replicate the problem of the poet in Sidney's *Apology* and to move us from the rarefied arena of aesthetic theory to the more pragmatic or material one of popular entertainment. These lines envision words as enemies, as things that are separate from the self and with which the self must contend. Words ("tongues") are something that affect the speaker but that are not exactly what he ("hearts") is.

This space between discursive representation and material experience appears frequently as an overt topic of rumination in Renaissance literature and can provide a means of connecting the subjective complications of "the sodomite" with broader constructions of power in the Renaissance; consider, for example, a text that has become central to "our" Renaissance—Shakespeare's *Hamlet.* In Act II Hamlet offers a description of man that has become one of the most famous of all Shakespearian quotations:

> What piece of work is a man, how noble in reason, how infinite in faculties, in form and moving how express and

[57]William Byrd, "When I was Otherwise than Now I Am," in *Elizabethan Verse*, ed. Edward Lucie-Smith (Harmondsworth, U.K., 1965), p. 2.

> admirable, in action how like an angel, in apprehension how like a god: the beauty of the world, the paragon of animals.[58]

Hamlet's presentation of man is frequently taken as one of the first great statements of emergent humanism in the Renaissance. No longer is man an inert unit suspended between the powers of the cosmos and the deferred promise of future felicity, as Boethius would have him to be. He is, rather, an *aesthetic* object, a "piece of work" that is noble, a "form" that is admirable. Yet the seemingly eternal man constructed here is, like a "piece of work," easily destroyed. For immediately following this exposition of man, Hamlet relabels him as "this quintessence of dust" and claims, "Man delights not me—nor woman neither, though by your smiling you seem to say so" (II.ii.308–310).

Hamlet's description of man presents simultaneously several combatant streams of thought that finally render the speech more obfuscatory than expository. As E. M. W. Tillyard notes, the speech is indeed an exposition of a new concept of man, but it is equally a borrowing from past languages, particularly those of the Middle Ages.[59] This rhetorical "man" is in many ways analogous to Hamlet's position in the play. Torn between a father who was king and a king who is now father, Hamlet is a character fragmented by past and future allegiances but lacking any very real present. Moreover, Hamlet's speech marks a distinction

[58]William Shakespeare, *Hamlet*, ed. Harold Jenkins (London, 1982), II.ii.303–307.

[59]E. M. W. Tillyard also makes a valuable point about the inherited language practices of the early Renaissance: "But though the general medieval picture of the world survived in outline into the Elizabethan age, its existence was by then precarious" (E. M. W. Tillyard, *The Elizabethan World Picture* [New York, 1960], p. 5). Tillyard does not specifically follow up on it, but this idea opens up the possibility that at least some of the languages of the era were ancestral practices being additionally stressed by the need to remain significatory in a world of new possibilities. Hence, I think it is possible to see in Tillyard's formulation some slight recognition of the rift between language and material practice that concerns my study. Of course, it is out of fashion to attribute any utility to Tillyard's work—and not without reasons; for a cogent outline of these reasons see Dollimore, *Radical Tragedy*, pp. 5–7.

between Man and men, for although a generic Man should in actuality include Hamlet himself—if only by rights of gender—Hamlet claims that "Man delights not me." The statement is very pointedly one of "*it* displeases me" and not "*my type* displeases me." For Hamlet, Man is a little less than kin and a lot less than kind. Finally, the speech is further complicated, for the final inclusion of woman moves from the transcendent realm of paradigmatic Man to the relational and social realm of men and women. Indeed, all of these tensions are encoded in Hamlet's phrase "piece of work." Is this work in the sense of human production, as in Ben Jonson's "plays" being collated into "works",[60] or is it work in the sense of divine creation, with all of Man and his world being a product of God and nature?

One could literally spend forever analyzing the divergent strains of this brief passage, for what is encoded within it is not so much a meaning as it is a space between language and meaning.[61]

[60]Cf. Richard C. Newton, "Jonson and the (Re-)Invention of the Book," in *Classic and Cavalier: Essays on Jonson and the Sons of Ben*, ed. Claude J. Summers and Ted-Larry Pebworth (Pittsburgh, 1982).

[61]The play as a whole is riddled with such interpretive rifts, but, following primarily in the steps of T. S. Eliot ("Hamlet and His Problems," in *Hamlet: An Authoritative Text, Intellectual Backgrounds, Extracts from the Sources, Essays in Criticism*, ed. Cyrus Hoy, [New York, 1963], pp. 176–180), criticism has usually attempted not to explain them as objects of analysis, but to explain them away as "problems." The juncture of Renaissance studies and postmodern theory in the current profession has led to several excellent inquires that counter this practice, three of which are particularly noteworthy. Francis Barker uses Hamlet and his "vaulting ambition" as an instance for analysis in a broader debate on the historical relationship between power, subjectivity, and the body (Francis Barker, *The Tremulous Private Body: An Essay on Subjection* [London, 1984]); René Girard sees the ruptures or logical discontinuities in the play as intentional critique of dramatic form that also interfaces with a type of character instability present in much of Shakespeare's drama (René Girard, "Hamlet's Dull Revenge," in *Literary Theory/Renaissance Texts*, ed. Patricia Parker and David Quint, pp. 280–302 [Baltimore, 1986). Finally, although it does not specifically relate to the issues of the subject that are my topic, Robert Weimann has pinpointed in the play "a deeply disturbing gulf between what is represented and what is representing" (Robert Weimann, "Mimesis in *Hamlet*," in *Shakespeare and the Question of Theory*, ed. Geoffrey Hartman and Patricia Parker [London, 1985], p. 277)—an analysis that clearly pre-

Hamlet here is trying on for size a certain language and finding it to be an unsuitable fit. In this sense, the real "meaning" of the speech is the ways in which it *cannot mean* for Hamlet. Hamlet's definition of Man is, in and of itself, remarkably thorough for so brief a speech. It sketches a human psychology of express and admirable form and moving; its similes of an angel and a god imply a theology in which Man is created in God's image; an Aristotelian biology is implied in Man's position as a paragon of a hierarchy of animals. It would indeed be possible to read this discourse as a full world picture, a sort of discursive psyche for the era—except, of course, that Hamlet tells us this is *not* possible. To do so would be to empower the intention of the discourse and to ignore the inability of the discourse to enact that intention.

Hamlet's speech perhaps provides us with the best answer to our original question, Can we speak of the sodomite? Yes, we can. But we must continually recognize that this sodomite—this potentiality for subjective inscription—is at best only tangentially related to the actual rhetoric that professes to inscribe it. Hamlet most certainly is a man, but he is also not "Man." Similarly, there is a sodomite, but he is not the stigmatized paradigm of Renaissance legal codes. For there is present in both Hamlet's speech and the sonnets I have examined a sense that the articulation of a paradigm does not directly inscribe its subject but, rather, creates a range of subjective possibilities—what I have called sub*junc*tivities—that fluctuate around the paradigm. To believe too much in the *contra naturam* buggerer is as much of a misreading as to believe too much in Hamlet's "Man." In both "Man" and "buggerer" there is a certain recognition that words say some things but not everything. These sonnets in the aggregate also begin to suggest that the sodomite is not something that is signified but something that is transacted or deployed. For although the sequences of Barnfield and Shakespeare differ in their strategies, on the broadest level they are both *negotiating* the sodomite, deploying the possibility of homoerotic subjectivity strategically and with a measured economy designed to gain

sages my own extended discussion about the rift between discursive theory and material representation in the Renaissance.

other meanings at a calculated expense. There is, in other words, a general acknowledgment in the sequences that one can speak the sodomite but to the end of saying something else altogether. In this manner the sodomite becomes something more than a mutant or deviant. He becomes a redaction of the very jousts of self and other, of being and nothingness, of all and none, of meaning and rupture, that characterize "Man" himself. If Hamlet broods on the problem, Shakespeare's sonnets make it pithy and eloquent, for, as the speaker tells us, "To giue away your selfe, keeps your selfe still" (16.13). "Still"—the cotermineity of all and nothing that marks both Man and sodomite; still—continuous and transitive through time; still—static and atemporal; still—to distill and reduce to an essence; still—a trace of stell, perhaps: the pen that traces the traces of presence . . . still.

CHAPTER 5

Milton's Sodomite

> Beneath the duality of sex there is a oneness. Every male is potentially a female and every female potentially a male. If a man wants to understand a woman, he must discover the woman in himself, and if a woman would understand a man, she must dig in her own consciousness to discover her own masculine traits.
>
> —Magnus Hirschfeld

> You know, God's kingdom, or Jesus' kingdom is for everybody. It's not reserved for pious heterosexual hypocrites. After all, Jesus was really one of the first social radicals. He didn't appeal to the "respectable" people of his time. . . . He ministered largely to outcasts.
>
> —James Purdy

Negotiating Gender

C. S. Lewis, in offering a questionable "resolution" to the problem of homoerotic prurience in Milton's canon, succinctly displays the complication encountered when the difference of the past is recuperated only in terms of the present.

> A certain amount of critical prudery . . . has been aroused by the account of what More had called "the amorous propension" of Milton's angels (*P.L.* VIII, 618–629). The trouble is, I think, that since these exalted creatures are all spoken of by masculine pronouns, we tend, half consciously, to think that Milton is attributing to them a life of homosexual promiscuity. That he was poetically imprudent in raising a matter which invites such misconception I do not deny; but the real meaning is certainly not filthy, and certainly not foolish. As angels do not die, they need not breed. They are not therefore sexed in the human sense at all. An Angel is, of course, always He (not She) in human language, because whether the male is, or is not, the superior sex, the masculine is certainly the superior gender.[1]

The possibility of homoerotic meaning in the canon is a non-possibility because, Lewis claims, Milton did not mean what we

[1] C. S. Lewis, *A Preface to "Paradise Lost"* (Oxford, 1961), pp. 112–113.

currently mean. And, hence, current meanings become atemporal, transhistorical, and absolute. The problem here has been intelligently summarized by Mary McIntosh in her groundbreaking essay "The Homosexual Role":

> Studies of English history before the seventeenth century consist usually of inconclusive speculation as to whether certain men, such as Edward II, Christopher Marlowe, William Shakespeare, were or were not homosexual. Yet the disputes are inconclusive not because of lack of evidence but because none of these men fits the modern stereotype of the homosexual.[2]

This is also the problem underpinning Lewis's assessment. If we were to label Barnfield "gay"; when we find a prescriptively gendered viewpoint in Shakespeare's poems; should we begin to worry about the sexuality of angels and, perhaps, of Milton: these are all stances that presuppose the same inscriptive directness of sexual discourses that we find in modern society.

Such statements, as Foucault has pointed out, play into a common theorization that constructs the seventeenth century as the historical genesis of both sexual repression and capitalistic bourgeois order.[3] This framework serves as the background for Foucault's own revisionist attitude that the discursive stigmatization of sexual behavior actually marks out "a general economy of discourses on sex in modern societies."[4] Such an "economy" becomes obvious if we consider briefly the textual world in which Milton's texts found an audience. At about the same time readers might have purchased their first editions of *The History of Britain*, they might also have been reading the sensational and popular compilation *The Arraignment of Popery*, which, among other items, recounts how the papists at Piedmont "cut of[f] a womans breast . . . and fried [it]; and eat [it]," and "cut off a mans privy members, and afterwards put a lighted-candle to the

[2]McIntosh, "Homosexual Role," p. 36.
[3]Foucault, *History of Sexuality*, p. 5.
[4]Ibid., p. 11.

wound."[5] While reading the joint publication of *Paradise Regained* and *Samson Agonistes*, readers might also have had in mind the broadsides circulating throughout London publicizing the celebrated trial "of the bloudie and unchristian acting of William Star and John Taylor of Walton," who, "being on horseback, [and] having at their heels some men in womens apparell on foot," bludgeoned four farmers who chanced upon their cross-dressed soiree.[6] And a glance at Milton's own commonplace book indicates that issues of sexual transgression other than that of "woman" clearly circulated within his mind:

> OF LUST
>
> Lust for boys or men. "What can be sacred to those who would debase the age that is weak and in need of protection, so that it is destroyed and defiled through their own lust?" Lactant. Book 6. c[hapter] 23.
>
> In our legends King mempricius is marked with the sin of sodomy[.][7]

The need to excise discussions of "deviant" sexualities from Milton's texts, then, is one sustained only by an ex post facto conception of Milton, not one demanded by the discursive remnants of the seventeenth century, for the textual world of Jacobean and Caroline England was one that was grappling with far more subversive issues than "whether the male is, or is not, the superior sex."[8]

These marks of repression, while they do indeed delineate and

[5]F. G. and E. H., *The Arraignment of Popery* (London, 1669), p. 96.

[6]*A Declaration of the Bloudie and Unchristian Acting of William Star and John Taylor of Walton* (London, 1670). Cf. *A Full and True Account of the Notorious Wicked Life of that Grand Impostor, John Taylor; One of the Sweet-Singers of Israel* (London, 1678).

[7]John Milton, *Complete Prose Works of John Milton*, ed. Don M. Wolfe, 8 vols. (New Haven, 1953–1982), vol. 1, p. 369.

[8]The difference between the "historic" Milton and the Milton constructed by literary history is interestingly described in Margaret W. Ferguson and Mary Nyquist, eds., *Re-Membering Milton: Essays on the Texts and Traditions* (London, 1988), pp. xii–xvi. See also Frank Kermode, ed., *The Living Milton* (London, 1960).

specify sexual activity, also mark the points at which these specified activities enter broader economies of power. Papists posed as much of a threat to monarchs as they did to genitals and breasts. John Taylor and William Star, when not riding with men in drag, lobbied for the acceptance of polygamy in opposition to Anglican principles. These statements, then, ostensibly mark the beginning of repression but also mark the entry of sex and sexuality into multivalent and overtly political economies of power. There is a sense in all of these, much as there is in the sonnets of Barnfield, that the articulation of deviance has very little to do with deviance itself, for the language of sex and sexuality always means otherwise; to borrow from French writer Renaud Camus, "Homosexuality is always elsewhere because it is everywhere"[9]—but for the purposes of the argument at hand we might just as easily ignore the "homo," for in these instances sexuality is always elsewhere.

Even a cursory glance at Milton's poems demonstrates that the categories of "truth" Lewis attempts to place on the canon betray the dynamics of the texts. And Lewis is not alone in his critical assumptions. There is strong idea within modern criticism that the Miltonic canon reveals the mind of a misogynist.[10] Based

[9]Quoted in Leigh W. Rutledge, *Unnatural Quotations: A Compendium of Quotations by, for or about Gay People* (Boston, 1988), p. 21.

[10]Throughout this synopsis of current critical stances I am summarizing points of view found in Maureen Quilligan, *Milton's Spenser: The Politics of Reading* (Ithaca, 1983); Diane Kelsey McColley, *Milton's Eve* (Urbana, 1983); Mary Nyquist, "Textual Overlapping and Dalilah's Harlot-Lap," in *Literary Theory/Renaissance Texts*, ed. Patricia Parker and David Quint (Baltimore, 1986), and "The Genesis of Gendered Subjectivity in the Divorce Tracts and in *Paradise Lost*," in *Re-Membering Milton: Essays on the Texts and Traditions*, ed. Margaret W. Ferguson and Mary Nyquist (London, 1988); Joseph Anthony Wittreich, *Feminist Milton* (Ithaca, 1987); Barbara K. Lewalski, "Milton and Woman—Yet Once More," *Milton Studies* 6 (1974: 3–20); and Joan M. Webber, "The Politics of Poetry: Feminism and *Paradise Lost*," *Milton Studies* 14 (1980): 3–24. Although these inquiries radically differ in the extent to which they read Milton's canon as either supporting or subverting patriarchal meanings, all of them attempt to adjudicate a place for Milton within the politics circumscribed by the man/woman polarity. As will become apparent in my argument, I am taking an opposite tack and placing the man/woman dichotomy within Milton's sexual politics. Reader's unfamiliar with the general terms of the debate on Milton and feminism should

largely on *Paradise Lost,* but also taking recourse to *Samson Agonistes* and *Comus,*[11] this argument generally runs that Milton uses the occasion of biblical exegesis to set forth a hierarchical program on the place of the female in domestic and social structures. The support for this argument is obviously and amply included in the poems. In *Samson Agonistes* the chorus claims that "wisest Men / Have err'd, and by bad Women been deceiv'd" (210–211), and in *Paradise Lost* man's "consort" (VII.529) first eats the fruit and Adam is figured as "the Patriarch of mankind" (V.506). There is, however, a revisionist view of this argument that claims, naturally enough, the opposite. In this argument Eve is viewed as a subtle exposition of the power of woman and a recognition of the more rarefied female essence resulting from this second try at creation: "O fairest of Creation, last and best / Of all God's Works" (IX.896–897). Dalilah similarly becomes a different woman, and the real culpability rests with Samson, a negative exemplum whose "marriage choices" we "cannot praise" (420). These polarities surface in critiques of all the poems: *Comus* becomes either a defense of or an attack on "the sage / And serious doctrine of Virginity" (786–787); "Lycidas" functions as either the emergence of a radical poetic voice or the reemergence of a voice terrified of "the *Lesbian* shore" (63); and the other poems and prose works eventually find their own bifurcated stances as misogynist and feminist polemics.

I would like to recast the premises of this debate using the brilliantly simple strategy Stanley Fish demonstrates in "Inter-

---

consult Nyquist, "Genesis of Gendered Subjectivity." Her article, incidentally, comes up on the "misogynist" side of the debate, but it is also particularly good at explicating the ideological implications in the debate as a whole and especially in the championing of Milton as a spokesperson for "mutuality." A much briefer but also helpful synopsis of the debate can be found in Ferguson and Nyquist, *Re-Membering Milton,* pp. xiv–xv. On the "feminist" side, a cogent rebuttal is to be found in Joseph Anthony Wittreich, *Feminist Milton* (Ithaca, 1987), pp. 1–43. See also Stevie Davies, *The Feminine Redeemed: The Idea of Woman in Spenser, Shakespeare, and Milton* (Lexington, Ky., 1986).

[11]All references to Milton's work, unless otherwise noted, will be from John Milton, *John Milton: Complete Poems and Major Prose,* ed. Merritt Y. Hughes (New York, 1957).

preting the Variorium"[12] and begin by assuming that the problem is really the point. For this debate in the aggregate attempts to skew a symmetry of options in the texts without really asking why the symmetry is present. For Milton, issues of gender, sex, and sexuality are more *negotiated* than articulated and are at play in a general economy of variable terms.[13] The strongest pieces of evidence on both sides of the debate always find direct counterparts that suspend judgment. For example, *Samson Agonistes* is generally considered to be an explication of the dangers of transgressing patrilineal decorum—an effort, in Manoa's words, to bestow on the "Father's house eternal fame" (1717). But the patriarchal values are counterbalanced by *Paradise Regained*, which was intentionally published together with *Samson Agonistes*. In the brief epic Satan claims, "I to thy Father's house / Have brought thee" (IV.552–553), a pronouncement that associates the Father's house with temptation and evil. Moreover, the conflation of fleshly father and Godly father that allows this phrase to be read as both a spiritual and misogynistic edict is separated in *Paradise Regained*, for the progenital overtones of the phrase are relabeled by Jesus as a simple casement, a "fleshly Tabernacle, and human form" (IV.599), and when Jesus withstands the final temptation he does not bask in the glory of the Father's house, but rather "Home to his Mother's house private return[s]" (IV.639).

Throughout the major poems the discourses of sex and gender (and they always happen in the plural) read more like syntagmatic units or extended phonemes than as transparent narratives in their own right; that is, various sexual discourses appear, but

[12]Stanley Fish, *Is There a Text in This Class? The Authority of Interpretive Communities* (Cambridge, Mass., 1980), pp. 147–173.

[13]Although the article appeared well after the terms of this argument were formulated, a very helpful analysis of the place of "negotiation" within "new historicism" can be found in Theodore B. Leinwand, "Negotiation and the New Historicism," *PMLA* 105, 3 (1990): 477–490. Leinwand develops the term as a means of reappraising the relationship between subversion and containment that has vexed much cultural materialist inquiry into the Renaissance, but his formulation also parallels and complements how I am using the term in relation to discourses of sex, sexuality, and gender.

only as sounds that must be taken together in order to determine a "content," "intention," or "meaning." The construction of various eroticisms and erotic meanings in the seventeenth century provided terms that, in turn, became circulated in many different systems of power, and sometimes in ways that undermine the intentions of the original construction. The mapping *of* this economy—rather than the mapping of a position *within* it—is the real object of analysis presented to us in Milton's canon. My primary means of mapping Milton's negotiations of gendered meaning will be, of course, Milton's sodomite.[14] As the seventeenth century progressed, homoeroticism and discourses associated with it, like these other discourses of deviation, became increasingly specified and stigmatized and concurrently gained importance not just as sexual categories but also as political tools. I would like to examine how this specification of homoeroticism is incorporated in exegetical literature from the later Renaissance and how the Miltonic canon in turn negotiates

[14]Strikingly little has been said about homoeroticism in the canon. The only major examination of the subject is the relationship between sodomy and *Comus* suggested by the Castlehaven scandal (Barbara Breasted, "*Comus* and the Castlehaven Scandal," *Milton Studies* 3 [1971]: 201–224; John Creaser, "Milton's *Comus*: The Irrelevance of the Castlehaven Scandal," *Milton Quarterly* 4 [1988]: 24–34; Leah Marcus, *The Politics of Mirth: Jonson, Herrick, Milton, Marvell, and the Defense of Old Holiday Pastimes* [Chicago, 1986] and "The Earl of Bridgewater's Legal Life: Notes toward a Political Reading of *Comus*," *Milton Quarterly* 4 (1988): 13–23.). Some other work, such as John T. Shawcross, "Milton and Diodati: An Essay in Psychodynamic Meaning," *Milton Studies* 7 (1975): 127–163, has approached the subject through Milton himself and an analysis of the poet's sexuality, but this is a project separate from mine. Edward LeComte, in an otherwise far-reaching analysis of sex in Milton's poetry, similarly addresses and dismisses homosexuality only as it might be attributed to Milton himself (Edward LeComte, *Milton and Sex* [New York, 1978], pp. 5–6). Claude Summers has been kind enough to share with me an as yet unpublished essay, "The (Homo)sexual Temptation in *Paradise Regained* (in *"Grateful Vicissitude": Essays in Honor of J. Max Patrick*, ed. Harrison T. Meserole and Michael A. Mikolajczak, forthcoming)," which also attempts to expand the parameters of the way we typically think through Milton's sexual epistemology. His essay complements mine well, for it traces epic traditions of sexuality, while mine focuses more strongly on a cultural contextualization.

these typical trends to alternative ends. I focus my argument primarily on *Paradise Regained* and its manipulations of pastoral and vernacular traditions, but I also suggest that the poem has broader implications for the historical study of gender practices.

Milton's Ganymede

In the brief epic, when Satan sets the table for the Son of God's banquet temptation, it is immediately apparent that the topic is not food but, rather, fleshly and sensual need. This idea is introduced in the poem through an antigesture when Satan rejects Belial's suggestion to "Set woman in his eye" (II.153). Satan's response, however, is revealed to be only a rejection of Belial's *limited* notion of sexual temptation, for when the banquet appears it is attended by nymphs, naiads, ladies of the Hesperides and "Tall stripling youths rich clad, of fairer hue / Than *Ganymede* or *Hylas*" (II.352–353). This allusion to myth pointedly introduces several traditions that subtextually inform the action of *Paradise Regained.* What Satan offers to Jesus—dominion, wealth, and fame—is essentially the identity of an epic hero,[15] and the offer of a Ganymede or a Hylas correspondingly posits the position of a Zeus or a Heracles—one godly, one mortal, the same identities for which Satan tests the Son. Moreover, the banquet is placed in "a woody Scene" that seems "to a Superstitious eye the haunt / Of Wood Gods and Wood Nymphs" (II.294–297). The Son must overcome not just the temptations of mortal flesh but also those of disparate genres (pastoral and epic) and disparate times (pagan and Christian).[16] These literary tradi-

[15]Cf. Stuart Curran, "*Paradise Regained*: The Implications of Epic," *Milton Studies* 17 (1983): 209–224.

[16]The invocation of pastoral here is ironically stressed, for immediately preceding the appearance of the banquet the narrator recounts that "Cottage, Herd of Sheepcote non he [the son] saw" (II.288). This antigesture, I think, is an example of *negatio*—that is, a feigned omitting—for it calls into mind the genre it is dismissing and sets the stage for the subsequent associations. I am grateful to Diane McColley for drawing this passage to my attention.

tions are certainly at work in the poem, but the construction of the banquet temptation is also distinguished by two specific rewritings of exegetical tradition. Through the manipulation of vernacular meaning and pastoral tradition, the temptation invokes a homoerotic component discordant with typical commentaries on the temptation. Additionally, it then separates homoeroticism from its traditional place in biblical commentary by making Belial the spokesman for heteroeroticism. I will examine these idiosyncrasies in order, using the first to place homoeroticism within *Paradise Regained* and the second to suggest some of the implications of this placement.

Vernacular Eroticisms and Pastoral Transformations

Seventeenth-century commentators commonly read Satan's temptation of Jesus as an allegory of Eve's temptation rewritten with good triumphing over evil. John Lightfoot's *Harmony, Chronicle, and Order of the New Testament* glosses *Luke*'s temptation in a representative manner:

> As our Mother *Eve* was tempted by Satan to the lust of life, . . . so by these [three temptations], had it been possible, would the same tempter have overthrown the seed of woman: for he tempted him to turn stones into bread, as to satisfie the longing of the flesh; to fall down and worship him upon the sight of a bewitching object to his eyes, and to fly in the air in pride, and to get glory among men. Luke for our better observing of this parallel, hath laid the order of these temptations answerable to the order of those.[17]

The assumption here is clear: the victory of Christ will rectify the problems that originated through the weakness of female flesh. The masculinist stance is strong, and, most important, it is a stance that Milton's poem interrogates through its invocation of Ganymede and Hylas.

As I have already demonstrated, both Ganymede and Hylas

[17]John Lightfoot, *The Works of the Reverend and Learned John Lightfoot D. D.* (London, 1822), p. 11.

led double lives—one in the world of mythology, one in the world of vernacular homoeroticism. Milton's awareness of the idiomatic subtext to mythology is apparent in his abstract for "Cupid's Funeral Pile," which calls for a choral description of the city:

> The first Chorus beginning may relate the course of the citty each eveing every one, *with mistresse, or Ganymed*, gitterning along the streets, or solacing on the banks of Jordan, or down the stream.[18]

As in the satires of Marston or Brathwait, this description defines *Ganymed* as the homoerotic counterpart to a mistress, a definition that suggests a vernacular subtext behind *Paradise Regained*'s allusion. Moreover, this double meaning is further signaled by the extent to which the allusion intermeshes with the broader schema of power in the epic. For if on a mythological level Ganymede and Hylas metaphorically represent the differential of power between God/hero and minion, the same differential is replicated in vernacular sexual meaning. Both Ganymede and Hylas are associated in lexicography with the specific sector of homoeroticism known as *paederastice*: man-boy love.[19] Hence the temptation is homoerotic, but it is also specifically a form of homoeroticism that supplies the power and dominion associated with an epic hero. These homoerotic connotations are, I will argue, intentionally transported into *Paradise Regained* as a means of critiquing conservative exegetical tradition. This intentionality shows strongly in the pastoral setting of the banquet, a generic choice that supplies an important key to understanding Milton's negotiations of homoerotic traditions. Although the setting of

[18]Milton, *Complete Prose Works*, vol. 8, p. 559. Emphasis mine.

[19]For a more thorough explication of the place of *paederastice* in Renaissance culture, see Orgel, "Nobody's Perfect." The tradition of *paederastice* has classical antecedents that undoubtedly inform Milton's allusion. Lucian, for example, is commonly claimed to have said that "marriage is open to all men, but the love of boys to philosophers only" (cf. E. K.'s gloss to Spenser's *Aegloga Prima*). On these classical antecedents see Dover, *Greek Homosexuality*, and Felix Buffière, *Eros adolescent: La pédérastie dans la Grèce antique* (Paris, 1980).

the banquet may be an attempt at generic totality, it also draws attention to the homoerotic implications of Ganymede and Hylas. The banquet appears in "a pleasant Grove, / With chant of tuneful Birds resounding loud" (II.289–290), accessed by

> alleys brown
> That open'd in the midst a woody Scene;
> Nature's own work it seem'd (Nature taught Art)
> And to a Superstitious eye the haunt
> Of Wood Gods and Wood Nymphs.
>
> (II.293–297)

To a certain extent this pastoral setting serves intertextual purposes. It casts the place of Jesus's first temptation as a recasting of the site of Eve's temptation, for Satan first views paradise as "A Silvan Scene," "a woody Theatre / Of stateliest view" (*PL.* IV.140–142). This echo recalls exegetical parallels between the temptations of Eve and the Son and also demonstrates that the poem is concerned with reworking the "common glosses" that establish an equivalence between these two episodes. However, the invocation of the pastoral is also empowered by an interpretive tradition of increasing specification of illicit male sexual behavior, and this tradition serves important disruptive purposes in *Paradise Regained.*

Pastoral has long been recognized as manifesting an almost schizophrenic relation to society, for while it is one of the most overdetermined genres, it is also the genre that has demonstrated the greatest ability to fluctuate in relation to local demands.[20] In

[20]In condemning Milton's *Lycidas*, Samuel Johnson provides a definition of pastoral that has, unfortunately, occupied a place of critical privilege: "Its form is that of a pastoral, easy, vulgar, and therefore disgusting" (Samuel Johnson, "The Life of Milton," in *Milton's Lycidas: The Tradition and the Poem*, ed. C. A. Patrides [New York, 1961], p. 56). However, this position—which in itself might be considered easy and vulgar—has, in the wake of William Empson's famous work, been reassessed and theorized. As Stuart Curran has perceptively claimed in a study of pastoral form and British Romanticism, "Nothing better exemplifies the intractability of generic definition than pastoral. As literary currency, the term predates and traverses the boundaries of most nations of the Western world; and yet its

the sixteenth and seventeenth centuries one of its primary interests is its participation in fields of sexual deviation and, by extension, its encoding of social responses to deviation. Richard Brathwait's several pastoral works embody the operative strategy. *The Shepheards Tales* use the occasion of the eclogue to display and critique examples of sexual transgression. Eclogue 2, which explicates Sapphus's love for Silvia, tells how "*Sapphus* woes *Silvia*, / Yet he thinks it ill, / To take to that, / Which he did never till."[21] Silvia refuses to fornicate with Sapphus out of wedlock, but the wedding that ensues is brought to an untimely end by the announcement by one of the guests that Silvia is pregnant and another guest's proclamation that Silvia is a "more familiar sort,"[22] that is, a whore. This scenario of multiple transgression is then abruptly ended by the intercession of the narrative voice with an unsatisfying moral: "Forts are won by foes assault, / If Maids yeeld, it is Mans fault."[23] The simplistic morality of the conclusion indicates an important facet of these sexualized pastorals: they are as much concerned with *displaying* prurience as they are with containing it; and the pastoral becomes not a simple narrative of rural purity but, rather, a genre constantly titillated by transgression.

These poems all mark out a complicated dialectic of sexual

---

value fluctuates from one culture to another, demanding continual adjustment to the local economy" (Stuart Curran, *Poetic Form and British Romanticism* [Oxford, 1986], p. 85). Annabel Patterson corroborates Curran's view when she notes that defining pastoral was "a cause lost as early as the sixteenth century, when the genre began to manifest the tendency of most strong literary forms to propagate by miscegenation" (Annabel Patterson, *Pastoral and Ideology: Virgil to Valery* [Berkeley, 1987], p. 7). I would differ from Patterson in that I would place the locus of miscegenation with Virgil and his conscious recontextualization and imitation of Theocritus. What seems certain, however, is Patterson's claim that "what people think of Virgil's *Eclogues* is key to their own cultural assumptions" (Annabel Patterson, "Virgil's *Eclogues*: Images of Change," in *Roman Images: Selected Papers from the English Institute, 1982*, ed. Annabel Patterson, pp. 163–186 [Baltimore, 1984], p. 163).

[21] Richard Brathwait, *The Shepheards Tales* (London, 1621), p. 190.

[22] Ibid., p. 193.

[23] Ibid.

containment/textual display, and the pattern becomes even more profound when we look at the genre's manipulations of homoeroticism. The two major models influencing Renaissance writers, Theocritus's *Idylls* and Virgil's *Eclogues*, both link the genre with homoeroticism. In Theocritus the primary passages of interest are from the fifth idyll, a competition between the shepherds Lacon and Comatas:

Comatas

I'm in no hurry; and yet I am terribly hurt that you dare to
Look me so straight in the eye, even I who instructed you
 when you
Still were an innocent boy. You may see just what gratitude
 comes to—
Might as well bring up a wolf cub as rear such a puppy to eat
 you!

Lacon

When can I even recall ever hearing or learning a single
Nice thing from you? What a jealous, obscene little mannikin
 you are!

Comatas

Once when I buggered your bum and you said that it hurt.
 You may hear
Nanny-goats bleat, but the billy-goat fucks them for all of
 their bleating.

Lacon

May you be buried no deeper than that penetration, you
 hump-back!
Crawl over here, I say crawl, and you'll sing your last pastoral
 ditty.[24]

Comatas

Don't you remember the time I was up you, and you with a
 grimace
Wiggled your bottom deliciously, holding on tight to that oak
 tree?

[24] Theocritus, *Theocritus: Idylls and Epigrams*, trans. Daryl Hine (New York, 1982), pp. 20–21.

Lacon

No, that is something I do not remember at all. When Eumarus
Tied you up here and then reamed you out thoroughly—that I remember[25]

In Virgil the major text is the second eclogue, a love lament by Corydon for Alexis prefaced by this contextualization:

A shepherd, Corydon, burned with love for his master's favourite,
Handsome Alexis. Little reason had he for hope;
But he was always going into the beech plantation
Under whose spires and shades, alone with his futile passion,
He poured forth words like these, piecemeal, to wood and hill.[26]

Although these incidents are relatively small portions of each collection of poems, their influence during the Renaissance is obvious. Not only did Barnfield take recourse to Virgil for a defense of his homoerotic pastoral themes, but Spenser's *Shepheardes Calendar*, the originary text in the great English pastoral tradition, immediately invokes and corrects the homoerotic legacy of Virgil and Theocritus. In the eclogue for January, Colin Clout is, as the argument says, "*enamoured of a countrie lasse called* Rosalinde"[27] who shuns his advances—a structure that necessarily recalls the lament of Corydon in Virgil's second eclogue.[28] To this typical tale of thwarted love, however, is added a seemingly gratuitous stanza:

It is not *Hobbinol*, wherefore I plaine.
Albee my loue he seeke with dayly suit:

[25]Ibid., p. 24.

[26]Virgil, *The Eclogues and Georgics of Virgil*, trans. C. Day Lewis (New York, 1964), p. 13.

[27]Spenser, *Poetical Works*, p. 421.

[28]The allusion to Virgil is also recognized by E. K.: "His clownish gyfts) imitateth Virgils verse, Rusticus es Corydon, nec numera curat Alexis" (Spenser, *Poetical Works*, p. 422).

His clownish gifts and curtsies I disdaine,
His kiddes, his cracknelles, and his early fruit.
Ah foolish *Hobbinol*, thy gyfts bene vayne:
Colin them giues to *Rosalind* againe.[29]

If this lament eclogue invokes its model, Virgil's second eclogue, then this stanza necessarily signals the sexual difference in the imitations; the stanza may be read as a narrative structure similar to Barnfield's ode in that it invokes homoeroticism in an effort to distance itself from it.[30] However, this easy explanation is complicated by the peculiar gloss to the name Hobbinol supplied by E. K.:

> [Hobbinol] is a fained country name, whereby, it being so commune and vsuall, seemeth to be hidden the person of some his very speciall and most familiar freend, whom he entirely and extraordinarily beloued, as peraduenture shall be more largely declared hereafter. In thys place seemeth to be some sauour of disorderly loue, which the learned call paederastice: but it is gathered beside his meaning. For who that hath red Plato his dialogue called Alcybiades, Xenophon and Maximus Tyrius of Socrates opinions, may easily perceiue, that such loue is muche to be alowed and liked of, specially so meant, as Socrates vsed it: who sayth, that in deede he loued Alcybiades extremely, yet not Alcybiades person, but hys soule, which is Alcybiades owne selfe. And so is paederastice much to be praeferred before gynerastice, that is the loue whiche enflameth men with lust toward woman kind. But yet let no man thinke, that herein I stand with Lucian or hys deuelish disciple Vnico Aretino, in defence of execrable and horrible sinnes of forbidden and vnlawful fleshlinesse, Whose abominable errour is fully confuted of Perionius, and others.[31]

The apology for "Hobbinol" again marks the peculiar and expected presence of homoeroticism in the genre; for the gloss

[29]Ibid., ll. 55–60.
[30]For a discussion of Barnfield's "Ode," see Chapter Four.
[31]Spenser, *Poetical Works*, pp. 422–423.

demonstrates not just a simple condemnation of *paederastice* but also a complicated range of meanings associated with it. *Paederastice* may be a form of "disorderly loue," but it also interacts in an exalted tradition of Platonism and heteroeroticism: it is preferable to "gynerastice." Homoeroticism here is a relative concept fluctuating around and within several different sexual schema.[32]

The tradition growing in the wake of Spenser—the tradition that informs *Paradise Regained*—devoted much energy to delineating and stigmatizing the *paederastice* that *The Shepheardes Calendar* accepts as a part of the range of sexual meanings inherent in the genre.[33] In 1649, when John Ogilby published his important edition of *The Works of Publius Virgilius Maro*, he, too, recognized the thematic homoeroticism of the second eclogue; as he glosses it in the argument, "Poor *Coridon* for fair *Alexis* burns, / Joy of his Lord, nor hopes for love-returns."[34] Yet rather than drawing on Platonic traditions or the relative merits of *paederastice* and *gynerastice*, Ogilby begins a tradition of explaining away the homoeroticism as the function of a pagan or naïve culture. As he notes in the margin of eclogue II,

> The Subject of Pastorals (saith *Scaliger*) is various; but the first and eldest Amatory, aswerr because Love is a Passion by Nature imprinted in all living Creatures, as because Men and Women promiscuously feeding their Flocks together were invited by their example: lastly the Musick of the Wood, the solitude of the Place, and quiet of that kind of Life advanced it

[32]Complementary, though not identical, readings of this passage can be found in Goldberg, "Colin to Hobbinol," and Orgel, "Nobody's Perfect."

[33]The importance of Virgil's *Eclogues* as a revisionary transmission from Spenser to Milton has been the subject of several interesting critical discussions. Richard Halpern discusses it especially in relation to the ways in which the fourth eclogue informs the Nativity Ode, and he uses it as an example of what he calls Milton's "fashion[ing] of a coherent poetic career" (Richard Halpern, "The Great Instauration: Imaginary Narratives in Milton's 'Nativity Ode'," in *Re-Membering Milton: New Essays on the Texts and Traditions*, ed. Margaret W. Ferguson and Mary Nyquist, pp. 3–24 [London, 1988], p. 3). See also Richard Neuse, "Milton and Spenser: The Virgilian Triad Revisited," *ELH* 45 (1978): 606–639.

[34]Virgil, *The Works of Virgil*, trans. John Ogilby (London, 1649), p. 5.

> much. *Virgil* not willing to omit a Theam so native and universal, feigns *Corydon* (under which name he veils himselfe) to fall in love with *Alexis*.

The interactions of Corydon and Alexis, Ogilby claims, become a mere metaphor for Virgil to explore the higher conceit of love—"natural" love as it is patterned in the procreative example of "Men and Women" and "Flocks." The poem, in Ogilby's view, *feigns* toward "natural" heteroeroticism, and the homoeroticism that covers a diverse range in Spenser's poem becomes increasingly specified and stigmatized.

The marked change between Spenser's and Ogilby's apologies for homoeroticism is best seen by looking forward to Dryden's 1697 edition of *The Works of Virgil*, which crystallizes the pattern of morality hinted at by Ogilby. Dryden's argument for the second eclogue clearly states the sexual intentions of Corydon, casting the lament in terms of courtship and amour:

> The Commentators can by no means agree on the Person of *Alexis*, but are all of opinion that some Beautiful Youth is meant by him, to whom *Virgil* here makes Love; in *Corydon's* Language and Simplicity. His way of Courtship is wholly Pastoral; He complains of the Boys Coyness, recommends himself for his Beauty and Skill in Piping; invites the Youth into the Country, where he promises him the Diversions of the Place; with a suitable Present of Nuts and Apples; But when he finds nothing will prevail, he resolves to quit his troublesome Amour, and betake himselfe again to his former business.[35]

The amour is "troublesome" not in that it is unrequited but, rather, because it is socially disruptive. In the preface to the pastorals Dryden specifies the moral stigma received in exchange for wasting time on Alexis:

> The Second contains the Love of *Coridon* for *Alexis*, and the seasonable reproach he gives himself, that he left his Vines half prun'd, (which according to the *Roman Rituals*, deriv'd a Curse

[35]Virgil, *The Works of Virgil*, trans. John Dryden (London, 1697), p. 6.

> upon the Fruit that grew upon it) whilst he pursu'd an Object undeserving his Passion.

Not content to let the love slip by as a metaphor, Dryden must exact a toll for transgression: misspent love results in cursed crops and a loss of revenue. The inventiveness of this solution stands in contrast to the original eclogue, in which Corydon does not lament crop damage but is irritated that he forgot the simple fact that "if you're brushed off by this Alexis, you'll find another."[36]

The movement from Spenser to Ogilby to Dryden, then, charts a course that progressively melds the pastoral tradition with the vernacular connotations associated with the names Ganymede and Hylas. This pastoral transformation is even more pronounced in handlings of Theocritus, primarily because the *Idylls* are more overtly sexual than the *Eclogues*. Accessible dissemination in English of Theocritus did not really happen until Thomas Creech issued his translation, *The Idylliums of Theocritus with Rapin's Discourse of Pastorals Done into English*, in 1684. However, Rapin's *Discourse*, written in 1659, found an ample audience in its Italian original, and the *Idylls* themselves had been a long-standing component of classical learning in the Renaissance and were available in several French coterie editions. Rapin's discourse also provides the bluntest explication of the most probable reason that Theocritus was ushered into England much later than his most famous imitator, Virgil. Creech's translation presents Rapin's analysis and also domesticates it for the English audience:

> As for the *Manners* of your *Shepherds*, they must be such as theirs who liv'd in the Islands of the Happy or Golden Age: They must be candid, simple, and ingenuous; lovers of Goodness, and Justice, affable, and kind; strangers to all fraud, contrivance, and deceit; in their Love modest, and chast, not one suspitious word, no loose expression to be allowed: and in this part *Theocritus* is faulty, *Virgil* never; and this difference perhaps is to be ascrib'd to their Ages, the times in which the

[36]Virgil, *Eclogues and Georgics*, p. 17.

latter liv'd being more polite, civil, and gentile. And therefore those who make wanton Love-stories the subject of Pastorals, are in my opinion very unadvis'd; for all sort of lewdness or debauchery are directly contrary to the *Innocence* of the *golden* Age. There is another thing in which *Theocritus* is faulty, and that is making his Shepherds too sharp, and abusive to one another; *Comatas* and *Lacon* are ready to fight, and the railing between those two is as bitter as *Billingsgate*: Now certainly such Raillery cannot be suitable to those sedate times of the Happy Age.[37]

It takes little interpolation to realize that Rapin's primary concern is not with raillery but with fornication, and this concern shows forth in many editions of Theocritus. For unlike Virgil, whose lament format included no specific sexual activity and could sustain allegorization, Theocritus's depiction of anal rape required immediate textual attention. Like Rapin, who rewrites the rape as raillery, Creech himself takes recourse to euphemism:

C. And do'nt you mind, when I—you know the trick—,
You wanton'd, laught, and clung to yonder stick:
L. Not that: but when your Master us'd to bind
And lash you there, I know; for that I mind.[38]

Rape becomes "lash" and intercourse "the trick," and homoeroticism—at least for those with no recourse to Greek originals—is now something hinted at in the text but hardly accessible through it.

The relative grace of Creech's excision was hardly standard, however. The anonymous French edition of 1688, *Les Idylles de Theocrite Traduites De Grec Vers Francois*, demonstrates the more standard sort of handling of Theocritian *paederastice*. Tellingly retitled as "Le Combat Bucolique" [The Bucolic Battle], the edition presents the passage with a vivid display of excision:

[37]Theocritus, *The Idylliums of Theocritus with Rapin's Discourse of Pastorals Done into English*, trans. Thomas Creech (Oxford, 1684), p. 67.
[38]Ibid., p. 35.

Lacon. Toy m'intruire! en quel temps? & comment te prie
Traistre, as-tu jamais dir rien de bon en ta vie?
Il ne m'en souvient pas, homme fourbe & malin,
Comate. C'estoit quand *********************************
****
****
Lacon. ***
****
** Viens icy; viens dis-je & chante enfin.[39]

The asterisks blatantly call attention to the fact that something is missing, and on the small chance that this is not enough, the translator also includes a lengthy note that derides the "baseness" of the excised lines:

> Il y a trois vers Grecs en cet endroit, que je n'ay pas traduits, parce qu'ils ne sont pas traduisibles, estant si obscenes, qu'il est impossible d'en pouvoir bien envelopper la pensee. Il seroit a souhaiter que les Poetes anciens fussent entierement purgez de ces grossieretez; & je ne puis m'empecher de croire quelquefois, comme je l'ay dit dans la Preface, qu'il faloit que les Grecs & les Latins n'attachons pas tout a fait a certains mots les idees que nous attachons a ceux qui leur repondent en notre langue.[40]
>
> [There are three Greek verses here that I have not translated because they are not translatable since they are so obscene that it is impossible to capture the sense of them. One would hope that the ancient poets shall be purged entirely of these grossnesses; and I cannot bring myself to believe sometimes, as I said in the preface, that the Greeks and Romans must not have attached the same ideas to certain words that our language does.]

If the concern is ostensibly to hide the debauchery of the text, the emendation betrays the cause, for although there is no anal rape

[39]Theocritus, *Les Idylles de Theocrite Traduites De Grec en Vers Francois* (Paris, 1688), p. 173.
[40]Ibid., p. 200.

present, there is an even greater sense of debauchery and transgression—a sense achieved by a translator who protests too much.

Such protestation became standard practice, and in 1767, when Francis Fawkes published *The Idylliums of Theocritus*, he took as part of his project the chastisement of Creech's less moralistic emendation. He states: "However Creech may have approved himself in Lucretius, or Manilius, I shall venture to pronounce his translation of Theocritus very bald and hard, and more rustic than any of the rustics in the Sicilian bard."[41] Although his rendition of the fifth idyll renames it "The Traveller," as if to excise the tradition of battle that had euphemistically replaced buggery, and claims that "the beauty of this piece consists in that air of simplicitie in which the shepherds are painted,"[42] Fawkes still cannot pass up the temptation to proselytize marginally on his choice to excise the rape: "There was a necessity in this place to omit translating four lines in the original, which are infinitely too indelicate for modest ears."[43] Fawke's edition appears past the midpoint of the eighteenth century, but the conscious invocation of the lineage of Creech and Dryden establishes it as the perfect example of the culmination of Renaissance dealings with the classical pastoral tradition. And this culmination is also a perfect example of *negatio* in the purest sense. For the history of textual practices with both Virgil and Theocritus also demonstrates a steady movement in extremity to the polar opposites of *negatio*: on the one hand, a steadily increased suppression of homoerotic meaning; on the other hand, a steadily increasing *noting out* of the meaning being suppressed—many times quite literally through notes.[44] Milton's choice to locate the banquet temptation within a

[41]Theocritus, *The Idylliums of Theocritus*, trans. Francis Fawkes (London, 1767), pp. ix–x.

[42]Ibid., p. 47.

[43]Ibid., p. 51.

[44]These translations' almost obsessive return to the elements they are excluding is reminiscent of the model of cultural formation discussed by Peter Stallybrass and Allon White: "A recurrent pattern emerges: the 'top' attempts to reject and eliminate the 'bottom' for reasons of prestige and status, only to discover, not only that it is in some way frequently dependent upon that low-Other . . . , but also that the top *includes* that low

pastoral setting, then, is also a choice to locate it within a tradition of increasing efforts to place a sexually normative framework onto the sexually disruptive genre of the Renaissance pastoral—a generic choice that firmly places Ganymede within Renaissance vernaculars of homoeroticism.

Milton's awareness of pastoral's ability to transport ulterior meanings surfaces earlier in his career and can be seen in the printed edition of *A Maske*. Milton's entertainment is, as critics have argued, inextricably linked with a social occasion of political power and sexual transgression,[45] and pastoral within the mask initially seems designed to rectify these problems of propriety. The most conventionally traditional exposition of pastoral—one that would have pleased Rapin himself—is seen in the person of the attendant spirit, whose transformation from transcendent entity to helper of the Castlehaven family is presented as a movement from divinity to pastoral shepherd: "I must put off / These my sky robes spun out of *Iris*' Woof, / And take the Weeds and likeness of a Swain / That to the service of this house belongs" (82–85). The expectation engendered here is that this shepherd will cultivate "the blind mazes of this tangl'd Wood" (181) into a happy garden and that pastoral will tame through simplicity the "*Chaos* that reigns" (334) in the demonic forest. However, like the Chaos of *Paradise Lost*, which divides into both heaven and hell, this wild wood is not replaced by the pastoral but is simply ordered into clearer meaning, for the matrix of the "good" pastoral provides a contrast that more clearly delineates the "bad" of Comus: "this have I learnt," says the spirit,

> Tending my flocks hard by i'th'hilly crofts
> That brow this bottom glade, whence night by night
> He and his monstrous rout are heard to howl
> Like stabl'd wolves, or tigers at their prey,

---

symbolically, as a primarily eroticized constituent of its own fantasy life" (Stallybrass and White, *Politics and Poetics*, p. 5). This model tacitly informs my overall argument.

[45]Cf. Breasted, "*Comus* and the Castlehaven Scandal," and Marcus, "Earl of Bridgewater's Legal Life."

Doing abhorred rites to *Hecate*
In their obscured haunts of inmost bow'rs.
(530–536)

From the perspective of the pastoral, the evil of Comus is visible and perhaps more easily avoided, but hardly eradicated. The disparate threats to chastity posed throughout the mask remain intact; as Edward Le Comte perceptively notes, "Comus's phallic wand—which fastens and fascinates the Lady—is never taken from him."[46]

The structure of *A Maske*, then, removes the Lady from the threat to her chastity but leaves the threat intact in the sylvan setting of the drama; hence, a space is engendered in the text from which to question the ultimate triumph of chastity over the threat of Comus. This space is highlighted in the printed editions of the mask, for after the dedication to The Right Honorable John, Earl of Bridgewater, in the 1637 edition, the text inserts the quotation "Eheu quid volui mihi! floribus austrum Perditus," and the 1645 text follows suit. Ironically, the quotation is from Virgil's second eclogue (which Le Comte boldly labels "homosexual"[47]) and recalls both a passage and a tradition that work against the ostensibly chaste goals of the mask:

heu heu, quid volui misero mihi? floribus Austrum
perditus et liquidis immisi fontibus apros.
quem fugis, a, demens.[48]

[46]LeComte, *Milton and Sex*, p. 2. This point is significantly expanded and contextualized within late Renaissance sexual thought in James Grantham Turner, *One Flesh: Paradisal Marriage and Sexual Relations in the Age of Milton* (Oxford, 1987), pp. 177, 180; its Freudian overtones have been amplified by William Kerrigan, who claims that "Sabrina consecrates the act of eating" and that "her ritual of undoing implies that the Lady, having figuratively drunk the potion of her tempter, is guilty" (William Kerrigan, *The Sacred Complex: On the Psychogenesis of Paradise Lost* [Cambridge, Mass., 1983], pp. 47–48).

[47]LeComte, *Milton and Sex*, p. 9.

[48]Virgil, *Eclogues and Georgics*, p. 16.

> [Alas, alas, what misery have I wished on myself? The south winds have made wretched my flowers, and the wild boars have sullied the clear water of my spring. Why do you flee, you demented man?]

The combination of this specific passage and the vernacular eroticisms associated with Virgil's second eclogue interface provocatively with the actual social occasion of the mask. Just a year earlier a nobleman had "made wretched the flower" of a young woman's virginity, and the peers of the realm had failed to enact Bridgewater's desire for a quick recompense to her.[49] Moreover, Bridgewater's relative, Touchet, had managed to "sully the water" of the family lineage through a display of "paederastice" that became memorialized in a series of broadsides more in need of textual expurgation than the lovesick woe of Corydon. While these specific intentions may have motivated the choice of the epigraph, the broader implication is the more interesting. For if the mask on one level uses the "purity" of pastoral to *purge* Bridgewater's persona, the inclusion reminds readers that pastoral itself is a genre that can also vividly *display* transgression. The exergue reminds readers to read not just the "good" pastoral of the shepherd but also the transgressive antipastoral of Comus, which shows in contradistinction; it becomes, in short, a retrospective means of suggesting to readers that such royalist efforts at purification are necessary only because of standing impurities.

In *A Maske*, then, transgressive pastoral is inserted through the epigraph from Virgil in order to reinsert the transgression the pastoral of the mask ostensibly seeks to elide. Homoeroticism here becomes a means of making the text speak otherwise and of signaling distances between text, intention, and tradition. This ironic use of pastoral (ironic in the sense of placing ironic stresses on the text) becomes a hermeneutic aid in deciphering *Paradise Regained*'s uses of the genre, for in a similar way the intersection of pastoral implications and vernacular homoeroticism in the

[49] Cf. Leah Marcus, "The Milieu of Milton's *Comus*: Judical Reform of Ludlow and the Problem of Sexual Assault," *Criticism* 25 (1983): 293–327, and "Earl of Bridgewater's Legal Life."

brief epic forms a temptation for Jesus that is more than food and more than woman: it is, rather, the temptation of sexual plurality—and, significantly, the temptation of a plural definition of male sexuality. Unlike "the common gloss / Of Theologians" (*PL*, V.435–436), *Paradise Regained* views the temptation of Jesus as an interrogation of male sexual temptation instead of as a correction of original female weakness. The sexual difference of this hermeneutic should not be undervalued, for if the task of most commentators was to refocus the temptation of Jesus as a further allegorical articulation of the problem of woman, then Milton's exegesis contradicts this norm and uses *Paradise Regained* to interrogate the problems of *male* gender weakness. This difference is even more pronounced when Milton's negotiations of pastoral traditions are placed within the broader context of Renaissance exegetical uses of homoeroticism.

The Exegesis of Sodom/y

If the intersection of pastoral implications and vernacular eroticisms signals Milton's effort to inscribe homeoeroticism within his exegesis, his desire to do so might be accounted for by the increased frequency with which exegesis confronted issues of male-male sexuality as the Renaissance progressed. Several biblical passages, including Luke's temptation (a point to which I will return in my argument), became key texts for debating homoeroticism, and the development of commentary on them displays a movement similar to that in pastoral translations. Milton's canon demonstrates a full awareness of this exegetical tradition—an awareness that becomes a key means of discerning *Paradise Regained*'s differences from standard modes of exegesis and gender construction, as well as the epistemological status of Milton's sodomite.

In presenting the epic catalogue of fallen angels in *Paradise Lost*, Milton also presents a full picture of fleshly sins. Moloch is the "horrid King besmear'd with blood / Of human sacrifice, and parents' tears" (I.392–393). Chemos is noted for "wanton rites" and "lustful Orgies" (I.414–15). Ashtoreth is associated with errant "Virgins" (I.441), Thammuz with amorous "Damsels"

(I.448). And those spirits not specifically figured with fleshly debasement are presented in debased fleshly forms: Dagon is "upward Man / And downward Fish" (I.462–463); Isiris, Isis, and Orus are "monstrous shapes" "disguis'd in brutish forms / Rather than human" (I.479, 481–482). Like Satan at the epic's opening, these spirits are fully associated with the flesh and its weaknesses, and this image is brought to its culmination in the picture of the last spirit, Belial: "a Spirit more lewd / Fell not from Heaven, or more gross to love / Vice for itself" (I.490–491). In perfect accordance with the traditions of his time, Milton chooses to depict this ultimate lewdness through an invocation of sodomy:

> In Courts and Palaces he also Reigns
> And in luxurious Cities, where the noise
> Of riot ascends above thir loftiest Tow'rs,
> And injury and outrage: And when Night
> Darkens the Streets, then wander forth the Sons
> Of *Belial*, flown with insolence and wine.
> Witness the Streets of *Sodom*, and that night
> In *Gibeah*, when the hospitable door
> Expos'd a Matron to avoid worse rape.
>
> (I.497–505)

This description involves two separate biblical episodes as referents for debauchery, the first being the story of Lot in Sodom, as told in Genesis 19, and the second being the story of the Levite who comes to Gibeah in Judges 19. The relevant passages from the King James Bible read:

> But before they lay down, the men of the city, *even* the men of Sodom, compassed the house round, both old and young, all the people from every quarter: And they called unto Lot, and said unto him, Where *are* the men which came in to thee this night? bring them out unto us, that we may know them. And Lot went out at the door unto them, and shut the door after him, And said, I pray you, brethren, do not so wickedly. Behold now, I have two daughters which have not known man; let me, I pray you, bring them out unto you, and do ye to

> them as *is* good in your eyes: only unto these men do nothing; for therefore came they under the shadow of my roof.[50]

> *Now* as they were making their hearts merry, behold, the men of the city, certain sons of Belial, beset the house round about, *and* beat at the door, and spake to the master of the house, the old man, saying, Bring forth the man that came into thine house, that we may know him. And the man, the master of the house, went out unto them, and said unto them, Nay, my brethren, *nay*, I pray you, do not *so* wickedly; seeing that this man is come into mine house, do not this folly. Behold, *here is* my daughter a maiden, and his concubine; them I will bring out now, and humble ye them, and do with them what seemeth good unto you; but unto this man do not so vile a thing.[51]

Milton's canon engages these episodes in several places. Not only does *Paradise Lost* directly invoke these texts, but the Trinity manuscript suggests that Milton planned a full-scale engagement of them. The listing of subjects for tragedies provides an outline for a tragedy about Sodom, *Cupid's Funeral Pile*, and also lists an idea for a tragedy about "Comazontes or the Benjaminitis Jud. 19. 20. &c. or the Rioters."[52]

The tradition engaged by the allusion to these episodes is outlined by a long history of Renaissance exegesis and replicates the movement to increased specification of homoeroticism present in versions of the pastoral.[53] Early translations and glosses tend to figure the incidents as examples of general debauchery

[50]Gen. 19:4–8.

[51]Judg. 19:22–24.

[52]Milton, *Complete Prose Works*, vol. 8, p. 556. For a perceptive discussion of the importance of Milton's proposed tragedy, see Michael Lieb, " 'Cupid's Funeral Pile': Milton's Projected Drama on the Theme of Lust," *Renaissance Papers* (Southeastern Renaissance Conference, 1977), pp. 29–41.

[53]Mieke Bal specifically examines the function of women in the Judges narrative in a way that interfaces productively with my argument. Her essential point, that Judges is enforced by a "countercoherence" strongly concerned with "the reality of gender-bound violence" (Mieke Bal, *Death and Dissymmetry: The Politics of Coherence in the Book of Judges* [Chicago, 1987], p. 5), again displays the affinity between Judges and the issue of sexual marginality.

and sin. Edmund Becke's 1549 edition of the Bible glosses the story of Lot as an example of "the fylthy lustes of the Sodomytes" and changes the translation to read, "Where are the men which came into thy house to nyght? bringe them oute unto us [that] we maye do our lust with them."[54] Although the emendation specifies a sexualized component to the debauchery, this pattern is inconsistent in the edition, for his rendition of Judges 19 retains the phrase "that we may knowe him," a euphemism that carries sexual overtones but that also opens a space for alternative interpretations, particularly since no gloss is supplied. The 1560 edition of the Geneva Bible also takes as its subject in Genesis 19 "the filthy lustes of the Sodomites," but in Judges 19 the headnote elides the primary topic of sodomy in favor of the fate of the concubine, taking as its topic how "at Gibeah she was moste vilenously abused to the death." Moreover, the entire story of Lot is viewed as a series of lustful exempla. The moral of the Sodomites' request to "knowe them" is that "nothing is more dangerous, then to dwel where sinne reigneth: for it corrupteth all." Lot's decision to offer up his daughters shows that "he deserveth praise in defending his guests, but he is to be blamed in seking unlauful meanes." The later incident in verses 37 and 38, where Lot's daughters conjugate with him to continue his line, offers the moral "Who as they were borne in moste horrible incest, so were they and their posteritie vile and wicked." The tale, then, is hardly about sodomy but is about all forms of debauchery, from lust to pandering to incest. This pattern shows most clearly in the 1568 annotated edition of *The Bishop's Bible*, prefaced by Thomas Cranmer, whose glosses present a clear pattern of interpreting specific incidents of transgression as general examples of debauchery. In Genesis 19 the Sodomites' request for the angels is glossed, "This one, fact declareth the *manifold wickednes of all the citie*,"[55] and Lot's solution also presents a scenario of transgression: "As the defence of the straungers was Godly, so this meanes to save them, was not good." The translation of Judges 19 calls the men of Gibeah "wicked" but then notes

[54]Edmund Becke, *The Holy Bible, with Notes and Commentaries by Edmund Becke* (London, 1549).

[55]Thomas Cranmer, *The Bishop's Bible* (London, 1568). Emphasis mine.

that the Hebrew original actually reads "Men of Belial: that is, geve *to al wickednesse*" (my emphasis) and also glosses the request to "knowe" the Levite as an example of "how horrible were these men geven over for reprobate mynde, whom neither [the] fears of God, nor regard of honestie or shame . . . restraine from open abomination." The primary concern here is debasement in the eyes of God, not specifically debasement through sodomy.

The generalized nature of these interpretations becomes clearer in relation to later Renaissance exegesis, which becomes increasingly fascinated with sodomy as a specific (male) entity in and of itself. The mammoth compilation *Annotations Upon all the Books of the Old and New Testament*, issued in 1645, rewrites the exegesis of Sodom as an exegesis of sodomy. The gloss for "know them" in Genesis 19 becomes an occasion to meld Genesis, Judges, and legal codes into a specific condemnation of sodomy:

> The Scripture in this word *knowing* modestly intimateth a most immodest meaning, not fit to be mentioned in plaine termes: see Gen. 4.1, Numb. 31.17. Judges 19.22. This sinne is from these men (men in shape though worse then beasts in their lusts, as the Angels in humane appearance were better then men) called *Sodomie* (as the buying of spirituall things from *Simon Magus* his offer, Act. 8.18. is called *Simonie*) and it is an abuse of either sexe against nature: see Levit. Chap. 18.22 & c. 20.13. Rom. I. 23, 24. wherein the Sodomites were most impudent, Isa. 3.9. and to their impudence was added violence, as by those sonnes of Belial, Judg. 19.22.[56]

Not only is sodomy fully inscribed in this commentary, but the inclusion of both sexes (which mimics legal codes of the 1640s) is undermined by the biblical citations. Following the substantiation of "know them" from Genesis to Numbers to Judges reveals a trend toward specification of male penetration. Genesis 4:1 relates how "Adam knew Eve his wife, and she conceived," and Numbers 31:17 is Moses' command to "kill every woman that

[56] *Annotations Upon all the Books of the Old and New Testament* (London, 1645).

hath known a man by lying with him," a sequence that clearly delineates "know" as sexual penetration and, by extension, tacitly defines the Gibeans' demand to "know" the Levite as a demand to penetrate him. Similarly, the two references to Leviticus focus on male sexuality: "Thou shalt not lie with mankind, as with womankind: it is abomination"; "If a man also lie with mankind, as he lieth with woman, both of them have committed an abomination."[57] The concern of this commentary is neither about general debauchery nor about both sexes; it is, rather, an exegetical commentary on male-male sexual intercourse. Moreover, the commentary to Judges 19 specifically refers the reader back to this exegesis of sodom/y, glossing "may know them" in Judges 19:22 as "a modest expression of their filthy lust, according to the scripture phrase. See Gen. 19.8," which is, of course, the story of Sodom.

By the end of the seventeenth century, the process of increased sexual specification progressed to such a point that Sodom was specifically and only male sodomy. In the most telling example of this change, George Lesly's dramatized *Divine Dialogues*, the exegetical play *Fire and Brimstone, or, the Destruction of Sodom* begins with an invocation of generalized vice similar to Elizabethan commentaries:

> Behold, how *Sodom* swaggers in its Pride,
> And Lust, and Gluttony! none is espied,
> That thoughts of Heaven have; or bowe a knee:
> But one poor Stranger, who adoreth me.
> My servant Lot: Whose holy Soul they vex;
> Because there's no distinction made of Sex
> Nor age, but all promiscuously do go,
> Like Goats and Leopards that all they may know
> Each other.[58]

However, the concern here is not so much in condemning all debauchery as it is in condemning debauchery that transgresses social divisions of sexual meaning ("no distinction made of

[57]Lev. 18:22, 20:13.
[58]George Lesly, *Divine Dialogues* (London, 1684), p. 33.

Sex"). Lesly himself constructs clear divisions, for the unmediated vice of early tracts becomes a highly specified diatribe against "buggary":

> *Sod.* Confounded Dog, bring forth thy handsome Guests
> Or by our great God *Priapus* we swear,
> That we thy Body will in pieces tear.
> *Lot.* . . . Neighbours be rul'd, this wickedness give o're.
> And if your Beastly lust cannot refrain,
> But that these strangers you with sin would stain,
> See here two Maids of mine who Virgins be,
> Use them at pleasure, and let them go free.
> *Sod.* Rogue, runagate, slave, think not that thou must,
> Make such exchanges to restraine our Lust.
> Who made the'a Judge? If we be rul'd by thee,
> Then must we bid adieu to Buggary.
> But hold, stand back, or we will break the Door.[59]

Sodomy is not longer part of a sexual economy of debauchery, a debased lust that can be satisfied by any trangressive action, but is rather a specific "taste" or sexual preference, one to which some refuse to "bid adieu."

The exegetical role of this specified sodomy grew in importance as the Renaissance progressed. The early beginnings of this trend linked sexual delineation with overt social and political concerns. The *Annotations* of 1645, for example, glosses the fact that "old and young" Sodomites joined in the assault against Lot as a lesson "that communitie in consent is no good argument of a good cause, for the whole Citie is assembled for a most wicked purpose against godly Lot, and his heavenly guests," and labels "sons of Belial" in Judges 19:22 as "most wicked men, or desperately wicked, who had quite shaken off all law, and the yoke of government." By the late seventeenth century, these political uses of exegetical sodomy had spread widely through popular publications engaged in anti-Catholic and royalist debates. The anonymous "Room for a Ballad, or a Ballad for Rome," for example, proudly states that

[59]Ibid., pp. 33–34.

> Our strict purity, is plain to each eye,
> That Catholicke Countreys views;
> For there to supress, the sins of the Flesh,
> Sodomy is in use and the Stews.[60]

The publication of *Sodom Fair: or the Market of the Man of Sin* in 1688 took the occasion to append a second part, entitled "The History of Fornication and Adultery," that attempts to trace licentious behavior to the papal decrees against marriage of the clergy—and one of its primary rhetorical tools is the derogatory invocation of sodomy:[61]

> For as *Huldericus* writeth, They [Roman clergy denied marriage rights under Gregory] accompanied not only with Maids, Married Women, and their own kindred, but with Mankind.[62]

> It is reported by *Roger* of *Chester*, that *Anselm* Archbishop of *Canterbury*, did forbid and condemn the lawful Marriage of Priests, in one *Synod*; but in the next was forc'd to make Laws against *Sodomy*; whereof eight Abbots, with a great crew of inferior Priests and Fraiars were found Guilty. *Huldericus* Bishop of *Augusta*, in the foresaid Letter to Pope *Nicolas* the first writeth, that whilst under a false shew of continency, the Church of *Rome* refused the ordinance of Marriage; their clargy COMMITTED INCEST, AND ABOMINABLE SODOMITICAL VILLANIES WITH MEN AND BEASTS.[63]

Milton's poetical exegesis, then, occurs at a historical juncture where an increased vocabulary for expressing homoeroticism—

[60]"Room for a Ballad, or a Ballad for Rome" (London, 1674).

[61]The mode here was also prevalent in the earlier Renaissance, and not just in relation to Catholics. Atherton, Lord Bishop of Waterford, for example, was claimed to have taken from the Devil "a male fiend to sodomize with him" (*The Life and Death of John Atherton, Lord Bishop of Waterford and Lysmore within the Kingdome of Ireland, borne neare Bridgewater in Somersetshire* [London, 1641], sig. A2).

[62]*Sodom Fair: or the Market of the Man of Sin* (London, 1688), p. 12.

[63]Ibid., p. 28.

if only in a negative fashion—merged with an awareness of the ability of homoeroticism to stigmatize diverse "unacceptable" categories of meaning. This merger, in turn, formed a trend toward sexually specific exegetical literature. If "common glosses" began, perhaps, with the goal of stigmatizing sodomy, they quickly became aware of how this goal allowed sodomy to become a multivalent sign of devaluation—and, in turn, likely became aware of the benefits accrued by sustaining the negative portrayal of sodomy. The movement toward sodom/y, then, becomes a standard against which Milton's sodomite—and Miltonic genders in general—must be interpreted.

This sustained attention to stigmatized sodomy also played a role in the development of commentary on the Son's temptation. Whereas a dominant tradition demanded, as did Lightfoot, that the temptation be restructured as a commentary on woman's weakness, a lesser but still significant tradition inscribed Luke's temptation within the debate on homoeroticism. Daniel Dyke's *Michael and the Dragon* presents a representative version of this type of exegesis:

> [We must learn to have] this same stoicall eye of our Saviour, that we may see eye-pleasing and tempting objects, and not bee moved and set a-gogge, . . . as he with the beauty of a young boy, to whom it was answered, that the Praetor must have continent eyes, as wel as hands.[64]

This tradition speaks differently from that of Lightfoot, but ultimately it speaks to the same end; in each case "this perfect man" envisioned in the Son must also be perfectly masculine, subject neither to the weakness of female flesh nor the prurience of deviant male flesh.[65] This tradition also signals the difference

[64]Daniel Dyke, *Michael and the Dragon, or Christ Tempted and Satan Foyled* (London, 1635), p. 218.

[65]The pattern of increased specification and articulation of homoeroticism in exegesis is by far the most prevalent one, but it is also countered by an alternative tradition. Nathaniel Crouch, for example, in glossing Judges, says only that "certain young men . . . were . . . ravished with her beauty," a rewriting that entirely erases the reference to sodomy by making the angel

of Milton's engagement of a homoerotic temptation, for if Milton's banquet temptation eschews the masculinist assumptions of Lightfoot's allegorization, it just as strongly disassociates itself from Dyke's mode of exegetical stigmatism, and this separation is achieved by assigning the patriarchal stances underlying both modes of exegesis to the voice of Belial.

Throughout the Old Testament, Belial appears as an embodiment of prurience, sexual transgression, and debasement from God. In Deuteronomy, "certain men" who "have withdrawn the inhabitants of their city, saying, Let us go and serve other gods," are called "the children of Belial."[66] When Eli accuses Hannah of drunkenness, she responds, "Count not thine handmaiden for a daughter of Belial,"[67] and Nabal, who is "churlish and evil," is "such a son of Belial, that a man cannot speak to him."[68] In all of these examples Belial functions as a referent for debasement, a convenient way of signaling a transgression of the ways of God. This function is clearly pointed out in the New Testament when 2 Corinthians strikes a binary opposition between the ways of Belial and Christ: "And what concord hath Christ with Belial? or what part hath he that believeth with an infidel?"[69]

Belial, then, would be the perfect spirit to suggest the sodomitical temptation of a Ganymede or a Hylas—the "more lewd" spirit from *Paradise Lost* (I.490) should join logically with the most lewd tradition of sodom/y. Indeed, this is the association firmly established by exegesis and by Milton's own allusion to

---

female. (Nathaniel Crouch, *Female Excellency, or the Ladies Glory* [London, 1688], p. 4.) However, this rewriting also supports my argument, for although the tradition I am analyzing established sodomy as the "other" *within* the text, exegeses that erase the sodomy (as, it should be noted, does Lewis's lit-crit gloss) establish it as the "other" *to* the text. In both cases sodomy is increasingly specified and stigmatized, albeit through the antithetical tropes of *copia* and *negatio*. I am indebted to Joseph Wittreich for drawing my attention to this countertradition and to an anonymous reader from *PMLA* for the contiguity of "common glosses" and Lewis's own commentary.

66Deut. 13:13.

67I Sam. 2:12.

68I Sam., 25:3, 17.

692 Cor. 6:15.

sodomitical biblical passages in *Paradise Lost*. But this expectation is thwarted in *Paradise Regained*, for Belial speaks the language of patriarchy, not the language of sodomy. Belial's suggestion of a sensual temptation and Satan's subsequent rejection accurately replicate the parameters of sexual conduct displayed in father-to-son advice epistles and commonplace books from the Renaissance. Woman, Belial claims, is "such object [that] hath the power to . . . / Draw out with credulous desire, and lead / At will the manliest, resolutest breast, / As the magnetic hardest Iron draws" (II.163–168). Removed from the poem, these words could be Leonard Wright's, who, in *A Display of Dutie*, warns young men that "most women by nature are sayde to be light of credite: lustie of stomacke: unpatient: full of words: apt to eye, flatter and weepe."[70] Alexander Niccholes's *Discourse of Marriage and Wiving* recognizes a similarly "lustie" woman and also brands her lust as "the Tyrant of the Night, the Enemy of the Day."[71] And in a most interesting textual parallel, Francis Meres, who claims that "the Flie that playeth in the fire is singed in the flame: so he that dallieth with women is drawen to his woe,"[72] uses the same metaphor as Belial: "As a Loadstone by a secrete in nature draweth Iron unto it, so a woman by a *Secret in nature* draweth men unto her."[73]

Belial's speech, then, is a moment of textual irony in which the words of temptation are actually the words of Renaissance patrilineal gender decorum. The masculinist assumptions of "common glosses" are here, but in the form of post-lapsarian sin.

[70]Wright, *A Display of Dutie*, p. 36.

[71]Alexander Niccholes, *Discourse of Marriage and Wiving* (London, 1615), p. 156.

[72]Meres, *Palladis Tamia*, p. 42.

[73]Ibid., p. 41. This pattern is sustained by a number of advice tracts. In addition to those cited here, see, for example, Walter Raleigh, "Advice to a Son," in *Advice to a Son*, ed. L. B. Wright (Washington, D.C. 1962), p. 26; Anon., *The Knowledge of the World: Or, the Art of Well-Educating Youth Through the Various Conditions of LIFE* (London, n.d.), sig. B1. Eugenius Theodidactus, *Advice to a Daughter* (London, 1658), p. 67, and George Savile, *The Lady's New-Year's-Gift: Or, Advice to a Daughter* (London, 1700), pp. 51–42, both, though ostensibly directed to women, still bear out the same patriarchal standards.

Satan's response to Belial also plays within these tropics. He claims that "these haunts / Delight not all" (II.191–192) and proceeds to describe the Son as one "wiser far / Than *Solomon*, of more exalted mind, / Made and set wholly on th'accomplishment / Of greatest things" (II.205–208). The Jesus whom Satan describes is very much the word made flesh—but the word here is the rhetoric of ideal Renaissance masculinity. In *Youth's Instruction* William Marty outlines the goal of filial advice. "The outward lineaments of the bodie," he claims, "are deprived of their choisest, and of their chiefest luster, if the inward parts and mind be not adorned, with such splendid virtues, as doe make a man to bee compleat, and consequentlie, a profitable member in the Common-weale."[74] The Son embodies just such "splendid virtues," and Satan knows that the temptation of woman is insufficient to make him *un*profitable, for, as Satan notes, "Beauty stands / in th'admiration only of weak minds" (I.220–221).

The irony of this construction is in what it implies about the language of Renaissance patrilineal gender decorum. For homoeroticism in this configuration is no longer the basely vice of the sons of Belial—that action that separates the good from the bad—but is now a demarcation of the point at which patrilineal decorum fails. The debate between Belial and Satan accurately replicates the actual language of young men's sexual indoctrination and furthermore notes that the Son is a perfect embodiment of the goals of patrilineal language. However, the construction of the banquet temptation further suggests that such language is an insufficient way to define the "perfect Man" (I.166). For once the temptation of woman is ruled out, Satan recognizes that "therefore with manlier objects we must try / His constancy" (II.225–226), and these "manlier objects" are figured homoerotically through the allusion to Ganymede and Hylas.

The point to be made here is that the use of Ganymede in this allusion is not a condemnation of homoeroticism—as it would likely be in an exegesis by, say, Drake or Lesly—but, rather, is a means of condemning patriarchal sexual decorum to a *limited* status. For if "common glosses" establish homoeroticism as the

[74]William Marty, *Youth's Instruction* (London, 1612), sig. A3.

other *within* patriarchal meaning, Milton's banquet specifies it as the other *to* patriarchy. Atypical handlings of homoeroticism appear in other places in the Miltonic canon, most notably in Milton's own exegesis of sodom/y, *Cupid's Funeral Pile*. For instead of "bidding adieu to buggary," Milton's outline remains ominously silent on the topic. There is no mass of men demanding "to know" the angels, only two youths and a priest who "inveighs against the strict raigne of melchizedeck." And while it is claimed that Lot "knows thire drift," there is no bargaining between buggery and virginity. Rather, the priest and youths "taxe [Lot] of praesumption, singularity, breach of citty customs, in fine offer violence."[75] Against a tradition of increasingly vivid display, the silencing of sodomy signals an exegetical difference—and this difference is replicated in *Paradise Regained*, when homoeroticism is divorced from the tradition of Belial and replaced with the language of patrilineal sexual orthodoxy.

Milton's Sodomite

It is worth considering the traditions of sodomy that inform both the pastoral and exegetical traditions behind *Paradise Regained*, for they begin to suggest some of what has been lost of Milton's canon in the lengthy historical process of explaining it. Indeed, in relation to the various trends and motifs I have delineated, Lewis's "criticism" seems more like a "common gloss," a logical continuation of the processes of stigmatization, segregation, and isolation that exemplify exegeses of the seventeenth century. Lewis—like many critics before and since—does not explain Milton's genders but empowers the tradition that gives them meaning through contradistinction. Moreover, these traditions and their relation to Milton's Ganymede indicate again that, for Milton, the sodomite, while in and of himself having a meaning, is more important for the ways in which he in turn *negotiates other* meanings—for the possibility of comprehensible homoerotic meaning in the banquet temptation both unwrites

[75]Milton, *Complete Prose Works*, vol. 8, p. 559.

the absolute otherness of the legal sodomite and suggests a space of meaning outside the heterocentrically prescriptive codes of ideal Renaissance genders. More precisely, *Paradise Regained* takes the position of otherness ascribed to homoeroticism by "the common gloss / Of Theologians" (*PL*, V. 435–436), removes the overt condemnation ascribed to it by separating it from the tradition of Belial, and then uses it as a position from which to signal a difference from common explications. The history of exegesis *constituted* sodom/y as a specified and condemned segment of sexual meaning—and Miltonic exegesis invokes this constitution as a means of *disrupting* orthodox languages.

Milton's sodomite, then, indicates a complex economy of meanings hiding beneath the actual sign; Milton's sodomite "means," but not *in one way*. Moreover, the complexity of signification encoded within Milton's sodomite branches out into the canon's entire conception of sex, sexuality, and gender—a conception clearly present in *Paradise Lost*. The epic begins with a hyperbolic description of Satan that has typically been associated with a mock-heroic construction. Resting "as far remov'd from God and light of Heav'n / As from the Center thrice to th'utmost Pole" (I.73–74), Satan's body is "stretcht out huge in length . . . / Chained on the burning Lake" (I.209–210):

> Thus Satan talking to his nearest Mate
> With Head up-lift above the wave, and Eyes
> That sparkling blaz'd, his other Parts besides
> Prone on the Flood, extended long and large
> Lay floating many a rood, in bulk as huge
> As whom the Fables name of monstrous size,
> *Titanian*, or *Earth-born*, that warr'd on *Jove*,
> *Briareos* or *Typhon*, whom the Den
> By ancient *Tarsus* held, or that Sea-best
> *Leviathan*, which God of all his works
> Created hugest that swim th'Ocean stream.
>
> (I.192–202)

Satan's great distance from God is associated with a great mass of flesh; this phenomenon also echoes the choral description of Samson at the depth of his despair:

> See how he lies at random, carelessly diffus'd,
> With languish't head unpropt,
> As one past hope, abandon'd,
> And by himself given over.
>
> (*SA*, 118–121)

The parallel between Samson and Satan is strong, and just as Satan is chained in Hell, Samson is destined "To grind in Brazen Fetters under task" (35). And in both cases the loss of proximity to God results in bondage in the flesh.

Milton's sexual epistemology, then, is informed by what might best be called an intense skepticism of the flesh. There is a lesson within the skepticism, for it suggests that our very effort to determine gendered meaning within the canon is already an entrance into an arena that Milton himself condemned. This lesson is also incorporated in *Paradise Lost* as a broad structural device. In the epic catalogue of fallen spirits in book 1, the narrative voice intercedes to tell how

> spirits when they please
> Can either Sex assume, or both; so soft
> And uncompounded is thir Essence pure,
> Not ti'd or manacl'd with joint or limb,
> Nor founded on the brittle strength of bones,
> Like cumbrous flesh; but in what shape they choose
> Dilated or condens't, bright or obscure,
> Can execute thir aery purposes,
> And works of love or enmity fulfill.
>
> (I.423–431)

Yet this description, which seems to liberate fallen angels from the fleshly conscription of the first portrayal of Satan, is ironically rewritten as a mark of indenture when Raphael later describes the conjugal practices of unfallen angels. As he states,

> Whatever pure thou [Adam] in the body enjoy'st
> (And pure thou wert created) we enjoy
> In eminence, and obstacle find none
> Of membrane, joint, or limb, exclusive bars:
> Easier than Air with Air, if Spirits embrace,

Total they mix, Union of Pure with Pure
Desiring; nor restrain'd conveyance need
As Flesh to mix with Flesh, or Soul with Soul.
(VIII.622–629)

The parallel between these two passages is obvious, and just as obvious is the superiority of unfallen spirits. For while the fallen spirits can range freely throughout the system of sex and gender, unfallen spirits can range freely *outside* of it.

This devalued notion of fleshly meaning shows most clearly in the recollection of the battle in heaven. Satan's divorce from God also progressively constructs a fall into fleshly sensation. Raphael prefaces his description of Satan's actions with an appositive that renames the archangel as

Author of evil, unknown till thy revolt,
Unnam'd in Heav'n, now plenteous, as thou seest
These Acts of hateful strife, hateful to all,
Though heaviest by just measure on thyself
And thy adherents: how hast thou disturb'd
Heav'n's blessed peace, and into Nature brought
Misery, uncreated till the crime
Of thy Rebellion?
(VI.262–269)

This origin of misery is specifically related to the origin of fleshly sensation, for Satan later notes, "But pain is perfect misery" (VI.462). Moreover, the central moment in the battle is when Satan first feels pain, and this moment is again played against the noncorporeal superiority of unfallen angels. When Michael "shear'd / All his right side; then *Satan* first knew pain" (VI.326–327). Satan is, of course, quickly healed—"th'Ethereal substance clos'd / Not long divisible" (VI.330–331)—for, as Raphael recounts in a speech that foreshadows his description of angelic intercourse,

. . . Spirits . . . live throughout
Vital in every part, not as frail man
In Entrails, Heart or Head, Liver or Reins,

Cannot but by annihilating die;
Nor in thir liquid texture mortal wound
Receive, no more than can the fluid Air:
All Heart they live, all Head, all Eye, all Ear,
All Intellect, all Sense, and as they please,
They limb themselves, and color, shape or size
Assume, as likes them best, condense or rare.
(VI.344–353)

Although this description accounts for Satan's quick recovery, his newly acquired *fleshly difference* from it is later highlighted, for Raphael is also careful to mention that the spirits "Not to have disobey'd" "stood / Unwearied, unobnoxious to be pain'd / By wound, though from thir place by violence mov'd" (VI.403–405).

At the farthest remove from God, at the lowest level in Miltonic epistemology, then, rests the level of experience that incorporates the entire critical debate on Miltonic gender and sexuality, including my own contribution to it here. In describing the sun's light as male and the moon's as female, Raphael also offers an insight that can give us a lesson in reading, for he calls these "which two great Sexes animate the World" (VIII.151). Yet there is, of course, another world—the world of the angels—unified with and in God. This unlapsed world assigns no meaning to "membrane, joint, or limb" (VIII.625), for it is a world in which the Word is still the Word and not the flesh. There is always, then, a greater "other" within Milton's epistemology, and the divisions which we view as inscriptive—such as man/woman, homo-/heteroerotic, deviant/normal—are all equally devalued, and therefore equally valid, units of negotiation in Milton's canon. Such a system of meaning indicates to us that the real question to be asking about Milton's genders—and, perhaps, all genders—is not *what* they mean but *how*. Throughout his career Milton was perplexed by this very question. As James Grantham Turner has rightly pointed out, Milton's sexual epistemology demands that

> forbidden heresies, sexual temptations, and even the frank pornography of Petronius and Aretino must be allowed to

> 'work' like homeopathic drugs; without their controlled absorption the soul cannot 'temper' good antidotes.[76]

Turner's thesis is perfectly borne out in *Paradise Regained*, for the topic in the banquet temptation is not homoeroticism but the ability of homoeroticism to disrupt the gendered traditions of exegesis. Regardless of how we adjudicate Milton's own attitude toward the homoeroticism Satan uses to tempt the Son, one thing is clear: the genderization of *Paradise Regained* neither accepts such easy meanings as "Man," "Woman" or, even, "buggerer" nor takes as its topic such conservative patriarchal questions as "whether the male is, or is not, the superior sex."[77] Rather, the text encodes a system of plural options—a "dissemination and implantation of polymorphous sexualities"[78]—that ascribes a certain sexual potentiality to everything from "fair women" to "tall stripling youths." The importance of this spectrum becomes even more important when we note that the articulation of purely patrilineal gender decorum is continually associated with post-lapsarian knowledge. For if Satan and Belial speak the language of conventional Renaissance gender, they also speak from an irredeemably fallen position. As Satan says, "This wounds me most (what can it less?) that Man, / Man fall'n, shall be restor'd, I never more" (I.404–405). Earlier the Son claims that "Man lives not by Bread only, but each Word / Proceeding from the mouth of God" (I.349–350). Satan, of course, can never know these words, for he is "lost / To be belov'd of God" (I.378–379). From this position of divorce from God, Satan speaks the system of gender difference, a system that articulates not just the roles of Ganymede and Hylas but also those of Man and Woman.

Reading Milton's sodomite in his vernacular and historical contexts demonstrates that *Paradise Regained* reveals gendered meaning in general to be a product of the fall, a system distinctive of a separation from God. It also demonstrates that although the sodomite that Lewis seeks to elide was, indeed, frequently devalued during the Renaissance, he was also constantly in play.

[76]Turner, *One Flesh*, p. 178.
[77]Lewis, *Preface to Paradise Lost*, p. 113.
[78]Foucault, *History of Sexuality*, p. 12.

Paradise Regained posits a bifurcated view of gender meaning, one that recognizes the ability of language both to make sexual meaning, as in the case of pastoral, and to unmake it, as in the disruption achieved by the intersection of pastoral and exegetical traditions. This system finds analogues in many different texts. We could look forward to the work of Julia Kristeva and claim that the brief epic and its presentation of the banquet constructs and critiques a "metaphysics of gender."[79] Or we could look back to a text Milton himself knew, Plato's *Symposium*, where Aristophanes labels the creation of individuated gender and sexuality as an act of godly punishment. And yet these analogues provide less compelling contextualizations than the very culture in which Milton lived and wrote. Within a culture grappling with papists, bodily mutilation, and cross-dressed marauders, the voice of patriarchy appears to be a weak voice, one desperately trying to instill itself but not quite succeeding. This view of patrilineal decorum is displayed in *Paradise Regained* when the language of patriarchy becomes the language of Satan and not the language of Milton. For Satan himself brands his image of fleshly temptation as "that which only *seems* to satisfy / Lawful desires of Nature" (II.229–230, my emphasis), and Belial calls his own imitation of patrilineal advice "credulous desire" (II.166), that is, desire in which we are too ready to believe.[80] There is space here, then, between the voice of patriarchy and the voice of the poet, and this space is highlighted by a critical practice that is able to read Milton's Ganymede; recognizing this space, I posit, offers the potential for a critical parity, if not a critical paradise, regained.

[79]Kristeva, "Women's Time," p. 33.

[80]The duplicity of this word is marked in Milton's canon also by the Lady in *Comus*, who labels her own chastity as "credulous innocence" (697).

CHAPTER 6

Coda: The Essential Sodomite

> Many will say it is a dream, and will not follow my inferences; but I confidently expect a time when there will be seen, running like a half-hid warp through all the myriad audible and visible worldly interests of America, threads of a manly friendship, fond and loving, pure and sweet, strong and life-long, carried to degrees hitherto unknown—not only giving tone to individual character, and making it unprecedentedly emotional, muscular, heroic and refined, but having the deepest relations to general politics.
>
> —Walt Whitman

> In an expanding universe, time is on the side of the outcast. Those who once inhabited the suburbs of human contempt find that without changing their address they eventually live in the metropolis.
>
> —Quentin Crisp

In the metatheoretical introduction to my argument, I alluded to a certain bifurcation in my stance. I would like here to acknowledge another split and offer a few words to address it. This is the split between my position within the academy and my position within the gay community. This book as a whole is empowered precisely by this rift, for while it works within academic discourses, it could never have been realized without the courage and commitment of our community—a community that has empowered me to name myself as a viable, competent gay male against a hegemonic discourse that has sought to label me as an outcast. This brief coda is entirely polemical and is designed to highlight some intersections of my theorization of historical sexual difference and our own present as gay people.

Edmund White, our most eloquent spokesman, has succinctly articulated the impact that the theoretical issues underpinning my study have on our own existence as gay people; as he says,

> revisionist gay theoreticians have prompted us to regard "the homosexual" as a false unity. . . . What this line of thinking suggests is that to fight for the rights of "the homosexual" is to struggle on behalf of a creature defined precisely so that he might be controlled. The paradox is that the only terms by which we can struggle for freedom are terms of servitude;

> after all, Victorian doctors first coined the very word *homosexuality* as a medical category, a "humane" stigma.[1]

White's reason for outlining this constructionist position is to suggest that it somehow misses the mark, especially for the volatile arena of identity politics and political self-construction. Few of us who lead active gay lives find it difficult to comprehend the impotencies of this line of thinking. After all, we seldom walk into a bar on a Saturday night and say to our friends, "I really hope I find a hot *false unity* tonight." I use this ludicrous example to stress a point: there is in many ways a discrepancy between how we theorize "the homosexual" and how "the homosexual" affects us as material people.

In some sectors this rift has led to a full-scale rejection of gay theory. How can we, it is asked, spend our time finessing the epistemological and historical contingency of difference when our people are attacked on the streets with bottles and knives, systematically annihilated by this government's genocidal response to AIDS, and socially debilitated by material constraints such as a denial of equal benefits and institutionalized job discrimination? This is a real and crucial question. It is also a question with a history, for it in many ways replicates our original rallying cry in the Stonewall riots, "Out of the bars and into the streets"—but "bars" are now theory, and "streets" are now activism. However, I also think that this response privileges a certain systemic power division that might work against our overall cause as gay people. There might be a more effective way to "think" ourselves, one that refuses to acknowledge, let alone privilege, the dichotomies of theory/praxis, of all/none, and, as I am trying to do with this coda, of "ivory tower"/"real world" that support Western (and, thereby, homophobic) power. Diana Fuss has, in this context, called for a rallying around "the radicality of [the] poststructuralist view which locates difference *within* identity,"[2] and herein rests the first place where my historical analysis provides some points of thought for our contempo-

[1]Edmund White, *States of Desire: Travels in Gay America* (New York, 1983), p. xviii.

[2]Fuss, *Essentially Speaking*, p. 103.

rary cause. In my argument about subjectivity in the sonnet tradition, we can find evidence that in a very real way what we think of as "normal" subjectivity takes as one of its very conditions of existence difference *within* identity. To make this even more explicit for our community, we need only think of the primary question that plagued a recent gay literature course I taught: Am I a *gay* person, or a *person* who is gay? This question inherently plays back into the tropics of origin I examine in my introduction and just as certainly serves to truncate political power. Renaissance sonnets and Fuss's argument demonstrate that this question is moot, for the difference it implies is not a hindrance to, but rather a *condition of*, being. In other words, the central premise of both postmodernism and Renaissance sonnets is that identity can never be firmly solidified as a quantifiable phenomenon. The desire to reify identity, I have claimed, can be seen as complicit with a certain set of dynamics that seek to constrain the subject—and it is this desire that we replicate when we attempt systematically to programatize the relationship between sexuality and the subject, either in the Renaissance or in our own times.

The second point to make here, and I think it is the more important, is that my extended historical analysis also offers a new way of thinking the constructionist/essentialist debate that is overt in gay theory and implicit in our community's political efforts. Lacanian feminist Jane Gallop has warned that "identity must be continually assumed and immediately called into question,"[3] and yet the dialectic necessary here inevitably breaks down when stressed across the axial of construction and essence. My analysis of Renaissance sodomy has suggested, I think, that this problematic can be erased if we stop to consider that power appears differently when viewed diachronically than when viewed synchronically. By this I mean that over the course of the Renaissance we can see that "sodomy" itself appears as a *construction*, an epistemological category that rebounds, mutates, fades, brightens, etc. It is clearly not essential; it is constructed. And yet we can also see that *at any point in time*, what is *constructed*

[3]Jane Gallop, *The Daughter's Seduction: Feminism and Psychoanalysis* (Ithaca, 1982), p. xii.

has an *essential force*. In Marlowe's *Hero and Leander*, in the poetry of Barnfield and Shakespeare, in Milton's banquet scene, homoeroticism is, first, comprehensible as something other than a "false unity" and, second, able to exert a force. It is, in these instances, not vacillating, fluctuating, disseminating, or pluralizing; it simply *is*. What over time changes can, in the present tense, *be*. This formulation also asks that we in many ways reassess what we mean by the terms "construction" and "essence." Within our own community discourse these terms most often are thought to be questions of etiology, a part of the prevalent but tired nature/nurture debate. I am suggesting that we need instead to view these terms in relation to the circulation of social power. We must think of these terms as indexes not of how things come to be but of how things exert power.[4] I think we can find in my historical analyses, therefore, a justification for assuming an essential political force—and for doing so with neither guilt nor paranoia. We can, I think, rally and rebel on *our* behalf, not on the behalf of a "false unity."

Happily, there are signs that our community is already merging praxis and precept in the way I am advocating. One such example is the emergence of the controversial activist group Queer Nation. A recent article in *The Advocate* describes the phenomenon: "In recent months, chapters of Queer Nation have sprung up around the country as a grass-roots, direct-action response to 'compulsory heterosexuality' and the invisibility of gays and lesbians. Militant and uncompromising, Queer Nation has the gay nation talking."[5] The rhetoric here is telling. The rallying cry against "compulsory heterosexuality" is drawn from Adrienne Rich's "Compulsory Heterosexuality and Lesbian Existence,"[6] one of the earliest and most influential efforts at lesbian theory. Moreover, its linkage with the term *queer* indicates the

[4]On this point see Jonathan Dollimore, "Homophobia and Sexual Difference," *Oxford Literary Review* 8, 1–2 (1986): 5–12.

[5]Robin Podolsky, "Birth of a Queer Nation," *The Advocate* 561 (October 9, 1990): 52.

[6]Adrienne Rich, "Compulsory Heterosexuality and Lesbian Existence," in *Women, Sex, and Sexuality*, ed. Catharine R. Stimpson and Ethel Spector Person, pp. 62–91 (Chicago, 1980).

extent to which the concerns of theory and the concerns of activism have merged: *queer* signals a sexual difference without inevitably linking it to gender difference as the terms *lesbian* and *gay* now do. Complementarily, the same issue of *The Advocate* also reminds us of the numerous ways in which activists have paved the way for the presence of gay, lesbian, and queer studies in the academy: "Queer students want to know more about who they are, where they come from, and where they're headed as gay men and lesbians. As a result, these student activists are demanding changes in their colleges' curricula."[7] The binary of theory and praxis in these instances becomes more annoying than inscriptive, for it is obvious not only that one helps the other but that one *is* the other. Indeed, this cotermineity can be seen clearly in my book, for while it is theoretical, it is also my own praxis, the material production and embodiment of my own position as a gay person in a social role.

These issues are, I think, the *essential* points to be drawn by our community from my analyses of sodomy and the sodomite in Renaissance epistemology. They do not, however, go very far in addressing the real frustration that arises from the struggle. Therefore, if I have asked us to re*think* ourselves through the terms of theory, I might now also ask us to re*empower* ourselves through the words of Quentin Crisp, for in an expanding universe, time *is* on the side of the outcast, and as our universe continues to expand ever more quickly, the ability to silence such outcasts will someday be lost.

[7]Karen Ocamb, "Gay Studies Make the Grade," *The Advocate* 561 (October 9, 1990): 40.

Works Cited

An Account of the Proceedings Against Capt. Edward Rigby, At the Session of Goal Delivery, held at Justice-Hall in the Old-Bailey, on Wednesday the Seventh Day of December, 1698, for intending to Commit that Abominable Sin of Sodomy, on the Body of one William Minton. London, 1698.

Allen, J. W. *A History of Political Thought in the Sixteenth Century.* New York, 1928.

Althusser, Louis. *For Marx.* Trans. Ben Brewster. Harmondsworth, U.K., 1969.

——. *Lenin and Philosophy and Other Essays.* Trans. Ben Brewster. London, 1971.

Ames-Lewis, Francis. "Ganymede on Dangerous Ground." *European Gay Review* 4 (1990): 128–134.

Annotations Upon all the Books of the Old and New Testament. London, 1645.

Aristotle. *Rhetorica.* Ed. W. Rhys Roberts. London, 1971.

Armstrong, Nancy, and Leonard Tennenhouse, eds. *The Ideology of Conduct.* London, 1987.

Attridge, Derek. "Puttenham's Perplexity: Nature, Art, and the Supplement in Renaissance Poetic Theory." In *Literary Theory/ Renaissance Texts.* Ed. Patricia Parker and David Quint. Pp. 257–279. Baltimore, 1986.

Axton, Marie. *The Queen's Two Bodies: Drama and the Elizabethan Succession.* London, 1977.

Bacon, Francis. *Cases of Treason.* London, 1641.

——. *The Essays.* Ed. John Pitcher. Harmondsworth, U.K., 1985.

Baines, Richard. "A Note containing the opinions of one Christopher Marly concerning his damnable judgement of religion and scorn of God's word." Brit. Mus. Harl. 6848: fol. 185.

Baker, Richard. *A Chronicle of the Kings of England from the Time of the Romans Government unto the Death of King James*. London, 1684.
——. *Variegatus, or Catoes Morall Distichs: Translated and Paraphras'd, with Variations of Expressing, in English Verse*. London, 1636.
Bakhtin, M. M. *Rabelais and His World*. Bloomington, IN, 1984.
Bal, Mieke. *Death and Dissymmetry: The Politics of Coherence in the Book of Judges*. Chicago, 1988.
Barker, Francis. *The Tremulous Private Body: An Essay on Subjection*. London, 1984.
Barnfield, Richard. *The Affectionate Shepheard. Containing the Complaint of Daphnis for the loue of Ganimede*. London, 1594.
——. *Cynthia. With certain Sonnets, and the Legend of Cassandra*. London, 1595.
——. *The Encomium of Lady Pecunia, or the Praise of Money*. London, 1598.
Barthes, Roland. *Image Music Text*. Ed. and trans. Stephen Heath. New York, 1977.
Becke, Edmund. *The Holy Bible, with Notes and Commentaries by Edmund Becke*. London, 1549.
Belsey, Catherine. *Critical Practice*. London, 1980.
——. "Disrupting Sexual Difference: Meaning and Gender in the Comedies." In *Alternative Shakespeares*. Ed. John Drakakis. London, 1985. Pp. 166–190.
——. *The Subject of Tragedy: Identity and Difference in Renaissance Drama*. London, 1985.
Berchorius, Petrus. *Metamorphosis Ovidiana moraliter a Magistro Thomas Walleys Anglico de professione praedicatorum sub sanctissimo patre Dominico . . .* Utrecht, 1960.
Blount, Thomas. *Glossographia: Or a Dictionary Interpreting the Hard Words of Whatsoever Language, now used in our refined English Tongue*. London, 1670.
Boswell, John. *Christianity, Social Tolerance, and Homosexuality: Gay People in Western Europe from the Beginning of the Christian Era to the Fourteenth Century*. Chicago, 1980.
Brathwait, Richard. *Natures Embassie: or, the Wilde-mans Measures*. London, 1621.
——. *The Shepheards Tales*. London, 1621.
——. *A Strappado for the Divell. Epigrams and Satyres Alluding to the Time, with divers measures of no lesse Delight*. London, 1615.
——. *Times Curtaine Drawne, or the Anatomie of Vanitie*. London, 1621.
Bray, Alan. *Homosexuality in Renaissance England*. London, 1982.
Breasted, Barbara. "*Comus* and the Castlehaven Scandal." *Milton Studies* 3 (1971): 201–224.

Breton, Nicholas. *The Good and the Badde, or Descriptions of the Worthies and Unworthies of this Age*. London, 1616.
Brink, C. O. *Horace on Poetry: Prolegomena to the Literary Epistle*. Cambridge, 1963.
Brodwin, Leonora Leet. "*Edward II*: Marlowe's Culminating Treatment of Love." *ELH* 31 (1964): 139–155.
Brown, Steve. "' . . . and his ingle at home': Notes on Gender in Jonson's *Epicoene*." Renaissance Society of America. Philadelphia, 21 March 1986.
Buffière, Felix. *Eros adolescent: La pédérastie dans la Grèce antique*. Paris, 1980.
Bushnell, Rebecca W. *Tragedies of Tyrants: Political Thought and Theater in the English Renaissance*. Ithaca, 1990.
Byrd, William. "When I was Otherwise than Now I Am." In *Elizabethan Verse*. Ed. Edward Lucie-Smith. Harmondsworth, U.K., 1965.
Cantalupe, Eugene B. "*Hero and Leander*, Marlowe's Tragicomedy of Love." *College English* 24 (1962): 295–298.
Castiglione, Balthazar. *The Boke of the Courtier*. Trans. Thomas Hoby. London, 1561.
Cecil. *Certain Precepts for the Well Ordering of a Man's Life*. Folger MS.
Chapman, George. *Ovid's Banquet of Sence*. London, 1595.
Charnes, Linda. "'So Unsecret to Ourselves': Notorious Identity and the Material Subject in Shakespeare's *Troilus and Cressida*." *Shakespeare Quarterly* 40, 4 (1989): 413–440.
Coke, Edward. *An exact abridgement of the two last volumes of reports, entitled the 12th & 13th parts*. London, 1670.
——. *The Third Part of the Institutes of the Laws of England*. London, 1644.
Collins, S. Ann. "Sundrie Shapes, Committing Headdie Ryots, Incest, Rapes: Functions of the Myth in Determining Narrative and Tone in Marlowe's *Hero and Leander*." *Mosaic* 4 (1970): 107–122.
Cooper, Thomas. *Bibliotheca Eliotae*. London, 1552.
——. *Thesaurus Linguae Romanae et Britannicae*. London: 1565.
Coote, Stephen, ed. *The Penguin Book of Homosexual Verse*. Harmondsworth, U.K., 1983.
Cox, C. B. "Bisexual Shakespeare?" *Hudson Review* 40, 3 (1987): 481–486.
Cranmer, Thomas. *The Bishop's Bible*. London, 1568.
Creaser, John. "Milton's *Comus*: The Irrelevance of the Castlehaven Scandal." *Milton Quarterly* 4 (1988): 24–34.
Cropper, Elizabeth. "On Beautiful Women, Parmigiannio, *Petrarchismo*, and the Vernacular Style." *Art Bulletin* 58 (1976): 374–394.

Crouch, Nathaniel. *Female Excellency, or the Ladies Glory*. London, 1688.

Cubeta, Paul. "Marlowe's Poet in *Hero and Leander*." *College English* 26 (1965): 500–505.

Cunningham, Karen. "Renaissance Execution and Marlovian Elocution: The Drama of Death." *PMLA* 105, 2 (1990): 209–222.

Curran, Stuart. "*Paradise Regained*: The Implications of Epic." *Milton Studies* 17 (1983): 209–224.

——. *Poetic Form and British Romanticism*. Oxford, 1986.

Davies, Stevie. *The Feminine Redeemed: The Idea of Woman in Spenser, Shakespeare, and Milton*. Lexington, Ky., 1986.

A Declaration of the Bloudie and Unchristian Acting of William Star and John Taylor of Walton. London, 1649.

Deleuze, Gilles, and Felix Guattari. *L'anti-Oedipe: Capitalisme et Schizophrénie*. Paris, 1972.

De Lille, Alain. *The Complaint of Nature*. Trans. Douglas M. Moffat. New York, 1908.

Derrida, Jacques. "White Mythology: Metaphor in the Text of Philosophy." In *Margins of Philosophy*. Trans. Alan Bass. Pp. 207–272. Chicago, 1982.

Dollimore, Jonathan. "Homophobia and Sexual Difference." *Oxford Literary Review* 8, 1–2 (1986): 5–12.

——. *Radical Tragedy: Religion, Ideology, and Power in the Drama of Shakespeare and His Contemporaries*. Chicago, 1984.

——. "Shakespeare, Cultural Materialism, and the New Historicism." In *Political Shakespeare: New Essays in Cultural Materialism*. Ed. Jonathan Dollimore and Alan Sinfield. Pp. 2–17. Ithaca, 1985.

Donne, John. *Complete Poetry and Selected Prose*. Ed. John Hayward. London, 1962.

——. *John Donne: The Complete English Poems*. Ed. A. J. Smith. Harmondsworth, U.K., 1971.

Donno, Elizabeth Story. *Elizabethan Minor Epics*. London, 1963.

Donzelot, Jacques. *The Policing of Families*. Trans. Robert Hurley. New York, 1979.

Dover, K. J. *Greek Homosexuality*. New York, 1978.

Drakakis, John, ed. *Alternative Shakespeares*. London, 1985.

Drayton, Michael. *Endimion and Phoebe. Ideas Latmus*. London, 1595.

——. *The Works of Michael Drayton*. Ed. J. W. Hebel. 8 vols. Oxford, 1961.

Duberman, Martin Bauml. *About Time: Exploring the Gay Past*. New York, 1986.

Dyke, Daniel. *Michael and the Dragon, or Christ Tempted and Satan Foyled*. London, 1635.

Eagleton, Terry. *Criticism and Ideology*. London, 1976.
Edward, Thomas. *Narcissus*. London, 1595.
Eliot, T. S. "Hamlet and His Problems." In *Hamlet: An Authoritative Text, Intellectual Backgrounds, Extracts from the Sources, Essays in Criticism*. Ed. Cyrus Hoy. Pp. 176–180. New York, 1963.
Ferguson, Margaret W. *Trials of Desire: Renaissance Defenses of Poetry*. New Haven, 1983.
Ferguson, Margaret W., and Mary Nyquist, eds. *Re-Membering Milton: Essays on the Texts and Traditions*. London, 1988.
Fineman, Joel. *Shakespeare's Perjur'd Eye: The Invention of Poetic Subjectivity in the Sonnets*. Berkeley, 1986.
——. "Shakespeare's *Will*: The Temporality of Rape." *Representations* 7 (1987): 59–89.
Fish, Stanley. *Is There a Text in This Class? The Authority of Interpretive Communities*. Cambridge, Mass., 1980.
Fletcher, Giles. *Licia*. London, n.d.
Florio, John. *A Worlde of Wordes, or Most copious and exact Dictionarie in Italian and English*. London, 1598.
Fone, Byrne R. S., ed. *Hidden Heritage: History and the Gay Imagination: An Anthology*. New York, 1980.
Foster, Donald W. "Master W. H., R.I.P." *PMLA* 1 (1987): 42–54.
Foucault, Michel. *The History of Sexuality, Vol. 1: An Introduction*. New York, 1980.
——. *Politics, Philosophy, Culture: Interviews and Other Writings*. Ed. Lawrence D. Kritzman. London, 1988.
Fowler, Alastair. *Kinds of Literature: An Introduction to the Theory of Genres and Modes*. Cambridge, 1982.
Fraunce, Abraham. *The Arcadian Rhetoric*. Ed. Ethel Seaton. Oxford, 1950.
——. *The Countess of Pembroke's Yvy-Church*. London, 1591.
Freccero, John. "The Fig Tree and the Laurel: Petrarch's Poetics." In *Literary Theory/Renaissance Texts*. Ed. Patricia Parker and David Quint. Pp. 20–32. Baltimore, 1986.
Frye, Northrop. "How True a Twain." In *The Riddle of Shakespeare's Sonnets*. Ed. Edward Hubler. New York, 1962.
A Full and True Account of the Notorious Wicked Life of that Grand Impostor, John Taylor; One of the Sweet-Singers of Israel. London, 1678.
Fuss, Diana. *Essentially Speaking: Nature, Feminism, Difference*. London, 1989.
G., F., and E. H. *The Arraignment of Popery*. London, 1669.
Gallop, Jane. *The Daughter's Seduction: Feminism and Psychoanalysis*. Ithaca, 1982.
Garber, Marjorie. "Shakespeare as Fetish." *SQ* 41, 2 (1990): 242–250.

——. "Shakespeare's Ghost Writers." In *Cannibals, Witches, and Divorce: Estranging the Renaissance*. Ed. Marjorie Garber. Pp. 122–146. Baltimore, 1987.

Girard, René. "Hamlet's Dull Revenge." In *Literary Theory/Renaissance Texts*. Ed. Patricia Parker and David Quint. Pp. 280–302. Baltimore, 1986.

Godshalk, W. L. "*Hero and Leander*: The Sense of an Ending." In *"A Poet and a Filthy Play-Maker": New Essays on Christopher Marlowe*. Ed. Kenneth Friedenreich, Roma Gill, and Constance B. Kuriyama. Pp. 293–314. New York, 1988.

Goldberg, Jonathan. "Colin to Hobbinol: Spenser's Familiar Letters." In *Displacing Homophobia: Gay Male Perspectives in Literature and Culture*. Ed. Ronald R. Butters, John M. Clum, and Michael Moon. Pp. 107–126. Durham, N.C.; 1989.

——. *James I and the Politics of Literature: Jonson, Shakespeare, Donne, and Their Contemporaries*. Baltimore, 1983.

——. "Sodomy and Society: The Case of Christopher Marlowe." *Southwest Review* 69 (1984): 371–378.

——. *Writing Matter: From the Hands of the English Renaissance*. Stanford, 1990.

Goldsmith, M. M. *Hobbes's Science of Politics*. New York, 1966.

Gouge, William. *The Workes of William Gouge in Two Volumes*. London, 1627.

Greenblatt, Stephen. "Fiction and Friction." In *Reconstructing Individualism*. Ed. Thomas C. Heller et al. Pp. 30–52. Stanford, 1986.

——. *Renaissance Self-Fashioning from More to Shakespeare*. Chicago, 1980.

Greene, Gayle. "Shakespeare's Cressida: 'A Kinde of self'." In *The Woman's Part: Feminist Criticism of Shakespeare*. Ed. Carolyn Ruth Swift Lenz, Gayle Greene, and Carol Thomas Neely. Pp. 133–149. Urbana, 1983.

Guattari, Félix. "A Liberation of Desire: An Interview by George Stambolian." In *Homosexualities and French Literature: Cultural Contexts/Critical Texts*. Ed. Elaine Marks and George Stambolian. Pp. 56–69. Ithaca, 1979.

Guilpin, Edward. *Skialethia, or, a Shadowe of Truth in Certaine Epigrams and Satyres*. London, 1598.

Halperin, David M. *One Hundred Years of Homosexuality and Other Essays on Greek Love*. London, 1989.

Halpern, Richard. "The Great Instauration: Imaginary Narratives in Milton's 'Nativity Ode'." In *Re-Membering Milton: New Essays on the Texts and Traditions*. Ed. Margaret W. Ferguson and Mary Nyquist. Pp. 3–24. London, 1988.

Hardison, O. B., Jr., Alex Preminger, Kevin Kercane and Leon Golden, eds. *Medieval Literary Criticism*. New York, 1974.

Hardwick, C., ed. *A Poem on the Times of Edward II*. London, 1849.

Hartmann, Heidi. "The Unhappy Marriage of Marxism and Feminism: Toward a More Progressive Union." In *Women and Revolution: A Discussion of the Unhappy Marriage of Marxism and Feminism*. Ed. Lydia Sargent. Boston, 1981.

Hawkes, Terence. *That Shakespeherian Rag: Essays on a Critical Process*. London, 1986.

Helgerson, Richard. *The Elizabethan Prodigals*. Berkeley, 1976.

Heywood, Thomas. *Oenone and Paris*. London, 1595.

Hindess, Barry, and Paul Hirst. *Modes of Production and Social Formation*. London, 1977.

Hobbes, Thomas. *Leviathan*. Ed. C. B. Macpherson. Harmondsworth, U.K., 1968.

Hocquenghem, Guy. *Homosexual Desire*. Trans. Daniella Dangoor. London, 1978.

Hotson, Leslie. *Shakespeare's Sonnets Dated, and Other Essays*. Oxford, 1949.

Howard, Jean E. "The New Historicism in Renaissance Studies." *ELR* 16, 1 (1986): 13–43.

Hubert, Francis. *The Life of Edward II*. London, 1628.

Huussen, Arend H., Jr. "Sodomy in the Dutch Republic during the Eighteenth Century." In *Unauthorized Sexual Behavior during the Enlightenment*. Ed. Robert P. Maccubbin. Pp. 169–178. Williamsburg, Va., 1985.

James I. *The Political Works of James I*. Ed. Charles Howard McIlwain. Cambridge, Mass., 1919.

Jameson, Fredric. *The Political Unconscious: Narrative as a Socially Symbolic Act*. Ithaca, 1981.

Jardine, Lisa. *Still Harping on Daughters: Women and Drama in the Age of Shakespeare*. Brighton, 1983.

Johnson, Samuel. "The Life of Milton." In *Milton's Lycidas: The Tradition and the Poem*. Ed. C. A. Patrides. Pp. 56–57. New York, 1961.

Jonson, Ben. *Ben Jonson: Works*. Ed. C. H. Herford and Percy Simpson. 11 vols. Oxford, 1925–1952.

Kantorowicz, Ernst. *The King's Two Bodies: A Study in Medieval Political Theology*. Princeton, 1957.

Kaplan, Cora. "Pandora's Box: Subjectivity, Class, and Sexuality in Socialist Feminist Criticism." In *Making a Difference: Feminist Literary Criticism*. Ed. Gayle Greene and Coppélia Kahn. Pp. 146–176. London, 1985.

Katz, Jonathan. *Gay American History: Lesbians and Gay Men in the U.S.A.* New York, 1976.

Keach, William. *Elizabethan Ovidian Erotic Narratives: Irony and Pathos in the Ovidian Poetry of Shakespeare, Marlowe, and Their Contemporaries.* New Brunswick, 1977.

Kelly, Joan. *Women, History, and Theory: The Essays of Joan Kelly*. Chicago, 1984.

Kermode, Frank, ed. *The Living Milton*. London, 1960.

Kerrigan, William. *The Sacred Complex: On the Psychogenesis of Paradise Lost*. Cambridge, Mass., 1983.

Kleinberg, Seymour. *Alienated Affections: Being Gay in America*. New York, 1980.

The Knowledge of the World: Or, the Art of Well-Educating Youth Through the Various Conditions of LIFE. London, n.d.

Kristeva, Julia. "Women's Time." *Signs* 7, 1 (1981): 13–35.

Lacan, Jacques. *Ecrits: A Selection*. Trans. Alan Sheridan. New York, 1977.

Lacqueur, Thomas. "Orgasm, Generation, and the Politics of Reproductive Biology." *Representations* 14 (1986): 4–16.

Lanham, Richard. "Sidney: The Ornament of His Age," *Southern Review* 2, 4 (1967): 319–340.

Laslett, Peter. *The World We Have Lost*. New York, 1965.

Laslett, Peter, ed. *Household and Family in Past Times*. Cambridge, U.K., 1972.

LeComte, Edward. *Milton and Sex*. New York, 1978.

Leech, Clifford. *Marlowe*. Englewood Cliffs, 1965.

——. "Marlowe's *Edward II*: Power and Suffering." *Critical Quarterly* 3 (1959): 181–196.

Leinwand, Theodore B. "Negotiation and the New Historicism." *PMLA* 105, 3 (1990): 477–490.

Lentricchia, Frank, and Thomas McLaughlin, eds. *Critical Terms for Literary Study*. Chicago, 1990.

Lesly, George. *Divine Dialogues*. London, 1684.

A Letter to a Member of Parliament: with two Discourses Inclosed in it. London, 1675.

Lever, J. W. *The Elizabethan Love Sonnet*. London, 1956.

Levin, Harry. "The Wages of Satire." In *Literature and Society*. Ed. Edward W. Said. Pp. 1–14. Baltimore, 1980.

Levin, Richard. "The Poetics and Politics of Bardicide." *PMLA* 105, 3 (1990): 491–504.

Lévi-Strauss, Claude. *The Elementary Structures of Kinship Arrangements*. Boston, 1969.

Lewalski, Barbara K. "Milton and Woman—Yet Once More." *Milton Studies* 6 (1974): 3–20.

Lewis, C. S. *English Literature in the Sixteenth Century Excluding Drama.* Oxford, 1954.
——. "*Hero and Leander.*" *Proceedings of the British Academy* 38 (1952): 23–37.
——. *A Preface to "Paradise Lost."* Oxford, 1961.
Licata, Salvatore J., and Robert P. Petersen, eds. *The Gay Past: A Collection of Historical Essays.* New York, 1985.
Lieb, Michael. "'Cupid's Funeral Pile': Milton's Projected Drama on the Theme of Lust." *Renaissance Papers* (Southeastern Renaissance Conference, 1977), pp. 29–41.
The Life and Death of John Atherton Lord Bishop of Waterford and Lysmore within the Kingdome of Ireland, borne neare Bridgewater in Somersetshire. London, 1641.
Lightfoot, John. *The Works of the Reverend and Learned John Lightfoot D.D.* London, 1822.
Lincoln, Elisabeth. *The Countess of Lincoln's Nursery.* Oxford, 1622.
Lindenberger, Herbert. *Historical Drama: The Relation of Literature and Reality.* Chicago, 1975.
Lodge, Thomas. *The Complete Works of Thomas Lodge.* Glasgow, 1883.
Maccubbin, Robert P., ed. *Unauthorized Sexual Behavior during the Enlightenment.* Williamsburg, Va., 1985.
Macpherson, C. B. *The Political Theory of Possessive Individualism, Hobbes to Locke.* Oxford, 1962.
Marcus, Leah. "The Earl of Bridgewater's Legal Life: Notes toward a Political Reading of *Comus.*" *Milton Quarterly* 4 (1988): 13–23.
——. "The Milieu of Milton's *Comus*: Judicial Reform at Ludlow and the Problem of Sexual Assault." *Criticism* 25 (1983): 293–327.
——. *The Politics of Mirth: Jonson, Herrick, Milton, Marvell, and the Defense of Old Holiday Pastimes.* Chicago, 1986.
Marlowe, Christopher. *Christopher Marlowe: Complete Plays and Poems.* Ed. E. D. Pendry and J. C. Maxwell. London, 1976.
——. *The Complete Plays.* Ed. J. B. Steane. Harmondsworth, U.K., 1969.
Marston, John. *The Metamorphosis of Pigmalion's Image and Certaine Satyres.* London, 1598.
——. *The Scourge of Villanie.* London, 1599.
Marty, William. *Youth's Instruction.* London, 1612.
Martz, Louis. "The *Amoretti*: Mostly Good Temperament." In *Form and Construction in the Poetry of Edmund Spenser.* New York, 1962.
Marx, Karl. "The Materialist Concept of History." In *Marxism: Essential Writings.* Ed. David McLellan. Pp. 3–19. Oxford, 1988.
Maus, Katharine Eisaman. "Horns of Dilemma: Jealousy, Gender, and Spectatorship in English Renaissance Drama." *ELH* 54 (1987): 561–582.

McCanles, Michael. *The Text of Sidney's Arcadian World*. Durham, N.C., 1989.

McColley, Diane Kelsey. *Milton's Eve*. Urbana, 1983.

McCoy, Richard C. *Sir Philip Sidney: Rebellion in Arcadia*. New Brunswick, 1979.

McIntosh, Mary. "The Homosexual Role." In *The Making of the Modern Homosexual*. Ed. Kenneth Plummer. Pp. 30–44. London, 1981.

Merchant, Carolyn. *The Death of Nature: Women, Ecology, and the Scientific Revolution*. San Francisco, 1980.

Meres, Francis. *Palladis Tamia, or, Wits Treasury Being the Second Part of Wits Commonwealth*. London, 1598.

Middleton, Richard. *Epigrams and Satyres*. London, 1608.

Middleton, Thomas. *The Blacke Booke*. London, 1604.

——. *The Works of Thomas Middleton*. Ed. A. H. Bullen. London, 1886.

Miller, Paul W. "A Function of Myth in Marlowe's *Hero and Leander*." *SP* 50 (1953): 158–167.

Milton, John. *Complete Prose Works of John Milton*. Ed. Don M. Wolfe. 8 vols. New Haven, 1953–1982.

——. *John Milton: Complete Poems and Major Prose*. Ed. Merritt Y. Hughes. New York, 1957.

Mintz, Samuel I. *The Hunting of Leviathan*. Cambridge, U.K., 1962.

Mullaney, Steven. "Strange Things, Gross Terms, Curious Customs: The Rehearsal of Cultures in the Late Renaissance." *Representations* 3 (1983): 53–62.

Neale, J. E. *Queene Elizabeth I: A Biography*. New York, 1957.

Neely, Carol Thomas. "The Structure of English Renaissance Sonnet Sequences." *ELH* 45 (1978): 359–389.

Neuse, Richard. "Milton and Spenser: The Virgilian Triad Revisited." *ELH* 45 (1978): 606–639.

Newman, Karen. "Renaissance Family Politics and Shakespeare's *The Taming of the Shrew*." *ELR* 16, 1 (1986): 86–100.

Newton, Richard C. "Jonson and the (Re-)Invention of the Book." In *Classic and Cavalier: Essays on Jonson and the Sons of Ben*. Ed. Claude J. Summers and Ted-Larry Pebworth. Pp. 31–55. Pittsburgh, 1982.

Niccholes, Alexander. *Discourse of Marriage and Wiving*. London, 1615.

Novy, Marianne. *Love's Argument: Gender Relations in Shakespeare*. Chapel Hill, 1984.

Nyquist, Mary. "The Genesis of Gendered Subjectivity in the Divorce Tracts and in *Paradise Lost*." In *Re-Membering Milton: Essays on the Texts and Traditions*. Ed. Margaret W. Ferguson and Mary Nyquist. Pp. 99–127. London, 1988.

Nyquist, Mary. "Textual Overlapping and Dalilah's Harlot-Lap." In *Literary Theory/Renaissance Texts*. Ed. Patricia Parker and David Quint. Pp. 341–372. Baltimore, 1986.

Ocamb, Karen. "Gay Studies Make the Grade." *The Advocate* 561 (October 9, 1990): 40.

Orgel, Stephen. "The Authentic Shakespeare." *Representations* 21 (1988): 1–26.

——. "Nobody's Perfect: Or Why Did the English Stage Take Boys for Women?" In *Displacing Homophobia: Gay Male Perspectives in Literature and Culture*. Ed. Ronald R. Butters, John M. Clum, and Michael Moon. Pp. 7–30. Durham, N.C., 1989.

Panofsky, Erwin. *Studies in Iconology: Humanistic Themes in the Art of the Renaissance*. Oxford, 1939.

Parker, Patricia. *Literary Fat Ladies: Rhetoric, Gender, Property*. London, 1987.

Patterson, Annabel. *Pastoral and Ideology: Virgil to Valery*. Berkeley, 1987.

——. " 'Under . . . Pretty Tales': Intention in Sidney's *Arcadia*." *Studies in the Literary Imagination* 15, 1 (1982): 5–21.

——. "Virgil's *Eclogues*: Images of Change." In *Roman Images: Selected Papers from the English Institute, 1982*. Ed. Annabel Patterson. Pp. 163–186. Baltimore, 1984.

Pequigney, Joseph. *Such Is My Love: A Study of Shakespeare's Sonnets*. Chicago, 1987.

Plowden, Edmund. *The Commentaries and Reports of Edmund Plowden*. London, 1779.

Podolsky, Robin. "Birth of a Queer Nation." *The Advocate* 561 (October 9, 1990): 52–53.

Pulton, Ferdinando. *A Collection of Statutes Now in Use, With a Continuation of the Statutes Made in the Reign of the Late King Charles the First of Blessed Memory . . . by Thomas Manby*. London, 1670.

Quilligan, Maureen. *The Language of Allegory: Defining the Genre*. Ithaca, 1979.

——. *Milton's Spenser: The Politics of Reading*. Ithaca, 1983.

——. "Sidney and His Queen." In *The Historical Renaissance: New Essays on Tudor and Stuart Literature and Culture*. Ed. Heather Dubrow and Richard Strier. Pp. 171–196. Chicago, 1988.

Quint, David. Introduction to *Literary Theory/Renaissance Texts*. Ed. Patricia Parker and David Quint. Pp. 1–19. Baltimore, 1986.

Rackin, Phyllis. "Androgyny, Mimesis, and the Marriage of the Boy Heroine on the English Renaissance Stage." *PMLA* 102, 1 (1987): 29–41.

Raleigh, Walter. "Advice to a Son." In *Advice to a Son*. Ed. L. B. Wright. Washington, D.C., 1962.

Rey, Michael. "Parisian Homosexuals Create a Lifestyle, 1700–1750: The Police Archives." Trans. Robert A. Day and Robert Welch. In

Unauthorized Sexual Behavior During the Enlightenment. Ed. Robert P. Maccubbin. Pp. 179–191. Williamsburg, 1985.
Ribner, Irving. "Marlowe's *Edward II* and the Tudor History Play." *Journal of English Literary History* 22 (1955): 243–253.
Rice, George P., ed. *The Public Speaking of Queen Elizabeth: Selections from the Official Addresses*. New York, 1951.
Rich, Adrienne. "Compulsory Heterosexuality and Lesbian Existence." In *Women, Sex, and Sexuality*. Ed. Catherine R. Stimpson and Ethel Spector Person. Pp. 62–91. Chicago, 1980.
Rodgers, Bruce. *Gay Talk: A (Sometimes Outrageous) Dictionary of Gay Slang*. New York, 1972.
"Room for a Ballad, or a Ballad for Rome." London, 1674.
Rousseau, G. S. "The Pursuit of Homosexuality in the Eighteenth Century: 'Utterly Confused Category' and/or Rich Repository?" In *Unauthorized Sexual Behavior During the Enlightenment*. Ed. Robert P. Maccubbin. Pp. 132–168. Williamsburg, Va., 1985.
Rouse, A. L. *Homosexuals in History*. New York, 1977.
Rubin, Gayle. "The Traffic in Women: Notes on the 'Political Economy' of Sex." In *Toward an Anthropology of Women*. Ed. Rayna Reiter. New York, 1975.
Rutledge, Leigh W. *Unnatural Quotations: A Compendium of Quotations by, for or about Gay People*. Boston, 1988.
Saslow, James M. *Ganymede in the Renaissance: Homosexuality in Art and Society*. New Haven, 1986.
Savile, George. *The Lady's New-Year's-Gift: Or, Advice to a Daughter*. London, 1700.
Scott, Janet. *Les Sonnets Elizabethains*. Paris, 1929.
Sedgwick, Eve Kosofsky. "Across Gender, Across Sexuality: Willa Cather and Others." In *Displacing Homophobia: Gay Male Perspectives in Literature and Culture*. Ed. Ronald R. Butters, John M. Clum, and Michael Moon. Pp. 53–72. Durham, N.C., 1989.
——. *Between Men: English Literature and Male Homosocial Desire*. New York, 1985.
——. "Tide and Trust." *Critical Inquiry* 15 (1989): 745–757.
S'ensuivent Les Blasons Anatomiques du Corps Feminin. Paris, 1543.
Sergent, Bernard. *Homosexuality in Greek Myth*. Trans. Arthur Goldhammer. Boston, 1984.
Shakespeare, William. *All's Well That Ends Well*. Ed. G. K. Hunter. London, 1967.
——. *Hamlet*. Ed. Harold Jenkins. London, 1982.
——. *Romeo and Juliet*. Ed. Brian Gibbons. London, 1980.
——. *Shakespeare's Sonnets*. Ed. Stephen Booth. New Haven, 1977.
——. *Troilus and Cressida*. Ed. Kenneth Palmer. London, 1982.

Shawcross, John T. "Milton and Diodati: An Essay in Psychodynamic Meaning." *Milton Studies* 7 (1975): 127–163.
Shepherd, Simon. *Marlowe and the Politics of Elizabethan Theatre*. Brighton, 1986.
Sidney, Philip. *An Apology for Poetry*. In *Critical Theory since Plato*. Ed. Hazard Adams. Pp. 155–177. New York, 1971.
——. *Miscellaneous Prose of Sir Philip Sidney*. Ed. Katherine Duncan-Jones and Jan Van Dorsten. Oxford, 1985.
——. *The Old Arcadia*. Ed. Katherine Duncan-Jones. Oxford, 1973.
——. *The Poems of Sir Philip Sidney*. Ed. William A. Ringler, Jr. Oxford, 1962.
Sinfield, Alan. "The Cultural Politics of the *Defence of Poetry*." In *Sir Philip Sidney and the Interpretation of Renaissance Culture: The Poet in His Time and in Ours: A Collection of Critical and Scholarly Essays*. Ed. Gary F. Waller and Michael D. Moore. London, 1984.
——. "Power and Ideology: An Outline Theory and Sidney's *Arcadia*." In *Essential Articles for the Study of Sir Philip Sidney*. Ed. Arthur F. Kinney. Pp. 391–410. Hamden, Conn., 1986.
Smith, Brian O. *The Crown and the Commonwealth*. Philadelphia, 1977.
Sodom Fair: or the Market of the Man of Sin. London, 1688.
Spenser, Edmund. *Poetical Works*. Ed. Edward De Selincourt. Oxford, 1912.
Stallybrass, Peter, and Allon White. *The Politics and Poetics of Transgression*. Ithaca, 1986.
Sterling, Brents. *The Shakespeare Sonnet Order: Poems and Groups*. Berkeley, 1968.
Stillman, Robert E. "The Politics of Sidney's Pastoral: Mystification and Mythology in *The Old Arcadia*." *ELH* 52, 4 (1986): 795–814.
Stone, Lawrence. *The Crisis of the Aristocracy, 1558–1641*. Oxford, 1965.
——. *The Family, Sex, and Marriage in England, 1500–1800*. London, 1977.
Stubbes, Philip. *The Anatomie of Abuses*. London, 1585.
Stubbs, John. *The Discovery of a Gaping Gulf whereinto England is like to be swallowed by another French marriage*. London, 1579.
Summers, Claude J. "The (Homo)sexual Temptation in *Paradise Regained*." In *"Grateful Vicissitude": Essays in Honor of J. Max Patrick*. Ed. Harrison T. Meserole and Michael A. Mikolajczak. Forthcoming.
——. "Sex, Politics, and Self-Realization in *Edward II*." In *"A Poet and a Filthy Play-Maker": New Essays on Christopher Marlowe*. Ed. Kenneth Friedenreich, Roma Gill, and Constance B. Kuriyama. Pp. 221–240. New York, 1988.
Sweeney, John Gordon, III. *Jonson and the Psychology of Public Theater: To Coin the Spirit, Spend the Soul*. Princeton, 1985.

Taylor, John. *A Briefe Remembrance of All The Englishe Monarchs*. London, 1618.
Tennenhouse, Leonard. *Power on Display: The Politics of Shakespeare's Genres*. New York, 1986.
Theocritus. *Les Idylles de Theocrite Traduites De Grec en Vers Francois*. Paris, 1688.
——. *The Idylliums of Theocritus*. Trans. Francis Fawkes. London, 1767.
——. *The Idylliums of Theocritus with Rapin's Discourse of Pastorals Done into English*. Trans. Thomas Creech. Oxford, 1684.
——. *Theocritus: Idylls and Epigrams*. Trans. Daryl Hine. New York, 1982.
Theodidactus, Eugenius. *Advice to a Daughter*. London, 1658.
Thorpe. *His Charge, as it Was Delivered to the Grand Jury at York Assizes, the Twentieth of March, 1648*. London, 1649.
Tillyard, E. M. W. *The Elizabethan World Picture*. New York, 1960.
Todorov, Tzvetan. *The Fantastic: A Structural Approach to a Literary Genre*. Trans. Richard Howard. Cleveland, 1973.
The Trial of Lord Audley, Earl of Castlehaven, For Inhumanely Causing his Own Wife to be Ravished, and for Buggery. London, 1679.
A True Relation of the Life and Death of Edward II. London, 1689.
Trumbach, Randolph. "Sodomitical Subcultures, Sodomitical Roles, and the Gender Revolution of the Eighteenth Century: The Recent Historiography." In *Unauthorized Sexual Behavior during the Enlightenment*. Ed. Robert P. Maccubbin. Pp. 109–121. Williamsburg, Va., 1985.
The Tryal and Condemnation of Mervin, Lord Audley Earl of Castle-Haven, at Westminster, April the 5th 1631. London, 1699.
Turner, James Grantham. *One Flesh: Paradisal Marriage and Sexual Relations in the Age of Milton*. Oxford, 1987.
Tuve, Rosemond. *Elizabethan and Metaphysical Imagery*. Chicago, 1947.
Van Leer, David. "The Beast of the Closet: Homosociality and the Pathology of Manhood." *Critical Inquiry* 15 (1989): 587–605.
Van Leer, David. "Trust and Trade." *Critical Inquiry* 15 (1989): 758–763.
Vickers, Nancy J. "Diana Described: Scattered Woman and Scattered Rhyme." In *Writing and Sexual Difference*. Ed. Elizabeth Abel. Brighton, 1982.
Virgil. *The Eclogues and Georgics of Virgil*. Trans. C. Day Lewis. New York, 1964.
——. *The Works of Publius Virgilius Maro*. Trans. John Ogilby. London, 1649.
——. *The Works of Virgil*. Trans. John Dryden. London, 1697.
Waith, Eugene M. "Marlowe and the Jades of Asia." *Studies in English Literature* 5 (1964): 247–268.

Watkins, J. W. N. *Hobbes's System of Ideas*. London, 1965.
Webber, Joan M. "The Politics of Poetry: Feminism and *Paradise Lost*." *Milton Studies* 14 (1980): 3–24.
Weeks, Jeffrey. "Discourse, Desire, and Sexual Deviance: Some Problems in a History of Homosexuality." In *The Making of the Modern Homosexual*. Ed. Kenneth Plummer. Pp. 76–111. London, 1981.
——. Preface to *Homosexual Desire*, by Guy Hocquenghem. Trans. Daniella Dangoor. Pp. 9–34. London, 1978.
Weever, John. *Faunus and Melliflora*. London, 1595.
Weill, Judith. *Marlowe: Merlin's Prophet*. Cambridge, 1977.
Weimann, Robert. "Mimesis in *Hamlet*. In *Shakespeare and the Question of Theory*. Ed. Geoffrey Hartman and Patricia Parker. Pp. 275–291. London, 1985.
Westling, Louise Hutchings. *The Evolution of Michael Drayton's Idea*. Salzburg, 1974.
White, Edmund. *States of Desire: Travels in Gay America*. New York, 1983.
White, Hayden. *Metahistory: The Historical Imagination in Nineteenth-Century Europe*. Baltimore, 1973.
White, T. H. *The Bestiary: A Book of Beasts, Being a Translation from a Latin Bestiary of the Twelfth Century*. New York, 1954.
Williams, Martin T. "The Temptations in Marlowe's *Hero and Leander*." *Modern Language Quarterly* 16 (1955): 226–231.
Wilson, Katherine M. *Shakespeare's Sugared Sonnets*. New York, 1974.
Wilson, Thomas. *The Arte of Rhetorique*. Ed. G. H. Mair. Oxford, 1909.
Winny, James. *The Master-Mistresse: A Study of Shakespeare's Sonnets*. New York, 1969.
Wittreich, Joseph Anthony. *Feminist Milton*. Ithaca, 1987.
Wright, Leonard. *A Display of dutie, dect with sage sayings, pythie sentences, and proper similes: Pleasant to reade, delightfull to heare, and profitable to practice*. London, 1589.

Index

Library of Congress Cataloging-in-Publication Data

Bredbeck, Gregory W.
Sodomy and interpretation : Marlowe to Milton / Gregory W. Bredbeck.
p. cm.
Includes bibliographical references and index.
ISBN 0-8014-2644-8 (alk. paper). — ISBN 0-8014-9945-3 (pbk. : alk. paper)
1. English literature—Early modern, 1500–1700—History and criticism. 2. Homosexuality and literature—England—History—16th century. 3. Homosexuality and literature—England—History—17th century. 4. English literature—Men authors—History and criticism. 5. Erotic literature, English—History and criticism. 6. Sodomy in literature. 7. Sex in literature. I. Title.
PR428.H66B7 1991
820.9′353′09031—dc20 91-55066